BROKEN

BROKEN OPEN

WHAT PAINKILLERS TAUGHT ME
ABOUT LIFE AND RECOVERY

WILLIAM COPE MOYERS

Hazelden
Publishing

Hazelden Publishing
Center City, Minnesota 55012
hazelden.org/bookstore

ISBN: 978-1-61649-997-6
Ebook ISBN: 978-1-61649-998-3

Library of Congress Cataloging-in-Publication Data

Names: Moyers, William Cope, author.
Title: Broken open : what painkillers taught me about life and recovery /
    William Cope Moyers.
Description: Center City, Minnesota : Hazelden Publishing, 2024. | Includes
    bibliographical references.
Identifiers: LCCN 2024012540 (print) | LCCN 2024012541 (ebook) | ISBN
    9781616499976 (paperback) | ISBN 9781616499983 (ebook)
Subjects: LCSH: Moyers, William Cope. | Drug addicts—United States—Biography.
    | Drug addicts—Rehabilitation—United States. | Recovering addicts—United
    States—Biography. | Opioid abuse. | BISAC: BIOGRAPHY & AUTOBIOGRAPHY
    / Personal Memoirs | SELF-HELP / Twelve-Step Programs
Classification: LCC HV5805.M68 A3 2024 (print) | LCC HV5805.M68 (ebook) |
    DDC 362.29092 [B]—dc23/eng/20240506
LC record available at https://lccn.loc.gov/2024012540
LC ebook record available at https://lccn.loc.gov/2024012541

Editor's notes
This publication is not intended as a substitute for the advice of health care
professionals.

Hazelden Publishing offers a variety of information on addiction and related
areas. Our publications do not necessarily represent Hazelden Betty Ford
Foundation's programs, nor do they officially speak for any Twelve Step
organization.

The stories shared in this book were used with the consent of the individuals
involved.

Cover design: Jon Valk Design
Typesetting: Percolator Graphic Design
Developmental editor: Marc Olson
Acquiring editor: Andy Lien
Editorial project manager: Cathy Broberg

To Henry, Thomas, and Nancy for sharing
this journey with me,
and to Nell and Jasper for joining us
along the way.

Our recovery alone is eloquent.

— Joan Larkin

Contents

Foreword

This is not a redemption story.

This is not even a singular story of addiction and recovery.

This is an honest account of a man and his complicated journey through the prison of substance use and misuse following a path that led to a fragile and precious sobriety (and a new understanding of that very word). The book is also a reflection on deep shame and what it means to face, embrace, and release it. Shame, and the destructive behavior that results from it, cannot be medicated, and the attempt to do so can destroy everything we hold dear, as William Moyers makes so abundantly clear.

William's journey also illustrates a more pernicious kind of shame that can hide behind the veneer of success, only to reveal itself in times of crisis or failure. There is an even more subtle element to that pattern of obfuscation, one which I myself struggle with and which William writes eloquently about: the fear of irrelevance and how it drives us to work too hard, polish our impeccable facades, and put our smoothly accomplished selves forward, all the while hiding exhaustion, loneliness, and a feeling of fraudulence.

For myself, that drive comes in part from a lifetime of trying to wriggle out from under the shadow of an iconic father, the lifelong search for my own authenticity, and the gnawing need to prove myself over and over, or, as William describes it, a "worthiness-hustling personality." As another child of an iconic father, William reveals that he, too, has desperately sought approval and recognition throughout his life, so much so that it has become part of his very character, even his cellular makeup. Yet I also see him as a light-bearer, bringing the glow of truth to painful, dark corners of self-torment and tunnels of emotional danger. He is like a modern Persephone, going into the underworld to retrieve his own unbroken spirit and bringing it to the surface to show those of us waiting by the entrance what it means to be truly alive—and to be truly alive means to find out who we are, in our fullness, in our essence, and at our core, and to understand that what constitutes fulfillment in one may be misery in another. What heals one person may deepen the wound in another. Recovery—and I use the word with a capital "R" in an all-encompassing sense, body, mind, and spirit—is different for every person. Every human being must find their own unique way, and that journey doesn't resemble the way forward for anyone else, where we each may encounter our bespoke moments of grace and revelation.

William's way was layered and painful, and yet all along included a persistent desire to help others. In every obstacle, in every confusing or tortured moment, there was something in him that knew the current experience could be of use to another suffering soul at a later date. That is a high calling—the path of a shaman.

William clarified something for me personally that has been deeply illuminating: there is no difference between the saved and the lost, and "when your fear of failure outweighs your faith in your essential worthiness, it will make you hide behind some kind of show." But he follows that insight with "you deserve better than that." We all deserve better. We all deserve the power of our own authenticity, the joy of being seen and known, with our imperfections only signaling our humanity, not telegraphing that we are "wrong" or defective.

William and I are both performers, albeit under different spotlights and on different stages. I don't crave drugs or alcohol, or carry the burden of addiction, but I certainly know what it is to crave numbness from pain. I have sought refuge in my work, in travel, in therapy, and in mindless distractions. Some of those things have led me to insight and relief, but some have just thrown a blanket over a gnawing discontent, fear, and chronic restless anxiety.

Of the many drops of wisdom and truth I found in *Broken Open,* some of the most enlightening were to be assured that our "defaults" of character are merely "unhelpful" traits. That our failures and imperfections have the resonance of authenticity—they are parts of our stories and our selves that deserve love and acceptance. That every moment is an opportunity to live a more honest life. That shame is a poison, and it is an ongoing, perhaps lifetime practice to flush it from our system. That "recovery" is individual—it can mean very different things to each of us at different times in our life. That our human concept of miracles is limited by our imagination, that service to others is liberating, and that real humility is a key to growth.

As William concludes, "Smoothing every story into a version that fits a single framework fails to do justice to the truth of our differences." There is so much freedom in that statement, so much to relax into. Our authentic selves are unique, and these totally individual and pristine creations deserve compassion and respect.

I felt moments of joy reading *Broken Open*. I felt the experience of being truly seen. I felt a sense of liberation by the permission William gives to not try so hard, to not avoid the truth of pain and shame, but to wander a path that is utterly authentic, even if it sometimes seems circuitous or slow. As William says, "Recovery begins the moment you first want to get well." I read "well" as "real," and I understand that recovery means to reclaim the lost parts of ourselves. We may travel separate roads, we may climb and fall, and start again, and we may shed old selves as we endeavor to release our authentic self into the world, but as Ram Dass once said, "We are all just walking each other home." William Moyers and his story make a great companion.

Rosanne Cash

Preface

A few weeks ago, a man I've never met left a voicemail on my office phone. His call came from a treatment center in Colorado. "My counselor told me to read your book because our stories really are all the same," he said, his voice quivering with emotion. "She was right. I feel I know you. If you can make it, maybe I can make it this time. Your book saved my life."

I am gratified that my first book, *Broken: My Story of Addiction and Redemption*, has stood the test of time. It continues to help people who are struggling for sobriety and looking for hope. It has also found an audience with family members who are desperate to find a solution for the person they love. And yet the book has stood still *in time* too. Like any memoir it is a snapshot—albeit a long one—of the first forty-six years of my life. In it I detail my decade and a half of drug use—a career that began with casual use of marijuana and alcohol as a teenager and progressed to a full-blown addiction to anything and everything (but mostly to cocaine) by the time I was thirty. I also describe what it took for me to find sobriety and figure out how to keep it. The stops and starts of my first attempts at recovery were punctuated by relapse after relapse and one treatment after another. The book ends in grateful triumph as I celebrate the clean and sober days and personal and professional successes that added up to a decade clean and sober.

I knew when I finished *Broken* that I had a long way to go in recovery, but I had absolutely no clue what obstacles I would run into in the years that followed. The futility of the fight to solve my wife's mental illness. My longing for intimacy and an ill-fated affair. A melanoma diagnosis, twice. The sorrow of love lost, divorce, and a family torn apart and left incomplete. The utter exhaustion and the ironic, intoxicating fulfillment of solo parenting three children who were all morphing into teenagers. And then love found when I least expected it.

Turning the pages that recount the years of my life, outlined in my journals, I relive the intimate experiences. Bad teeth and well-meaning dentists. Chronic pain and pill prescriptions in the middle of a national opioid epidemic. My recovery journey no longer guided simply or solely by the well-worn pathway I learned in Alcoholics Anonymous (AA). Shame and blame from people who have dedicated their lives to smashing stigma. Missteps and messes. Euphemisms, half-truths, and outright lies. Disasters with my own footprint smack dab in the middle of the nastiest of them.

In those years I came face-to-face with a stealthy shadow that had kept pace with me, stride for stride, for two decades. Twenty years after I left a crack house for the last time, addiction found me in the pharmacy. This time, with these powerful pills at work on my mind and body, my tried-and-true routes to recovery disappeared in confusing weeds or led to abrupt and unexpected dead ends. I was lost and alone, scared, uncertain where to turn next. I felt estranged from people who had walked with me for so many years, cut off from the movement I had committed my life to serving. I felt the sting of stigma, the slashes of guilt, and there were far too many times when I was convinced I could not find the strength or the courage to go on.

Broken was published in 2006, before any of this, the rest of my life, happened. In the years since, I have met many people who thank me for that book's candor. "That must have been really hard to write about," they often say. A few even call me "brave." Though I am careful to acknowledge and even affirm their compliment, I've never seen it that way. For me, writing about the gritty and outright ugly incidents I experienced under the influence, the futility of relapse, the hurt I caused others, and the toxic shame that is the main ingredient in the insanity of addiction was easy because it was in the past. That was the story of who I was once, before recovery made me into someone new and better.

In this way every addict's memoir I've read, including mine, has been V-shaped. The stories begin with a downward slide and head south quickly to new depths of despair before bottoming out. The low point becomes a launching pad for an upward climb to a substance-free life, happily ever after. Some version of "V for Victory" is always the last line, written in the bright blue sky of redemption, hopefully on the way to becoming a bestseller. "I was lost but now am found," our narratives of falling and rising rarely follow any other pattern.

As satisfying as redemption stories are, and as helpful as they can be in providing assurance and hope to people who think they're beyond helping, their usefulness is limited. I have come to believe with all my heart that for most of us who survive our addictions, an ongoing life of recovery cannot be described by—and should not be expected to match—the endlessly upward streak that completes the V.

Recovery from my addictions to cocaine and alcohol was the end of the book I wrote in 2006, but it is not the end of my story. My life since *Broken* has been a roller coaster of ups and downs, a crazy-quilt of intimate heartbreak and heartfelt thrills, a handful of jaw-dropping close calls, and always the relentless rush of interactions when helping others in crisis surely saved me from my own dark and dangerous crisis. All of these events and experiences have driven the evolution of my journey. Today I understand that there is more to my healing and well-being than simple sobriety. Recovery is the ongoing and rewarding challenge of the life I get to keep living.

The book you are holding in your hands or are viewing on a screen or are listening to right now doesn't follow the V-shaped pattern because the rest of my life hasn't followed it. This book doesn't offer a new pattern. Instead, it explains openly what I have come to believe through what I have lived—up close and personal—and what I stand up for professionally as a national advocate for treatment and recovery today. I don't know if this next chapter of my story will save anybody. I hope it does. At the very least I hope it offers each of you permission to imagine that there is a way for every one of us to recover our lives from the debilitating disorders of addiction—even if we have failed or flamed out or been turned off time after time.

A few years ago, I gave a speech at an urban treatment

center in New Orleans. A man rushed to the podium when I was done. "Damn man, I want what you have," he practically shouted, his burly arms reaching out to enfold me in a bear hug. "Someday I know I'm gonna get there, I promise."

I hugged him back and told him I believed in him. And, like I always do, I pulled a card from my back pocket with my email address and phone number on it. I urged him to stay in touch. For a moment I wanted to add "Be careful what you ask for. There is way more to me and my journey than you know." But there were others waiting to greet me—and besides, what would I say? I was still a long way from figuring out what it was that I had, where I was going, and how the heck to explain it all.

■

1

Broken

1989–2006

I show my scars so that others know they can heal.
— RHACHELLE NICOL'

"Here hon, let me fix you up so you look the part." A makeup artist covered in tattoos gently interrupted my pacing and guided me to a chair so she could work her magic. For a few minutes she applied a bunch of creams, serums, and powders to my face—products I'd never heard of, let alone used. This included something amazing that made the bags under my eyes disappear. As she leaned closer, she whispered, "I'm in recovery too, baby. I'm proud of you."

It was early in the morning on Monday, September 25. The year was 2006. My agent had landed a prime-time, live interview for me on *Good Morning America* the same day my memoir was officially released in Barnes & Noble bookstores across the country. *Broken: My Story of Addiction and Redemption* was on its way into the world—and people were interested.

I showed up that morning dressed in a jacket and tie, but I was ragged. Hesitating nervously in the greenroom's doorway,

I had looked less like a recovery success story and more like a guy who had partied too hard the night before. Excited and terrified by the prospect of being in such a spotlight, I had barely slept. The magic woman's skill and kindness worked their miracles. I smiled, and even without the makeup, I bet I would have looked better. I felt better. I breathed deeply. I was ready to go.

I could hardly believe it—seven uninterrupted minutes of free airtime one-on-one with journalist Chris Cuomo of ABC television and, in the next days and weeks, dozens of radio and TV interviews, including with Terry Gross at NPR and Larry King on CNN. *People* magazine had bought exclusive rights to my story. This kind of national media attention—short-lived as it always turns out to be—is every author's dream. And it was happening to me.

When I heard the news about the magazine feature earlier in the year, I called my coauthor Kathy Ketcham, who had just rafted the Colorado River and was sound asleep in a motel. "We got *People* magazine!" I shouted, for she seemed so far away. "*People*?" she repeated. I imagined her sitting up in the motel bed, smiling ear to ear. All those months of hard work were paying off. "This is big, William! Really, really big."

It *was* big—at least it felt that way to me. By the time the three-page spread filled with photos of my family and me appeared in September 2006, my life resembled the chart of a twelve-year stock market bull run. The upward trajectory was thrilling and hard to believe all at once. I was the author of a hardcover book that felt utterly satisfying to grip in my hands—347 pages of my life story to share with millions of people. *Broken* was in the world not just to sell books—though I surely hoped a lot of people would buy it—but to help others who were broken in their addiction and without hope find the inspiration to get well too. After so many years of disaster and failure, and another decade-plus of hard work, trial-and-error learning, and growth in recovery, I finally felt like I had earned the good things that were coming my way.

THERE WAS NO WAY to conclude that my journey was anything other than inspiring. In so many predictable ways, the stories I shared in *Broken* told a tale no different from what you hear in the rooms of recovery or read about in the genre of addiction memoir, whose authors are usually addicts and alcoholics with celebrity followings or notorious backgrounds. I was neither famous nor notorious, though my last name was well known and respected—my parents are the journalists Judith and Bill Moyers.

What made my story stand out is that, unlike most authors in recovery, I waited more than a decade after I stopped drinking and smoking crack to write it. I wanted to tell the world about the redemptions of recovery as well as the loss and despair that always come with addiction. I wanted to use my story and my platform to dispel the stigma that continues to harm people with substance use disorders. I wanted to show readers that recovery was and is possible.

Growing up, I had dreamed of being an author. For years after I found sobriety, I resisted the urgings of friends and colleagues to turn my story into a book. In those first years of recovery what did I know? All I really knew was I didn't know enough to have a convincing, authentic, and credible perspective. Only with time and space, and only in the context of knowing my life free from it, would I really understand what my addiction meant. Only then would I feel confident enough to chronicle my journey and share it with the world.

The years between my final stint at treatment and my appearance in that kind makeup artist's chair at the television studio were filled with hundreds of Twelve Step meetings, many weekend retreats focused on working the Steps, and day-by-day living in the capital city of St. Paul, Minnesota—which happens to be home to one of the largest communities of people in recovery in America. All this helped to solidify my appreciation for the blessings and the challenges of rebuilding a life after addiction.

What I learned and did during those years worked for me. I stayed sober, one day at a time. As Bob C., my sponsor in Atlanta, counseled me so many years ago—back when I was listening to but not living the wisdom he shared so freely—I stayed "in the middle of the bed," wrapped in the support of my AA community, guided by the Steps and principles we shared, shaped by the weeks and months and years I counted as free from the drugs and drink that could have, should have, killed me. I was grateful to be alive and proud of my recovery.

I was also proud of my day job. I had gained credibility as a public policy advocate with years of down-in-the-trenches work and up-at-the-podium speaking across the country, pushing federal lawmakers to expand access to treatment. I did this work for the Hazelden Foundation (now the Hazelden Betty Ford Foundation), a nonprofit institution of worldwide renown with a decades-old mission of helping people like me. Ironically, I had relapsed twice after attending their treatment center, first in 1989 and then again in 1991, when I walked out against the advice of my counseling team. Only a handful of years later I was becoming one of the organization's public faces.

I GAVE MY FIRST public talk in 1997 at a Rotary Club luncheon in St. Paul about a year after I started working at Hazelden. My prepared remarks were full of what I thought were compelling statistics about the impact of addiction in the workplace and in society, but just minutes into my speech, I noticed to my horror that I was losing my audience. People were yawning and dozing off, glancing at their watches, and surreptitiously slipping away from the hotel ballroom. I realized I had to say something different if I was going to save the moment.

I abandoned my typed pages and said, "This disease is alcoholism and drug addiction. And I have it. I am a drug addict and an alcoholic. This is what one looks like. Take a good look at me."

The room fell silent. Forks froze in midair as the energy changed from bored indifference to keen attention. A few men who were about to exit stopped to listen. I sensed that my words shocked them. I didn't fit their perception of someone who might be susceptible to addiction or in recovery from it. When I finished my talk, there were a few moments of silence. Then a few claps. Then sustained and standing applause.

In the days that followed I got a few phone calls from people who had heard my speech, including from a father who was sick with worry about his teenage son and a business owner who told me how each of his colleagues around the table were deeply moved by my talk, but none of them knew he was an alcoholic in recovery. "Your speech got me thinking that maybe I should tell them my story too," he said.

After that presentation for the Rotary Club, I realized that my personal story didn't have to stay private. Going public—being honest about my experience and my journey—was the most effective way I saw to break through the stereotypes and smash the stigma that causes so many people to hide their problems, live in secrecy and shame, and avoid getting help.

Since that morning—for better or worse—my life and work have been entwined, guided by the belief that when we addicts and alcoholics stand up and speak openly about how addiction affects our lives and how recovery—in truly miraculous and unforeseen ways—has changed our lives for the better, we can help others see that a new life is possible. We offer ourselves as evidence. We share our lived experience through stories that testify not only to the severity of the problems addiction poses but also to the solutions that are available and the victories that can be achieved. In doing so, we chip away at the layers of confusion and misunderstanding that accompany this disease. Addiction can affect anyone, but recovery is possible for everyone too. People of all colors, religions, socioeconomic backgrounds, and political persuasions can find hope and help. With support and luck and work, we can all get well.

What started as a job at Hazelden became a community for me. Here I had found a place to learn more about addiction and its treatment than I could possibly have anticipated, as well as a mission within which I could discover and practice what I soon came to see as my vocation. All the bad years of my life and my story—my failures and flaws—could be used for a purpose that was both noble and of life-or-death importance. As I had been rescued and redeemed, I could offer that same grace to others. And I could do this all the time! I was the happiest I have ever been while I was on the road giving speeches, in my office or at home taking phone calls, and responding to letters and emails from people in crisis. The higher-ups at Hazelden supported me every step of the way. It was a perfect fit.

We also fought stigma together—a fight that continues. Even today, only one in ten people with a diagnosable substance use disorder seeks treatment for it. People are ashamed to admit they need help, and even those who do get treatment and find recovery are often reticent to share their stories with people outside their inner circles or the halls of the fellowship. Shame has kept too many of us too quiet for too long. Supporting and defending drug addicts and alcoholics while pleading for the need to provide intensive, ongoing care for the disease of addiction has never been a popular vocation in a world where people with addiction are frequently viewed with suspicion at best, and contempt or disgust at worst.

This work became my passion, rooted as it was in my own story of catastrophe and redemption. And when things weren't going well at home, or I was consumed with worry or regret or troubled by old shame or feelings of inadequacy and self-doubt, I could always turn toward someone who needed and wanted what I had to give.

When people come to me for help, prompted by hearing a talk I gave, seeing an interview in the media, or reading one of my books, I see myself in them. I hear my own voice in their words. Their pain and despair resonates with the deep memory of my own. I understand the fear and helplessness they feel. I recognize the hesitations and silent spaces in their speech. I also remember the hands that have been held out to me. I remember the faith that others have placed in me when I had none in myself—the unswerving belief that I could make it. I don't know how to say this without sounding a little bit crazy, but when people reach out to me, in my mind and heart, we are not two but one. We're united by a need we share because of our disease. In my efforts to help them, I am also trying to save myself.

From the crack houses of New York City, Atlanta, and Washington, DC, to a role as a recovery champion at a place like Hazelden to a six-figure advance for my first memoir and a multi-page photo spread and feature story in a national magazine, the upward trajectory of my successes felt stunning. This stretch of time, with all the excitement and anticipation and applause—all the productivity and promise of my public and professional careers and the sense of personal purpose I had found in helping people—should have been one of the most thrilling periods of my life. But it wasn't. The strands of my life, so carefully woven during these rich years, were starting to unravel.

IN OCTOBER OF 1994, I lay on my side on the floor of a detox center in Smyrna, Georgia. We had been in Atlanta for three years, brought there by a dream job at CNN. It was my fourth attempt at treatment, this time following a four-day cocaine binge that I had hoped would kill me. I was alone, wretched, sick in body, mind, and spirit. There was nothing left in me to give or to take. In the stillness that accompanied that empty moment, I was able to listen. And then I heard. *St. Paul.* A whisper. I looked around and no one was there. *St. Paul.* Where did those words come from? I always thought of the whisper as divinely inspired—a God moment.

I knew somehow, in that split second, that I had to walk away from my journalism career, sell our house, and move my wife and two baby boys back to Minnesota. It was clear that my way of trying to stay sober wasn't working and someone, somewhere—who knew what or when or why or how—was telling me to go to the place where my wife and I first met, the place where the two of us had tasted success at staying sober. We could start over again in St. Paul.

The Moyers family left Atlanta in the spring of 1995. Allison flew to Minneapolis with the boys while I brought the car. As I drove north, the green landscapes of Tennessee and Missouri gave way to the dark, still-melting fields of Iowa, and I remembered how excited we had been back in 1992 when we crossed these same fields headed south. Allison grew up beneath the Bermuda sunshine and I was a Texas boy. We had never made peace with the Minnesota winter, and yet here we were, heading back to the land of icy sidewalks and early sunsets, sober but jobless. Hopeful but hazy on the details of how we'd make it.

Was it folly? Naivete? Probably. We arrived in St. Paul with wide eyes, big dreams, and vague plans. We knew where we wanted our new life to take root, but that was about it. We spent a big chunk of our savings on a grand-but-crumbling house with a wraparound porch, one of many like it that rose atop the city's Summit Hill in the 1880s, when the men whose last names now label landmarks and streets were making their fortunes.

I doubted I'd make a fortune in St. Paul (or have a street named after me), but I knew this was where I had to be. By the time we moved into our house, I had been out of treatment for less than a year. Within days we were anchored back into the local AA community. I had my old sponsors, Bob B. and Paul L., and a home group in the basement of a church a few blocks from where we lived. As 1995 came to a close, sobriety was my priority: go to meetings, read the literature, visit the county detox, and hang out with people just like me. When I wasn't involved in some AA activity, I was pursuing my most challenging and rewarding role ever: being a sober dad to toddler Henry and baby Thomas. I was awake and aware and at ease for the first time in decades.

Beyond my family, those Twelve Step meetings were my life. The Twin Cities is flush with AA and NA and Al-Anon groups. On the St. Paul side of the Mississippi, nearly every church hosts a meeting, and the neighborhood coffee shops are gathering spots for people in recovery. It seemed like no matter where I went or what I was doing, I always crossed paths with people I recognized from AA. We started to re-alize that these "fellow travelers" were doing the same thing as us: raising kids, working jobs, running errands, and living life, all while staying sober. It was amazing and affirming and reassuring. No matter how I felt or what I had on my plate in those days, I knew in my bones that I wasn't alone in it. There was a spring in my step. I was grateful to be alive.

Some who have followed my story have opinions about our choice to come back to this city. "It was your 'safe place,'" a friend once said, "far away from the temptations you found in New York and Georgia." What my friend forgets is that I had gotten high in St. Paul, too, between my two treatments at Hazelden. Though perhaps not as notorious as the intersection of Boulevard and Ponce de Leon in Atlanta, the spot where Selby Avenue crosses Lexington Parkway used to be a reliable place to score. On a cold night in the winter of 1991, I hid inside a closet in a dingy apartment on that corner while my distraught father searched for me. He had flown in when Allison called to say I'd disappeared. They had been looking for me for days.

Another landmark from that sad week of my life is a little further away. Charles Avenue runs north of and parallel to University. In the 600 block, just west of Dale, there's a gray duplex with loose gutters and a sagging chain-link fence. I recall how cold it was there as dawn broke on February 15, 1991, and I remember the bitter shame I felt when my credit ran dry and my bullshit bravado stopped working with the people I had paid to help me buy and use cocaine. This is the place where I finally called home, on a borrowed landline phone, and asked Allison to come pick me up.

"Oh, William," she said, exhausted. "Where are you?" I gave her the address and waited in the frozen light that filtered through the plastic-wrapped front window. I felt empty and angry and alone.

The intersection of Lexington and Selby is about a half mile from the home we bought together in 1995. That house on Charles in the Frogtown neighborhood is a five-minute drive from our stately neighborhood on the hill. About a month or two after we moved back to St. Paul, I was driving—probably to the hardware store for some supply or tool that one of the endless house projects required in those early days—and decided to drive past these places, plus a few more. Bars where I drank. Corners where I met a dealer or someone else who had a hookup. Houses in which I smoked crack and freebased cocaine.

Many of the places in which I used drugs also housed kids and other family members—people whose lives were linked with or even depended on an addicted parent or son or daughter. Usually these people passed beneath my notice, fixated as I was on the needs of my disease. They were watching me, though. Years after I had returned to the city, in a hallway beside a restaurant, a teenager stopped in his tracks when he saw me. "Hey mister, you're the man who was with my sister a few years ago—on Charles." I was stunned for a second, then stammered, "Are you Janette's brother?" I didn't recall his name, one of a pack of kids who seemed to outnumber the adults in that house. "Yeah, that's me. I remember because you were the only White man who came around and didn't cause us trouble." He told me that his sister, who was pregnant when we were smoking crack together, had given birth to a baby girl. "She's beautiful," he said with a smile. "They're fine!"

I don't know precisely why I returned to these locations in the late 1990s, but I do know it wasn't because I craved the drugs I had used there. Perhaps I was testing my resolve—like an experiment with the ice on a lake in winter. Would the sobriety I had been given be enough to bear the weight of my walking again in this city? Maybe I wanted a kind of rite of passage in which I literally passed through the neighborhoods of my shame—the valleys that still contained shadows of death—and went on to demonstrate to myself and the world that I was an honorable homeowner and a productive member of society by purchasing drywall screws and lightbulbs at the Ace Hardware on Grand. Maybe it was journalistic curiosity or a grungy nostalgia for the simpler, if starker, demands that era made on me.

Today, I believe that I traced those old routes to remind myself that those days were real and that they were and would be a part of me forever. I could grow and change, but my identity would always include the marks and the memories of my past. I'm not the type of person who can make neat distinctions between the person I was in previous chapters of my life and the person I am today. I'm told that some of us have brains that work in this way: there's no "Old William" and "New William." For me, there's just me—just William. There are probably events and experiences I don't remember clearly, of course, but for the most part—and without deciding to do so—I carry my past right along with me in the present. In the same way, the people and places I've encountered along my journey continue to matter, even as what they mean to me—and how I tend the memories they left with me—evolves and transforms as I do.

I HIT BOTTOM as a thirty-year-old alcoholic crackhead in the sticky New York City summer of 1989. I started keeping a journal shortly thereafter—in a three-subject Mead notebook purchased by my mother. Though faded a bit with the passage of years, its $1.79 price tag remains affixed to the cover. My family was shocked when my secret life was revealed. They did not know what to do, except follow the emergency advice of a trusted family doctor. To keep me out of the crack house and off the streets, I was admitted to a locked psychiatric ward of St. Vincent's Hospital in Greenwich Village. A few days later, my mom came to visit. She brought along salty snacks and bottled water, hoping that these things would help to restore my ravaged body. She also gave me that cheap spiral-bound notebook, with the suggestion that writing on its blank pages might be a good way to sharpen my scrambled brain. She hinted that maybe someday I'd want to look back on what I had written.

At first I had neither the energy nor the guts to consider the disaster my life had become under the influence and no way to put words to my anguish, never mind my hopes and dreams. Finally, four days after I was admitted to the unit, hateful and sad, bored, angry, and desperate to get high again, I opened the notebook and started to write.

I haven't stopped.

On the opening page in that initial journal was a draft "To Whom It May Concern" letter intended for the administration of St Vincent's. In it, I thank them for helping me get "back on my feet" (after four whole days of restless and involuntary sobriety) and politely request a transfer to another program. I cite "differences of opinion with members of the staff" as evidence that this was not the place for me.

I wish I could say that this early composition was the only time I penned absolute bullshit into one of my journals. It's not. My entries over the thirty-plus years since that summer of 1989 describe a journey of stops and starts, reflecting various states of mental and emotional health—the vagaries of a recovery that didn't "take" for a handful of years. The notebooks and hardbound journals that fill an entire shelf of my home library include a written record of the lies I convinced myself to believe as well as trenchant observations, borrowed quotations, and mundane-but-also-poignant details that would otherwise be forgotten.

It's here in my journals, more than anywhere else, that I consider the big human questions. Who am I (and *why* am I like this)? What's my purpose in this life? I explore my recovery. I appeal to God—and not just when I feel lost or alone but also when I find myself overwhelmed with gratitude for this gift of my life. It feels therapeutic to get these things onto the page. Then the noise in my head doesn't seem so loud.

What began with a spiral-bound notebook handed to me by my mother so many years ago continues to this day. I write in my journal almost every morning. In the winter or on cold fall or spring mornings, I do so in a chair by the fireplace with a side table where my journal and meditation books are stacked beside the latest edition of the *New York Times Magazine*. I light the gas fire, start the coffee, feed the cat and dog, and unload the dishwasher. Then I sit down and write, in silence and solitude, reflecting on the events of the day before and looking forward to the challenges of the day ahead. When the weather is warmer, I sit on my front porch and watch the sun rise or wave to neighbors and strangers on their morning walk or run.

I treasure my journals because they offer a remarkably unbroken narrative of a life that is pocked with fractures and false starts as well as moments of wonder and triumph. It's completely biased, of course. There's grandiosity and self-indulgence in my journal entries, side by side with honest self-assessment and evidence of a soul in search of meaning. Some entries are just bullet points or a few sentences or a quote that seems relevant to the moment. When I have the time or there's a lot rattling around inside me, I might write long paragraphs, but entries are rarely more than a page or two.

I've lost and found a lot of things since the summer I landed in St. Vincent's Hospital. My journaling habit has stayed with me. But that Mead notebook wasn't the only life-changing gift I received in August of 1989. The community room in the locked ward of that now-demolished medical center was also the place I first encountered the Twelve Steps.

Beginning with the mandatory group meetings at St. Vincent's—meetings I resented from the start because I was among people with whom I felt I had nothing in common—the program of Alcoholics Anonymous was presented as the only path to my recovery from addiction to crack cocaine and alcohol. In each of the four times I pursued treatment, from 1989 to 1994, the Twelve Steps—documented in the blue book with the blank cover that insiders know as the Big Book, but what is officially titled *Alcoholics Anonymous*—showed me how to stop using the substances that were killing me. The testimonies in the Big Book taught me that it was possible to stop *need-*

ing these substances. They showed me that my problem was more fundamental than drinking and using—that my addictions crouched on top of deeper wounds caused by my inability and unwillingness to live life according to life's terms. Their stories also offered hope that I could start living a better life—a life of connection and service and gratitude and joy.

It took a few years and repeated lessons for me to "get it," but finally I did. Since that moment, I have never doubted the value of AA and the fellowship of people like me that it has freed from the hells of addiction. Without these things, the past three decades of my life would have been miserable. I'd probably be dead from the effects of my illness.

Of all the self-help books and recovery memoirs I've collected over the years, it is only the Big Book that I continue to read over and over. I read it to discover and understand those themes of commonality that explain, in uncomplicated prose, the complexities of my addiction, why my problems are so similar to the stories of others, and what I can do to get better. With chapters like "There Is a Solution," "How It Works," and "Into Action," the Big Book combines inspiration and wisdom, how-to advice and hopeful promises. With few edits and updates, it has stayed in print since before World War II and remains an infallible guide for millions of people in America and around the world who consider themselves members of Twelve Step groups.

The Big Book is perhaps the earliest example of a collection of personal stories about alcoholic debauchery and futility. It's unique in that it was assembled *by* alcoholics *for* alcoholics, with the express purpose of explaining what life was like, what happened, and what it is like now for Bill Wilson and his friend Dr. Bob Smith. Several dozen other early AA members added their stories as well, all in an effort to help individuals who suffered from the same illness of alcoholism.

The Big Book was the first book I ever read that describes what it means to be an alcoholic and how to stop being one. I've collected several copies, one for every time I went to treatment, each time wanting desperately to believe that those stories of fresh starts and spiritual awakening could also be my story. The dog-eared hardback on my shelf is the first one I ever owned. I received it at Hazelden.

On August 28, 1989, I left New York City for a place called Minnesota. Under my own power and willingly, though with nervous anticipation, I walked past the admissions portico at Hazelden. *"Read this* and you'll understand why you're here," a counselor told me that day, handing me this book. *"Live this* and you'll never need to be here again." The Big Book is to many alcoholics or addicts what I always assumed the Bible is to people who go to church. It isn't enough to read it. You've got to let it work on you and in you. You have to understand and apply what's in it to day-to-day life.

At the time, I couldn't *live* the path outlined in the Big Book and explained by the kind counselors who wanted to help me change. Applying its principles and practices was beyond me in the fall of 1989. After spending a month in residential care and four more at Hazelden's halfway house in St. Paul, I would end up in treatment again (and again and again), demonstrating by example how embodying the Big Book's wisdom is a lot harder than reading it.

Finally in 1994 the words fell in. The Twelve Steps, and the communities of care and practice and peer support they continue to form, saved me. As I pursued my recovery in St. Paul, these things became the fixtures around which I ordered my days. The people in the rooms where we read the Big Book together and told our own stories of "the way we used to be, what happened, and the way we are now" were brothers and sisters to me. We accompanied each other through highs and lows, comings and goings, births and deaths. We walked our walks along a tried-and-true pathway of self-examination, forgiveness, and surrender. The Steps promised progress—a slow but sure journey from the dark horrors of addiction to the robust beauty and wonders of everyday life. We lived by a simple and sacred truth: use drugs again and they will kill you. Drink another drop and you're dead. Maybe not today or tomorrow, but under the influence the horrors will certainly return. And when they do, every good, decent, honorable part and piece of you will be eaten alive.

These beliefs, supported and sustained by the practices and rituals of AA, provided the unassailable foundation for my life in the 1990s and beyond. I worked the Twelve Steps to keep at bay my proclivity for substances. I followed their guidance so I could live as someone who was continually striving to become a better person. They helped me check myself when I wandered toward dangerous ground. For many years I believed that my ongoing survival was contingent on constant acknowledgment of my powerlessness and rigorous application of the Steps.

These things were sacred to me, in the sense that they were to be treated carefully, tenderly, respectfully. I was taught that *recovery* is about maintaining *sobriety,* which depended on *abstinence.* As I understood it, this required a combination of humble hard work, selfless service, and constant vigilance. The stakes were so high! Life stood on one side, and death on the other. Life offered the possibility of happiness, of goodness. The other option was a slippery slope back to all the evils that accompanied addiction—all the guilt, shame, and despair that for so long had hurt people I loved and made my existence unbearable.

I wasn't just a believer. I became an evangelist—fluent in the language of recovery and increasingly comfortable sharing it in front of a crowd. Armed with the hard-won wisdom of my experience in AA, cheered on by a community who embraced me as a champion and advocate, and handed a platform by Hazelden, I spread the news about addiction and redemption. Well before my story became a book, I was becoming known among policymakers and journalists as well as the general public as somebody who had figured out how to make it in recovery and who knew how to help others do the same. By the time *Broken* was finding an audience, many understood that I knew a few things. Beyond being a reliable source for a pithy quote about addiction and recovery, I was a person you could point to or look at and be assured that getting and staying clean was possible, that the program worked. My story showed the world that even a serial loser like me could turn his life around step by step and become a sober success.

IN THE NEARLY two decades since the *People* photograph was taken, I have only looked at it twice. When the article was published, I took in the whole of it: my wife, my children, and me, right in the center. Our family. My family. In that moment, I wanted to believe that everything I had worked so hard and so long to put back together and build into the perfect example of recovery had been achieved. It had come to be, and *I* had come to be. Here, on these public pages, was my proof.

Today I reach with trepidation into a cardboard banker's box on a high shelf of the closet where I store important things. The box holds photo albums, colorful pictures the kids scrawled on special days growing up, letters from my parents, and four copies of the magazine. A copy for each of the kids and one for me. I never gave my children theirs because I worried they would feel like I do now, as old wounds open up to reveal the raw pain of regrets and lost opportunities.

The photograph shows our family, intact, posing confidently at the base of the grand staircase in our home in St. Paul. My son Thomas, then twelve, has his arm around me. My right arm rests on fourteen-year-old Henry, our firstborn. Allison stands next to me, her arm resting on the carved banister, her hand lightly touching the back of my head like a blessing. Next to Allison stands our nine-year-old daughter, Nancy Judith, with her arm wrapped securely around her mother's waist. In the picture we hold on to each other; we are connected, intertwined, unbreakable, a family whose very existence is indebted to the reality of recovery. We are living evidence that the promises can come true.

"We have nothing to hide," the captioned quote from Allison proclaims.

STANDING IN THE quiet hallway beside my family's unboxed mementos, looking at the photograph, I remember the words I first heard in the rooms of recovery: "Beware those times when your outsides don't match your insides." No one could see that the smiling man sitting up so straight and tall—so grateful to be surrounded by the people he loved best in the world—was ravaged by a violent thrash of emotions, struggling to square what was happening to him. The camera didn't capture my sense of futility or my powerlessness. *This can't be happening this way* became a silent mantra that I repeated to myself a dozen times a day. I was drowning and it seemed there was nothing I could do to stay afloat, that I was just not strong enough to swim against the crosscurrents that propelled me further and further from what I wanted and needed my story to be.

■

2

Breaking Up

2005–2008

We have been compelled to abandon
the ship, which is crushed
beyond all hope of ever being righted. . . .
It is hard to write what I feel.

— ERNEST SHACKLETON, OCTOBER 27, 1915

Since the first anniversary of my sobriety, October 12, 1994, I've kept my recovery chips in an old jewelry box. Over time it has filled up with the medallions marked in Roman numerals that are commonly given at AA meetings. I have received one of these coins for each of the years I've been free from the grip of alcohol and drugs. By the time *Broken* was transforming from a collection of anecdotes and reflections into an actual book, I had ten medallions to mark my own decade of sobriety, plus a handful of special chips handed down to me from fellow travelers along the way. In the years since, I've dropped many more into the box.

Marked with slogans and symbols intended to inspire perseverance and remind recipients of the lifesaving grace of day-by-day sobriety, those milestone medallions tell one story about my life. They don't tell the whole story. They say nothing about who I am as a father to my kids or how I show up as a son to my parents. They don't testify to my qualities as a neighbor or a friend or committed employee, nor do they reveal the shape of my inner life. They also don't say anything about what it's like to be married to me.

AS FALL GAVE WAY to winter in 2005, not long after receiving my eleven-year token, I had an affair. It was a mess. I was stupid and selfish. Worse, I was stone-cold sober. I knew what I was doing even if I couldn't understand why I was doing it.

Over the course of the next three years, even as Allison and I continued to mark recovery anniversaries alongside our kids' birthdays and other milestones, the marriage we shared would crumble, despite the things we tried to do to preserve our family.

My affair was brief and regrettable. It ended almost as quickly as it began. And though its lingering effects contributed mightily to the unraveling of our relationship, it was itself a symptom of deeper chaos and unease within and between Allison and me. My wife was struggling with mental illness—a complex diagnosis that warranted stays in residential treatment facilities far from our home in the Midwest. By the time the leaves had fallen off the trees along the Mississippi's limestone bluffs that autumn, Allison had been physically away from us for months. Emotionally she had been missing for far longer.

Left to manage the demands of day-to-day home life with three busy kids (Henry nearly thirteen, Thomas eleven, and Nancy eight), along with my fast-paced job and the exhilarating but overwhelming challenge of writing and delivering *Broken* to my publisher, I was running ragged, plagued by a perpetual headache. I squeezed in AA meetings when I could and tried to keep up with journaling, but most of my prayers seemed like some version of *Help!* And my attempts at "conscious contact" with the God of my understanding were few and far between. I was emotionally absent as well, awash in worry and resentment while trying to keep it all together.

There are countless ways to explain or justify seeking intimacy beyond one's marriage, but there is no excuse for infidelity. On lonely late-night walks around the neighborhood or bathed in the glow of my desk lamp in the hours after the kids went to sleep, I attempted to square what I had done with the values I claimed to hold. I came up lacking. I imagined my character defects emerging on my face like pimples. Shame surged within me, and because shame has always been intolerable for me, so did my defensiveness and self-pity. I hadn't yet embraced consistent therapy and had no friend who seemed close enough to trust with such a burden.

I took the kids to Arizona to visit Allison over the Thanksgiving break. Though we had worked to keep Henry and Nancy and Thomas in touch through weekly phone calls and regular packets of notes and drawings sent through the mail, my children hadn't seen their mother in the two-plus months since she had left Minnesota for treatment. The counseling staff agreed a visit was a good idea. She needed to see them, and they needed her. We would celebrate the holiday together.

The reunion was painful. Allison was subdued and distracted. I played the cheerleader, tripping over myself to make sure everyone was upbeat, but my smile was plastic. I felt hollow.

The kids were baffled by my attempts to pretend like things were normal and unsure how to interact with their mother in this unfamiliar setting. We ate turkey and potatoes and cake in the cafeteria. After three days of strained and fumbling together-ness, which included a couple of family counseling sessions, attempts at Ping-Pong, a hike in the desert, and an outing or two to the nearby mall, it was time for us to say goodbye.

That's when we broke.

I will never forget the scene: five of us standing in a parking lot in the desert outside Tucson as my children wailed and my wife wept and the sun set. Thomas cried like I had never heard him do before, his arms wrapped around Allison's waist. Nancy held tight to her leg, unwilling to accept yet another goodbye. Henry hovered beside me, clenched and trembling. The oldest, he had been taking his cues from my behavior all weekend— trying to make everything okay. Now his face was streaked with tears. He suddenly lurched forward, pressing his thin, tall frame against his mother. The four of them huddled together in the failing light, heaving and shuddering like a single body.

I stood apart from them, telling myself that I was letting Allison have her moment, hiding behind my appointed role as sad-but-stoic father, my heart lodged in my throat. Witnessing the anguish of these people I loved was torture. That I was powerless to change any of it was pure agony. It seemed surreal to be here, like this, all of us shattered. A year prior we had been fine, whole, happy. Part of me wanted to scream "No! This can't be! Not them! Not us!" But I stayed silent, shamed by my own secret, scared of what echoes the dark canyons around us would throw back at me.

The kids and Allison gulped air and held on tight. They said "I love you" to each other again and again, repeating the words to extend their leaving and delay the pain of being separated once again. As the last of the light faded behind the jagged mountains in the west, I gently pried Nancy from Allison and guided her toward the rental car. The boys followed. We drove away in heavy silence. The car's headlight beams seemed ineffective against the desert's deep darkness. We were a tiny lifeboat on a midnight sea.

Twenty minutes later, a few blocks from where we were staying, I pulled over beside a convenience store that advertised "scoop ice cream" on a hand-drawn poster in the window. A young woman behind the counter next to the register explained that the options were limited to chocolate, vanilla, or mint chip. Back in the car Thomas and Henry began to banter as they compared their cones, offering each other a taste. Nancy silently attacked hers. I felt myself breathing again.

Later that night, the exhausted kids asleep in the hotel beds beside me, I wrote in my journal: "If today is the bottom, then maybe now Allison and the kids and I can begin to rebuild our sandcastle existence. If today wasn't the bottom, then we are all in deep trouble."

THE FOUR OF US came home to a weirdly warm December in which the snow held off for weeks before falling heavily in the last days of the month. The Moyers family Christmas in St. Paul that year—it was just the kids and me—felt similarly unseasonable. Allison had always been our chief decorator and hostess, the hub of the wheel that spun out holiday magic. We did our best without her. I tried to re-create the look and feel of a classic Christmas, ensuring each child had piles of presents beneath the tree, but I was out of my lane. I knew it, and so did my children. We ate spiral ham and smoked turkey from Vermont that my brother had sent. Henry helped make his favorite Stove Top stuffing from a box. There must have been a couple of store-bought pies. We did our best to stoke the spirit with a few rounds of board and card games, but Allison's absence weighed on all of us. Their godparents, Ellen and Peter Brown, lived across the street and were a godsend to them and to me.

Try as I did to stay present with my kids that Christmas, my attention was elsewhere. I was worried about Allison, alarmed by how compromised she had been in November, and I was perplexed and increasingly paranoid about how I could put back together what was still falling apart. The slow motion of the holidays felt like the calm before a speeding up storm that was going to wreck us all.

Henry, Thomas, and Nancy spent the remainder of their Christmas break with my parents in New York. They were excited to go, and my mom and dad were eager to have the time with them. The kids left on the twenty-sixth, giving me a handful of days by myself. I spent those confused days pacing through the empty house, eating leftovers while watching college football, and dreaming of ways to undo or escape or at least minimize the damage I had done.

I also went to meetings.

The week between Christmas and New Year's Day—like most of the winter holiday season—is a boom time for Twelve Step groups. Many people depend on holiday-adjacent meetings to help them stay sober. AA meetings during this time of year—when overindulgence and alcohol are often portrayed as essential to celebrations—provide a substance-free place to be merry and bright. People are usually happy, even as appreciation and thanksgiving for another year or month of sobriety can sit side by side with painful or embarrassing memories from Christmases past.

I made a point to visit the meeting at Hazelden's Fellowship Club, where so much of my early recovery had its roots. Sitting in that safe place in the dimming days of 2005 offered me an hour or two of respite from the taunts and terrors of my life. *I still have this,* I told myself. *I belong here.* We affirmed each other. Swapped gratitude. I gave hugs and shook hands. Applauded and encouraged others wholeheartedly, even as I kept my shame and my still-too-raw wounds to myself.

In AA, we learn that holding secrets can be like walking around with stones in our shoes. Left to shift and rub, they make moving forward painful if not impossible. Even little ones can cause blisters over time. My affair was no small stone. I felt its presence every day, with every step I took. My usual distractions—work or exercise or the unending labors of solo parenting—provided no real relief. I was stuck in a kind of limbo, as maddening and pathetic as my now-vacant family home.

If this was "life on life's terms," it felt intolerable. I hated what was happening to my family. I wanted to stay married, and I wanted to stay sober; my affair had threatened both. I knew I had to get my shit together. I had to empty the rocks from my shoe. I looked to the Twelve Steps for a path out of my pain. I needed a way to set right the harm I had done to

Allison and to our marriage—to fix it, and thereby regain the comforts of serenity. *Then,* I thought—*then* I would be able to share these comforts with the people I loved. *Then* I could get back to imagining that I was a good man and working like hell to make myself match that image. I had to come clean with my wife, whom I loved.

On the first day of the new year, I flew west again. This time I was by myself. Instead of returning home as we had anticipated, Allison had moved even farther away, deciding to pursue more specialized care, this time in California. I supported this move at first, but the longer she was gone the more my silence was hurting us both. So off I went. My visit came shortly after she had moved into a facility near San Diego. She got permission for a long weekend off-site. I booked a hotel room not far from the beach.

On the plane, I pondered how I would tell Allison about what had happened. It wasn't complicated. I did what I did. It was wrong. I was wrong. I was sorry. There was no other way to spin it or say it. And I *was* sorry, to the bottom of my heart. I was ready to make amends and start rebuilding the trust I had damaged and the marriage I valued. Rigorous honesty was the only solution, I reminded myself. "Half measures," the Big Book counsels, "avail us nothing."

As the plane descended, I could see a sliver of ocean below, where the Pacific met the land. The slim swath of blue grew larger, along with the golds and greens of the hills around the airport. Allison had seemed so changed when I saw her over Thanksgiving, filtered and slowed at times, prickly and abrupt at others. I was descending toward an unknown future, getting closer to the ground and to the reality that awaited me there. I had confidence in the aircraft I was riding in, but I didn't yet know what was in store for my family—whether our landing would be controlled or catastrophic.

I told Allison everything over dinner. She cried. She bit her lip, knotted her hands, clenched her fists. For a moment I saw the woman I had met sixteen years earlier, both of us sharp and awake, riding the bright days of early sobriety. Now her face flashed bolts of anger, then sagged into furrows of sadness. Her eyes searched out mine and locked on. I was transfixed. There was nowhere else for me to look because there was nowhere else for me to go. I didn't move. She shook her head. Was it disbelief or disgust? She asked me why, then answered her own question: "It doesn't matter, does it, William? You did it. I knew it—I suspected it whenever we talked on the phone this past month. You seemed so distant." She stopped talking.

"I'm sorry, Al. I am sorry." I said it again and again. And even though I meant the words, the whole thing felt anticlimactic. Here we were in a rented room, so far from the home we had made together, both of us exhausted by our separate struggles. Too spent to know what to say or what to do next. There wasn't a fight in either one of us, and we had nowhere to run. It felt as though we'd ridden a lifetime of roller-coaster ups and downs in the months that led to this moment.

We made love later that night. Over the weekend we spent together, we ate meals I don't remember. We took a few walks in the breezy sunshine. I answered emails while she napped. We spent several emotional sessions with Allison's counselor, who helped us process what I had revealed and take a few early steps toward the acceptance and reconciliation we both said we wanted. I flew home after a couple more days, relieved that Allison remained in a place where she had people to help and support her healing. I felt lighter for having unburdened myself of a secret and hopeful that we could recover. But I was already second-guessing my visit, worried about having saddled our already-tenuous relationship with this new weight.

Even as I was comforted by Allison's willingness to forgive me for what I had done, for a long time I was plagued by shame about what I had *not* done—as a man who prided myself on having a decade of steady sobriety—to avoid the situation in the first place. I often told myself, *Moyers, sober people just don't do shit like that.*

In the years since the fall of 2005, I've come to learn that most people are not so different from those of us who tend to ascribe our mistakes and failures to the problems we have with substances. Author Beverly Conyers notes that even people who are committed to recovery can be separated from their values and ideals—lured by the charms of what she calls "a quasi-conscious existence." Writing for addicts and their families, she warns, "Our desire to live a sober, more thoughtful life doesn't protect us from slipping into a life of diminished awareness—from taking the path of least resistance." It wasn't a warning that reached me during these years; I'm not convinced I would have listened even if it had. The paths of least resistance are awfully attractive when we're exhausted and unmoored. For the longest time I found it easier to blame my infidelity on what I called "my humanness" than accept it as part of my sobriety—as if the two were separate things.

ALLISON FINALLY RETURNED to St. Paul in February, after five long months away. I stood in the foyer beside the suitcases and watched my family come back together. The kids mobbed their mother with eager updates about their grades in school and what books they were reading. They pulled her toward the stairway so they could show her their clean rooms. In those first happy hours, the house felt full again, complete. Allison was home. We could get back to our lives and our life together. A little later that night, as we held each other close, I marveled at how far we had traveled and how many challenges we had overcome. "We are going to make it," I said. "I know we are." I believe both of us thought it was possible.

At first it seemed easy. We resumed the roles and duties that had always made ours a vibrant, noisy, and mostly orderly household. Allison reclaimed her place as conductor. She took the kids to school and brought them home after. She made sure their clothes were clean and that they had what they needed each day. She planned our meals and cooked them—her forte. With my wife and partner back at the helm, I was able to focus on my work at Hazelden with renewed hope and an ambitious schedule.

After a few weeks of smooth sailing, the persistent realities of our situation troubled the waters. Allison had arrived home changed. She was hurting, despite her brave face, and I was worried, despite my attempts to pretend that all was well and normal. The issues that had led her to seek help in the first place still lurked like rocks just beneath the surface of our lives, made sharper, perhaps, by my breach of her trust.

Allison had returned to St. Paul with an aftercare plan, and she had supports available. We started to see a marriage counselor who offered us strategies for rebuilding our relationship, but it wasn't long before sparks of conflict flashed between us. The buzzy busyness of our family's life was a welcome distraction on some days. On others, it was an excuse to feel overwhelmed and lash out or withdraw from each other.

I had changed as well, in the time she was away. We stepped back into the routines and division of responsibilities that had once been such an effective way to keep house and raise the kids, but before long I realized I wasn't as relieved by her return as I had hoped to be. I found myself missing the days when it was all up to me. Allison's absence had required me to imagine and then endure life without her in the mix. To my surprise, I had learned to appreciate and to pull off—albeit in my own style—the work required to run a family and a home as a solo parent. Matching socks and folding laundry while watching football on television, having shared mealtime conversations, tackling chores on Saturdays, attending church on Sundays followed by brunch at our favorite restaurant on Grand Avenue—these things had become meaningful and reliable parts of a routine for the kids and me.

Though the house looked the same as it had when she left, Allison returned to a home that had been altered by her absence. Everything was recognizable, but it didn't quite fit together as it had in the past. Our world had tilted on its axis. Both of us struggled. Allison with her mental health and me with a long-held conviction that didn't seem true anymore—an often-quoted theme from one of the stories in the Big Book: "Acceptance is the answer to *all* my problems today." I had shared and cited this claim for years. I had found guidance and comfort there, as well as in the pious reminder that comes a few sentences later: "Nothing, absolutely nothing, happens in God's world by mistake."

Bullshit, I thought. These words now felt false and cruel. My life was loaded with mistakes and messes, and it seemed as though God were taking a hands-off approach to the welfare of my wife and family. It's easy to apply acceptance retroactively, to remember past times of turmoil and struggle through the rosy glow of serenity and equanimity, but when the building is actively on fire—when it's coming down around your ears and threatening everything you hold dear—platitudes about acceptance and adjusting your attitude ring hollow. My wife was becoming a stranger in "God's world." My kids were watching their mom and dad float away from each other and from them in "God's world." Our happy household was a half-truth at best. My successful sobriety was stretched thin over all kinds of hurt. The life I had worked so hard to build and maintain was fraying and falling apart. Quoting the Big Book from memory didn't help. The pile of medallions in my keepsake box just sat there. Even my work—so long a source of pride and productivity—seemed futile and overwhelming all at once. What good were these achievements when my family was in so much pain?

The answer to my problems wasn't acceptance—it was fighting! I was scared and angry—angry with myself, angry with Allison, angry that nothing I did seemed to help. All the things I tried, all the ways I sought to make my wife happy and show my kids that our family was okay, somehow seemed to end up hurting us. I hated the idea of failure because I knew how it felt.

I refused to accept that our marriage could die on the vine. I refused to accept what was unacceptable to me.

I had failed at being married before. My first marriage began when we were quite young, and it was saddled from the start with my undiagnosed addiction. *That* marriage was a casualty of my broken brain and bottomless hunger—*that* marriage, and my ability to be the husband Mary needed and deserved, was destroyed by alcohol and drugs. *This one was different.* Allison and I came together through recovery! We had already been through hell and back! How could our story end up like this?

AS THE WINTER of early 2006 slowly gave way to spring, it seemed like *Broken* had a chance to make a big impression. Though it wasn't scheduled to be released until September, my publisher was heavily promoting the book and it was garnering early attention. The reviewer at *USA Today* had asked to preview the book. At the time that paper was ubiquitous, reaching readers from coast to coast. Major television news outlets were showing unusual interest in a title by a first-time author; no doubt my last name was attracting their attention. Positive reviews from these powerhouse media could introduce my book to millions. My agent, Amy Williams, had urged me to write *Broken* for years. When *People* magazine reached out wanting to do a feature on it, she told me that the book could be a bigger hit than any of us anticipated.

This part of being an author excited me. Sharing my story at events, conferences, and interviews with reporters was where I shined. Because of what was happening at home, I was eager to feel productive elsewhere. I told myself that making *Broken* a bestseller would benefit my family—and I knew it had the potential to help a lot of people who shared my experience of addiction. Investing in the success of the book with my time and energy became a welcome occupation. Yet as the attention mounted and the release date approached, I started to get scared too, worried that the tale of redemption I had narrated was already outdated and painfully aware that I might be asked questions I wasn't equipped to answer.

The photo shoot for *People* happened on a sticky, gray day in July. Allison and the kids and I dressed like we were going to a family dinner, each of us sweating in our not-quite-summer clothes. We dabbed at our faces. Smiled when the photographer asked us to. It felt like we were playing roles in a perfect family.

IN THE INTRICACIES of a long relationship between two people, what breaks can never be fully restored. Whether it is small shards or bigger chunks that fall away, what's left of the whole is altered forever. For the next three years, Allison's and my attempts to repair and rebuild our relationship ebbed and flowed. Long periods of peace ended with eruptions of anger. Light days of easy companionship followed dark nights of recrimination and remorse. Months of marriage counseling sessions produced torrents of tears or chilly indifference or careful progress. Heartfelt apologies, vows to be better, threats of self-harm—we experienced them all. Over and over, we were seared by flashes of pain and disappointed by too many mirages masquerading as hope. Both of us were exhausted.

On the home front, Allison found stability and satisfaction

in the kitchen she loved, cooking scrumptious meals for the kids and me. She made sure every one of their birthdays was better than the last with amazing cakes. She supplied us with batches of chocolate chip cookies—usually still warm from the oven as they disappeared into our eager mouths.

I kept up my end of the routines and traditions of family housekeeping. Chores had always been an important assignment in our family, as it was in mine growing up. Whether it was cleaning rooms, mowing the lawn in summer, raking leaves in the fall, or staying on top of shoveling the Minnesota winter snow, each of the kids had their jobs. I'd often find an excuse to help. Working together gave me time to bask in the company of my daughter and sons. It also provided space for us to talk.

My children were trying to understand what was happening to our family. "Are you and Mom going to stay together?" "What's going to happen if you guys get a divorce?" "Why can't the two of you just be happy again?" The pain behind their questions matched the pain I felt by not being able to give them a reassuring answer. "I don't know" is all I could say. "We're doing our best to make it work."

I could see in their faces what I knew in my gut: all of us were scared. We found ourselves living a reality that our previous experience as a family hadn't prepared us for. Despite the routines we tried to maintain, we were awash in an uncertain sea—sometimes stormy, sometimes placid, but always fluid. It felt like the kids were lashed to a barrel, with me swimming alongside, frantically doing my best to keep them upright and safe, all the while struggling to keep my own head above water.

One miracle throughout those hard days was the ongoing

gift of my sobriety. Certainly, this helped keep our family afloat. Craving for alcohol and cocaine never returned, thank God. Not once during the early days of disappointment and drama, not during the years in which Allison and I struggled to put the pieces back together—nor even later as we navigated separation and divorce—did I think a shot or two of warm whiskey or an afternoon at the crack house would make any of it better. There were times I wanted desperately to be free from the mess my life had become, but even at my lowest I knew that the old escape routes were paths to destruction.

In this choppy and swirling season, wherever I was and whatever I was doing, my recovery was a life preserver—its sturdy support buoying me up for the task at hand or offering moments of rest. When I was exhausted or in despair, I knew enough about myself to understand that the only thing harder than going through this sober would be doing it drunk or high. I kept to the path I had been told to follow since my first AA meeting at St. Vincent's: "Don't drink, go to meetings, get on your knees and pray for God's will and the power to carry it out." It worked. On more days than I can count, the habits formed through years of abstinence, daily prayers, and responding to messages and calls from people who needed help kept me from giving up and going under.

On other days, my personal-and-public sobriety felt like an added burden. Trying to live up to an image of success meant hiding flaws and refusing to admit failure. As my marriage frayed and my family flailed and suffered, rarely did I allow myself to lean on things and people who might have helped me. I just held tighter to the ropes I thought could hold everything together. In these moments, being a recovery representative—an inspiring and encouraging example of contended sobriety—seemed less like a lifesaver and more like an anchor; the combined weight of expectation and assumption attached to all those milestone medallions just another heavy thing pulling at me while the barrel bobbed and tilted and rolled among the waves.

IT WAS DURING this period that I first willingly went to an Al-Anon meeting. I have my sponsor Bob B. to thank for that—or rather his wife, Lynda.

Twelve Step recovery is built on a foundation of autonomy—there are no leaders in AA, neither elected nor appointed. Basic respect is freely given; authority is earned by experience. That being said, some members of the community stand out by virtue of their wisdom and their willingness to share it with others. Lynda and Bob are such people. This is true not only in the Twin Cities—they live a few blocks from me in St. Paul—but also around the world.

Both Lynda and Bob are in demand as speakers, sought out to tell their stories at international conventions, treatment centers, small intimate weekend workshops, even annual banquets of Twelve Step chapters in cities and towns throughout the Midwest. Rarely do they decline an invitation to give away their experience, strength, and hope. Bob quit drinking in July of 1967. A month later, Lynda joined Al-Anon. A few days after they married the following December, Bob gained sustainable sobriety that has never been interrupted. Together, their braided stories describe some of the myriad ways addiction impacts and alters everyone in a family. They're unabashed advocates of family recovery, underscoring the vital need for each member of a family affected by this illness to find their own path to healing and well-being.

Over the three-plus decades that I've pursued recovery, Bob has saved my sobriety countless times. He can defuse a crisis with a solid perspective or tame an inflamed ego with a well-timed and perfectly aimed truth bomb. In the early days, Bob's gruff love helped me get up again when I stumbled or when I lapsed into self-pity or despair. He once flew from Minnesota to Atlanta to spend all of twenty minutes with me after a relapse had sent me back to treatment. "Get your head out of your ass," he counseled, advice that was blunt but invariably on point. Now it was Lynda's turn to wade in and throw me a lifeline.

Although I had no desire to get drunk or high in those days, as I came to learn, I was nonetheless under the influence of forces that can be just as potent, just as toxic, and just as debilitating. I was tied up in knots trying to save my marriage—encouraging Allison to do this or not do that. Because I knew what I wanted, I assumed I also knew what was best for her. I became obsessed with what she was feeling. If she was happy, so was I. When she was sad, I despaired. When she expressed anger, I urged her to "let go." When she seemed lost, I extolled her to "hold on." I craved control in the drama that was our family's life and so took on the roles of producer, director, understudy, supporting cast, lighting tech, sound engineer, and usher, convincing myself that I could save our remarkable story from becoming a tragedy with a few rewrites and a new vision. We could do it, I was certain, if only she—and everybody else—would just do as I told them.

One afternoon in the spring of 2008, I met Lynda at a local coffee shop. I was a mess.

"Damn it, Lynda, this is impossible," I spilled it out. "She's crazy, I'm crazy, we're crazy. I don't know what to do. Letting go of crack and alcohol was easier than this. I love Allison—she needs my help, but she won't take it!" Lynda said nothing, just let me roll on. "I know she can get better. I know we can make it and stay married—I know it! If only she'll do what I say, follow my advice, give us a chance. Why is this so hard? Yes, I made a mistake but that was almost three years ago now, and . . ."

My voice trailed off as Lynda's lips formed a rueful smile behind her cup. By this point, gossip about my affair had long since made the rounds of the recovery community. She sighed and brought her mind-reader's gaze up to meet mine. I could almost hear her thoughts. She was just like Bob. Being in their presence was both calming and unsettling. I knew whatever was about to come out of her mouth was what I needed to hear. Bob was a bull. He could be downright harsh in what he said, even as he'd bear-hug you after. Lynda was smooth as silk. Both were no-nonsense.

"This is the challenge we all face," she said quietly. "Being able to love and respect a person without interfering or trying to control them—that's what is at stake now." She took a sip of her coffee. "You have to allow Allison to find her way, to make her choices and come to her own conclusions. This isn't about you, William. It's about her. But how you deal with it? Well, the learning is often painful, and it doesn't always work out the way you want. It always works out the way it is meant to be. It will—if you take care of yourself."

She paused. I knew she was giving me a chance to let her words sink in. She's a patient woman and I'm a slow learner. Months earlier, in an attempt to placate Allison, I had attended a retreat without her at a center in Pennsylvania. The focus of the weekend was the topic of "codependency," a term I had heard before but had always resisted self-applying because I thought it suggested a weakness I didn't want and a problem I didn't have. Besides, as an alcoholic and addict in long-term recovery, I figured I could find all the answers I needed in Alcoholics Anonymous—not at the spouses' table.

But here I was, at my wit's end and suffering, gripping the ropes around that barrel I imagined held my family, trying in vain to make it go where I wanted. The very fact that I had signed up for that retreat thinking it would help Allison get over her issues with me and save our marriage proved Lynda's point. In reality, there was nothing I could do to help Allison heal or make her change. My attempts to do so—working to create the perfect conditions in which everything would magically snap back to the good old days—had begun to dominate my thinking and, worse, my behavior. I did not like the man I was under the influence of this impossible project. Saving our marriage wasn't a thing I could achieve by force of will. All I could do was save me—a task that seemed both baffling and impossible. Lynda reminded me that I didn't have to do it alone. There were people who could help.

A few days later, on her recommendation, I went to an Al-Anon meeting in St. Paul. My stomach was in knots as I parked outside the pale stone church. Descending a dimly lit stairway, I followed the signs toward the designated room. Having tried

Al-Anon a few times after getting home from the retreat, my expectations were low. The only meetings I had found back then were attended almost exclusively by women, and I very quickly realized the issues they discussed frequently featured men who sounded a lot like me. Each time it was all I could do to keep from sneaking out of there. After a couple of attempts, I gave up looking for another group. But now I was trying again, this time with a meeting exclusively for men, as Lynda had suggested.

As I reached the door of the community room, I could hear chatter and laughter inside. I felt more at ease. Even if I wasn't sure exactly what to expect, at least I knew I wouldn't be the only guy in the place. I stepped through the door and was stunned by who I saw among the men in a large circle of chairs. About two-thirds of the men were people I knew from AA meetings. These were people I respected—some with decades of sobriety! These familiar faces had long ago "let go" of the substances that they could not control and that were destroying their lives, yet here they were, in a different meeting, sharing their various struggles with the same kind of problems I was carrying. In that moment, I knew I wasn't alone. I had the company of an understanding community. Through the fellowship and support I found in those Monday night meetings, I started to learn how to understand and tolerate myself a little better.

AUGUST 30, 2008
Allison tells me she loves me.
We embrace. I am filled with joy.
And then I wake up. It is a dream.

Three weeks before I made that wistful entry in my journal, Allison told me our marriage was over. She was standing in the kitchen, her scratch-made macaroni and cheese in process on the cooktop in front of her. As I entered the room, she turned toward me and, without emotion, said, "I don't think I want to be married anymore." Then she turned back to the stove to add the cheese to her noodles.

I couldn't make a sound. Even if I had known what to say, the words wouldn't come. Instead, I turned and went into the backyard.

It was a fine afternoon in late summer. In the Upper Midwest, this is usually the best time of year to be outdoors. I walked past the patio furniture and onto the lawn, where I lay down on my back. After a few moments, the family housecat, Nimbus, appeared. She strolled around my head, delicately cat-sniffing my face and forehead as I lay there staring into the sky above. Amoeba-like clouds morphed into peculiar shapes on the invisible currents of air. The cat began to lick my hair. I blinked and noticed that my mouth was open. I noticed, also, that I was out of breath even though I wasn't doing anything to exert myself. I felt my heart beating erratically—a new sensation for me. My fingers felt cold. I absently considered whether I was having a heart attack and decided that possibility didn't seem so bad. I wondered if my obituary would make the *New York Times*.

I didn't get up. Instead, I let gravity take me, feeling its force hug me into the ground until I felt oddly secured, anchored into the spot. I began to slowly pull in air through my nose, hold it for a few seconds, then exhale steadily out of my mouth. It might have been the first time I ever put into real-life practice what I had learned from the half dozen or more meditation sessions that had been part of my treatment experiences so many years earlier. This breathing pattern seemed to connect with my beating heart in a comforting way. I closed my eyes and kept breathing deliberately. The cat climbed onto me and settled on my chest.

When I opened my eyes again the expanse above me was bluer than it had been a few minutes earlier, the sunlit drifts still making their way slowly across my field of vision. I remembered something I had read about mindfulness, that we could try being the sky instead of the constantly shifting clouds. My heartbeat felt normal again, but I still wasn't ready to get up. "Everything will be okay," I softly recited a few times. Nimbus purred in response. I reached up to stroke her fur. "I know everything will be okay," I said. I would tell myself this again and again in the months that followed. Sometimes I was able to believe it.

A FEW DAYS after the macaroni and cheese event, Allison announced that she was returning to Bermuda to help a friend who was dying of cancer. Although she had traveled back and forth to her homeland a handful of times over the previous three years, I couldn't understand her decision to leave this time. It felt like she was choosing somebody else over us. She said she planned to stay a week but was gone for three, leaving me to manage the start of the school year. Henry was beginning his sophomore year in high school, with Thomas one class behind. Nancy was entering the fifth grade.

Allison checked in periodically, calling every few days, but she seemed disconnected from what was happening at home. I didn't want to fight on the phone, so I simply left things unsaid. I harbored a secret hope that she would have a cathartic experience while tending to the needs of her dying friend, and maybe—just maybe—she might change her mind. She didn't, and when she finally came home, we separated.

We decided to rent one half of a duplex that was available down the street. At first the plan was that we'd take turns in the duplex, with one parent staying with the kids in the house. Then Allison wanted to be in the duplex full time. Her relocation lasted one day; the next morning she arrived in tears at the front door, saying she couldn't stand to be so close and yet not at home with the kids. "Okay, I'll move out and use the other place," I offered, but I was wary of what that meant, given her history of precipitous decisions and departures. I was right. Her back-and-forth treks to Bermuda continued.

Whenever she departed, I'd pack my bag and drag my wardrobe of suits back to our house. Sometimes I'd stay for a week, sometimes longer. The reunion with the kids was sweet, and it felt reassuring—for them and for me—to be together again under one roof. But every time Allison returned, it was out the door once more, with suitcase filled and wardrobe in the car trunk.

Later, Allison and I agreed that telling the kids about the divorce was perhaps the hardest thing we had ever done. Trying to emphasize that we'd still be a team when it came to being their parents, we did it together at dinner around the table in the backyard. We assured them of our love for them and promised that we'd do holidays together. We even emphasized how convenient the duplex was—just down the alley, in the same neighborhood. But it didn't matter to the kids. All they heard was their mom and dad didn't love each other anymore.

ALLISON FLOATED AWAY from us. It took another handful of months to formalize our divorce and finish dividing all the things we once shared. She left us to return to Bermuda and live by herself. I moved back into the house, taking up the mantle of single dad and solo parent.

"Where's Mom?" Nancy asked, over and over again, always with a flood of tears.

"Dad, don't you think we can all try to get back together again?" pleaded Henry.

"What happened to Mom and you?" Thomas begged to know. Later, after it was clear she wasn't coming back, Thomas said the words that nearly broke my heart. "It's as if she is dead."

I didn't have answers for my children, because nothing made sense to me either. Where, what, why, when, and how—the journalist's quest for answers always starts with these questions, but stories of heartache and heartbreak respond with an aching silence. I couldn't explain to my children what I didn't fully understand myself.

■

3

Breaking Out

2006–2009

*I find it a hopeless undertaking indeed
to keep up with people's expectations of me.*

— BILL WILSON

There was a time—pretty much the entire 1980s—when I didn't do much good in the world. It's not that I didn't have opportunities. My upbringing and education, my family's connections, and my natural talents positioned me to be a contributing member of society. My addictions got in the way, however. My inability to consume alcohol like "normal" people—which means knowing when and how to stop drinking—and my insatiable pursuit of the released-from-reality high I experienced from smoking everything from marijuana to crack cocaine never seemed to affect my pleasant manners, but it certainly put a crimp in my capacity for reliably decent citizenship. It also destroyed dozens of personal and professional relationships, cost me my first marriage, and derailed what might have been a satisfying and productive career in journalism.

My addictions not only prevented me from doing good things; they also induced me to do bad ones. It's difficult to overstate the shame that addicts and alcoholics like me hold on to because of who we became and what we did under the influence of the substances or behaviors that dismantled our wills and directed our actions. We lied and stole. We wasted energy and opportunities and resources. We spent money we didn't have and made promises we wouldn't keep. We manipulated others with excuses and evasions. We hurt our loved ones and ourselves and then tried to convince everyone that it didn't matter. Waking up to the reality of these failures is painful, and confessing them is often an agony, no matter how compassionate or kind the person who finally hears us out.

These feelings might fade beneath the grace of forgiveness or be admitted and amended via processes like the Twelve Steps, but most of us continue to carry a sense of obligation that doesn't go away even with the passage of time. We, who for so long were useless to many of the people who loved us or needed us or wanted to rely on us, want to be useful. We want to somehow make right what was wrong. For many of us, myself included, fulfilling this desire to make good what we once made so bad becomes a part of the way we stick with recovery; sometimes it leads us to jobs and careers in professions that help or heal.

In their book *Beyond the Influence,* my friend and confidant Kathy Ketcham and her coauthor William Asbury write eloquently about the crisis that feeds this impulse among many recovering people.

> If you are an alcoholic, during your drinking days you only took in; if you are like most alcoholics, you took everything you could get from anyone who was willing

to give it to you. Rarely did you give anything back. The anguished insight that so much was taken and so little was given in return is the source of the alcoholic's most profound spiritual distress.

The most difficult spiritual work in recovery is to understand that the source of your anguish is not the desire to get back what you have lost, but to give back what you have taken.

If my work at Hazelden offered me an opportunity to pay back the debt I owed to the miracle of recovery, *Broken* provided a kind of vocational promotion. The book's popularity with readers and the attention it got from the media gave me a new and bigger way to be useful. My story of addiction connected me to millions of other stories that shared its familiar and destructive shape, even if our details were different. My story of redemption offered these people some hope that they, too, could get better. Through *Broken* I became part of the solution for people who were still suffering with active addictions or slogging through the early months of recovery as well as those who loved them. Publishing and promoting the book opened the door to people who wanted my help and gave me a way to connect with and help others. What I shared with the world seemed to matter. It seemed to make a difference. It seemed to meet a need.

Even during my first attempts at treatment, when I desperately wanted to believe how different I was from the junkies and drunks around me, I sensed that sitting with others who were in the same boat was significant. Eventually I realized that this kind of connection and fellowship was also a reliable way for me to stay sober. Focusing on someone else's struggle pulled me out of self-pity and navel-gazing. Being useful—even to one other person—affirmed that I was worthwhile. And it distracted me from my search for other things that might make me feel better. I was persuaded by the "one alcoholic helping another" simplicity of AA. We can't recover in isolation. When we try, we will nearly always fail. This insight continues to guide and shape my recovery, and it is a core part of the healing and hopeful message I help the Hazelden Betty Ford Foundation share with the wider world.

I wish I could say that the self-serving/other-serving generosity of the Twelfth Step was the sole reason I wrote a memoir and got it published, but I'm not that kind of saint. I had a desire—a need—to help others. I also wanted to be famous. My early life had given me a taste for celebrity—completely unearned by me—and my career since getting sober had put me somewhere on that map, this time for my own sake. I liked the way audiences responded to my speeches and presentations. I was gratified when journalists called me for comments or had me as a guest on their shows. Being a player in the corridors of power and a public representative of a noble cause made me feel good. My hunger for the kind of respect and admiration my father has achieved and enjoyed through his storied career has always been part of what drives me. The expectation that I live up to my name and my potential was stitched into my psyche from my earliest days and has dogged me for decades. Insecurity about my ability to do this—to measure up—colors my life and influences my choices to this day.

Because it was a story that could help others in need,

Broken was an act of service. To borrow the metaphor from *Beyond the Influence,* it was payment toward the debt I owed for the gift of recovery. Because it became a bestseller, the book also gave me a place in the sun. Its critical and commercial success, and the attention it drew to me as a person, offered hope that I might finally break out from beneath my father's long shadow and achieve the rewards of recognition and regard and approval that would satisfy my own deep need to feel like I mattered. As I tried to keep all the pieces of myself and my life together during the years my marriage was falling apart, these twined impulses continued to work in me, sometimes for the better and often for the worse.

IT WAS SEPTEMBER 24, 2006—a warm Sunday evening in Manhattan. My six minutes of fame on *Good Morning America* would take place the next morning. *Broken* was on its way into the world. After the next day's interview, I was scheduled to attend my first-ever book signing at the big Barnes & Noble on Broadway. That event would kick off a tour that would land in forty cities over the course of two months. My publisher had flown me to New York for the interview and put me up in a swanky place in Midtown. I had invited my parents to dinner at the hotel's restaurant, intending it to be celebratory—a victory lap in the epic story of recovery and redemption that we shared. What I had to do instead was tell them about my affair and the sorry state of my marriage.

My mom already knew. Some weeks earlier, while she was visiting us in St. Paul, I told her what had happened and how afraid I was about what it could mean if the press caught the scent of scandal just as my star was beginning to rise. Always my cheerleader and strongest support, my mother offered reassurance. "What we learn from the inevitable mistakes we make in a marriage," she had told me quietly, "can strengthen us for the tough times and the better times that keep coming." She counseled honesty and hard work.

Here in Manhattan, my dad greeted me with a hug. If he noticed my fast heartbeat, he didn't mention it. There was anticipation and pride in his eyes. This night mattered to him. Along with my mom, Dad had been a front-row witness to the events I narrated in *Broken,* and a main character in the story. My journey had coincided with my parents' own. Through the years, they had become deeply knowledgeable about the illnesses of addiction and codependency and their corrosive effects on families. Like so many who commit to their own healing while supporting an addicted child, parent, or sibling, they had survived and recovered alongside me.

The restaurant had tables on the sidewalk. We perused the menu and placed our orders. My father, who is no stranger to the book tour circuit, asked me about the next day's interview and the logistics of the events that would follow. I answered his questions readily, even as I calculated when and how to direct the conversation to the subject I dreaded.

Mom had been so supportive, concerned as she was about Allison and the kids. She had named the affair for what it was: a mistake that could be endured. It didn't need to destroy our lives. I felt as though Dad would understand what I was about to tell him as well, even if the news hurt him. Maybe the hopefulness of this evening, with the energy and success of the book's release and my upcoming tour as a published author, would outshine the disappointment I was about to unleash.

After the server took our dinner orders, I leaned in. "There's something I have to tell you that's not good," I said. Dad noticed my change in tone and sat back in his chair. I told him about what had happened the previous year. That the affair was short and over. I shared how hurt Allison had been but that she had forgiven me, how we had been regrouping as a family. I told him that the higher-ups at Hazelden were in the loop and that I had maintained my sobriety. I shared my fear that news of the affair, which had become an item of gossip and speculation in the St. Paul recovery community, could have implications for the publicity that was part of this moment.

As the details poured out and piled up on the table between us, I watched the pride and the excitement in my father's demeanor battle with the crestfallen realization of what I had done and what it might mean.

In his long life, Bill Moyers has worn many hats and had many careers: compassionate minister, curious journalist, frustrated father, concerned grandpa, media mogul, press secretary to the president. From across the table that night, I saw these roles cycle behind his eyes as he considered what he was hearing. He landed on damage control.

"Well, you need to go home. Cancel the tour. Tonight."

I don't know what exactly I expected, or even what I had hoped for, but this wasn't it. Our meal arrived, allowing us each to look away from each other for a moment. The silverware clinked. The traffic beside us flowed past. I sipped from my glass of water. Another memory rose up. I was sitting with my father at a different table, years earlier. He had come to see me in Atlanta. Over our cafeteria trays, I told him I was resigning from CNN and would be moving my family to St. Paul. Dad had been incredulous at the time, even as he eventually came to understand and appreciate my choice. His questions were practical: What would I do for a living? How would I support myself and my family?

My father's fears were unfounded then, I assured myself, so they were overblown now too. Things would work out. This was too important to cancel. I looked up from my plate and told them I had already made my choice. I would fulfill my obligation to my publisher and to Hazelden. I was ready for this tour. This book—this mission to which I had devoted years of work—meant so much. I wanted it to succeed. I wanted *me* to succeed. I said I appreciated his concern, but I wasn't going home to hide. My family would be okay, I said. "We'll get through this."

Dad looked away. I could tell he was horrified. To his credit, he didn't push. Mom smoothed the napkin in her lap. I felt my jaw clench. We allowed ourselves to be distracted by our food. Somebody changed the subject. A little later, my parents and I hugged each other in the echoing lobby as we said goodbye. They'd watch me on television the next morning.

Back in my room that evening, I wandered from the window to the bathroom and back to the bed. I couldn't sleep. Hours slipped by. I felt less confident than I had at dinner. I can count on one hand the times that I've directly defied my father. I suddenly felt sick to my stomach.

I was spinning. Seeing Dad's fallen face again and again.

Hearing his words. Reliving my refusal to follow his advice. *You have to go home.* Was it advice or was it an order? *What if he's right? I know what I'm doing. Do I? I should get some sleep. Why can't I sleep? I need to sleep!*

I put my head on the pillow of that big empty bed, but even today I don't recall if I slept at all. By the time the alarm clock began beeping to rouse me, I was a bleary mess. Even the bags under my eyes had bags.

But I had work to do.

I showered and dressed. A car came for me at 6 a.m. Two hours later, after the makeup artist's deft work made me passably presentable, millions of people had seen my face and heard my story. When the light above the camera went out, I wasn't sure exactly how the interview had gone. They cut to a commercial, and I was ushered to the edge of the set. There, a big bearded man wearing headphones came in close to retrieve the microphone and its wires from under my jacket. "I'm a friend of Bill's too," he said softly, tending to his task without meeting my eye. "I could never do what you just did. Thank you." He squeezed my shoulder and walked away as someone else came up to shake my hand.

Suddenly I didn't feel as empty inside. My fears about the future could wait. The cameras were rolling now, and people were paying attention.

I was off and running.

THE PROMOTIONAL TOUR for *Broken* began immediately. I left the *Good Morning America* interview to climb into a limousine and head to my first book signing event. I was due at Barnes

& Noble in just over an hour. My cell phone began buzzing almost immediately. It was my dad.

"Wow!" he said. "That was the best natural interview I've ever seen you do." I could hear his excitement, and I felt my heart swell with relief. My father had just praised me for being on television. He had recognized a skill that he knew something about—probably as much or more than anybody else who tuned in that morning. He wanted me to know that he was watching and that he appreciated what I was doing. He was proud of me, and it felt so very good.

I'm the firstborn son of self-made and successful parents. My mom and dad were born in the midst of the Depression in the 1930s. They raised my siblings and me to value excellence in others and to strive for it in ourselves. In my young mind, this translated to an imperative that I should constantly *do* more in order to *be* more. Their expectations set a high bar. From my ninth-grade year, I participated in sports all three seasons of the school year, played trombone in both the band and orchestra, and worked a job on weekends as well as part of every summer. Despite my academic efforts, however, I never seemed to get grades that met the Moyers standard. I was a B student in a straight-A household—never quite good enough, I believed, for my parents and, thus, for me. That day in the limo, however, through the small speaker on my flip phone, I heard my dad assigning me an A.

He offered another round of congratulations before passing the phone to my mother. She was also elated and wished me luck at the midday book signing. My parents would join me in the afternoon. Together, we'd take the train to Washington, DC, where the Smithsonian Associates would host the three of us for a panel discussion the following evening about my book and our family's story. The event was going to be broadcast live on C-SPAN, moderated by Jim Bohannon.

As the car moved slowly uptown, I was flying high. No more talk of going home and hiding. I took my parents' endorsement of my performance as a broader endorsement of what I was doing. *You're right to stay the course,* I told myself. *You need to be out here.*

The limo deposited me at the curb, and I walked into the store prepared for popping flashbulbs and paparazzi. Reality reasserted itself in the more humble form of a folding table, a stack of books, and rows of empty chairs. There was nobody waiting. By the end of the afternoon, a whopping six people had attended my first-ever book signing.

AFTER A DECADE of giving speeches for Hazelden, I was a seasoned veteran of public events. But nothing I had done prepared me for what *Broken*'s launch required of me. I was used to the steady pace of the long-distance run. During the two-month tour, each day felt like a sprint. Nearly every stop included a bookstore visit, where I'd read an excerpt—usually a passage from the prologue—and answer questions from audiences of varying sizes. That first event in Manhattan with only a handful of people turned out to be an outlier. Many of the events drew dozens. I was surprised and thrilled that there were so many people who took the time to show up and hear my story—and then spend their money to buy a book for me to sign my name in. Most of my previous public events had been speeches or presentations. During those talks I had some distance from the audiences, even as I stayed to shake hands or meet people afterward. On the book tour, in contrast, everybody who bought a book and stood in line had my attention for a minute or two. With my pen ready to inscribe their book, I'd ask their name. More often than not what poured out was some explanation of why they were there. Nearly every interaction came with an account of somebody's pain or loss or hope or joy.

I was gratified, if a little baffled, by the intensity of these brief interactions. In that first week, shuttling from New York to Washington, DC, and back to the Twin Cities, I realized that it wasn't exactly me that drew these people. I was a first-time author, recognizable for my last name, perhaps, or noteworthy because of the organization I worked for. These people didn't know me—most of them hadn't even read my book yet. The women and men who showed up to these events were after something they felt I represented: a beacon of hope, an avenue toward help, another chance—each person had some need. I had navigated these kinds of encounters before, but now, as my memoir garnered more and more public attention, they were ongoing, up close, and often very personal.

I had appeared on *The Oprah Winfrey Show* with my parents back in 1998. At the time, we were promoting a PBS miniseries about addiction and recovery. When Oprah asked me that afternoon how people in need could get help, I rattled off the toll-free phone number for Hazelden. Within the hour, more than 2,000 phone calls overwhelmed the resource center in Minnesota. Unlike that onetime spike, the 2006 tour—and the paperback tour that followed in 2007—generated daily flows of emails, calls, and queries, both to Hazelden and to me personally.

After a week or two, the book events got crowded enough that my publisher arranged to have a representative stand beside the table at each signing to help keep the interactions short and the lines moving. Even so, people wanted to share, and I wanted to hear and help. I handed out cards or took down contact information. By the time I got back to the hotel after a reading or stepped aboard an airplane headed to another city, my email inbox was usually stacked with fresh follow-ups. I never felt like I could ignore these messages or queries and did my best to respond with at least a short note. "If not me, who?" I asked myself. By putting my story into the world as a book and thereby stepping into the public spotlight, I had made myself available, I reasoned. People wanted what I seemed to have: a solution to their problems with addiction.

"I read your book on my sobriety anniversary this year and I will read it every year from now on because your journey inspires me in mine to stay clean and sober," a woman from Florida wrote.

Others asked for direct help: "Dear Mr. Moyers: Help, my son is dying. I read your book that says to hate the disease, not the person. But so help me God, I hate him more than I love him right now. . . . I am begging you, if there is any way my son can be helped, please help me to find it. You are my last hope."

So many stories of hope, so many stories of loss, and a relentless rush of appeals from people who needed someone on their side and saw me as a person who could provide guidance.

AT ONE OF the early events on the 2006 tour, a woman with streaked gray-and-black hair pulled back in a ponytail and wearing a homemade-looking flower-print skirt arrived at the front of the line without a book. Her own arms stacked with a dozen or more bracelets, she slipped a loop of Tibetan prayer beads onto my wrist. I don't remember her name—I can't even picture her face—but I recall the clear sound of her voice. "I can tell you could use these," she said. I remember her tenderness.

She didn't know exactly what was happening in my current life, but she seemed to understand that I needed some kind of help. She saw past the polish and the ready-for-the-receiving-line smile I wore. Perhaps she sensed how out of kilter I was, how far from a sense of grounded gratitude I had spun.

Her gift stayed with me. Touching the beads or stretching the band through my fingers became a daily part of my connection to God on that tour. This simple act helped get me out of my head, where the stresses and tensions of the day ricocheted from neuron to neuron to the point where it was hard for me to pay attention to anything else. The beads returned me to a simple truth. *I was not alone.* I could get through whatever was ahead, no matter what obstacles confronted me.

GOD WAS NOT my only company on the tour.

Being on the road, traveling from one city to the next, meant that I was always on the move and often alone in hotel rooms. Not knowing how easy it would be to find meetings on each stop, I had made arrangements with a group of friends and fellow travelers to stay connected by phone. Once a day, usually in the morning, I joined a conference call with a half dozen men. A few were members of my home group back in Minnesota. The others phoned in from as far away as Texas. All were in recovery, and all knew at least a little about what was going on for me at home.

"We're with you every step of your way," they'd remind me at the start of every call before we shared what was happening in our lives at that moment. They said it again as we said our goodbyes. These friends listened to me more than they talked about themselves because they knew how grief-stricken I was about the wreckage of my once well-ordered life. Telling my story—being heard by people who knew the larger story—helped me stay sane as well as sober. Not once was I tempted to check out the hotel rooms' minibars, though the attractively packaged bottles they were loaded with surely had my name on each label.

Some days—usually evenings after an event or early mornings in a new city—I was able to find and attend actual meetings. "Hello, I'm William, I'm an alcoholic and a drug addict," I'd say. In unison the enthusiastic response from the other people in the room—strangers who nevertheless knew me intimately because I was just like them—would remind me why I was there and assure me that I had the support of people who had felt what I was feeling and who didn't judge me for it. AA kept reminding me that I was part of something bigger than me and was never alone.

As the weeks progressed and I continued to turn up at random meetings at various tour stops, however, I noticed a new dynamic. Sometimes—not all the time—people recognized me. Occasionally, someone would recall seeing me on television, or might even have attended a book signing, and they would ask me about it—aloud and in front of the group. Even in the rooms of anonymity, I was getting called out by name—by full name. This troubled me because it felt like the scale got tilted away from what the meeting promised and what the fellowship depended on. I didn't want to be noticed in that way—not here. I didn't go to meetings to sell books or give speeches. What I needed was to be just another alcoholic sitting in the shelter of anonymity and enjoying the grace of mutual acceptance and support—just like anyone else in that room. This new development felt like a loss. It made meetings tricky, and meetings shouldn't be tricky.

Broken made it to #13 on the *New York Times* bestseller list. It came out in paperback in 2007 and has stayed in print since. I don't know what my career might have looked like if I had never written or published my story. What I do know is that my life and my vocation were forever changed by the way this book found its audience.

THE BOOK TOUR ended, and the following Monday saw me back in the office at Hazelden. Returning to the duties and demands of my external relations and advocacy work reminded me that, for all the attention that *Broken* had generated, my single story was still only a tiny part of a nationwide picture of addiction and the way people find—or fail to find—help and healing.

Much of my work centered around educating the public. Ours is a culture that hasn't traditionally chosen to view alcoholics and addicts with much kindness. Shunning and judgment seem to go along with drug and alcohol problems. Stigma fostered by ongoing misunderstanding or outright intolerance keeps suffering people quiet about their condition.

There are still people who believe that addiction is a choice some people make or that it's evidence of poor moral character or some other weakness of will or spirit. Despite decades of medical science demonstrating that addictions are illnesses—on par with cancer or diabetes or hypertension—these ignorant myths persist. Beyond the kind of shaming and blaming that happens within families and between individuals, the bias against addiction and people who have it extends to how we choose to write and enforce laws and policies too.

Hazelden had been active in fighting stigma since its founding. Having encountered so much ignorance about and intolerance toward people with addictions, Hazelden's early leaders envisioned a transformation of public perception that went beyond their primary mission to heal and help addicts and alcoholics. Proponents of the Minnesota Model, which recognized that people with addiction deserved to be treated professionally and with dignity and respect, understood the fight against stigma as a battle of good information versus outmoded myths. This included presenting and championing the most current science, the most accurate information, and the most persuasive stories to policy makers, the medical community, scientific researchers, and the news media. This direction continues to animate the Hazelden Betty Ford Foundation's mission today.

For decades, the discrimination against addicts and alcoholics was painfully evident in the way health insurers limited or denied care and treatment for people with substance use disorders. The project that kept me running upon my return from the book tour was advocating and organizing for passage of the so-called healthcare parity bill. As proposed, the parity law would help millions more people get help by requiring most insurance companies to treat—and pay for—mental health care and addiction treatment at the same rate as any other medical condition.

This change in the nation's laws had been Hazelden's signature policy and advocacy focus for nearly a decade, beginning before I joined the staff in 1996. By 2005, I had developed enough cachet as an ambassador for our field that I was trusted to lead this effort, so I was on lots of planes back and forth between St. Paul and Washington, DC.

Moving the parity bill forward was a long process. We were up against well-funded opposition from the alcohol industry (*Why should our best customers stop drinking?*), the health plans (*Mandates never work*), big business (*Premiums will rise*), and even elements of the criminal justice systems (*We'll have less to do if people stop misbehaving under the influence*). These powerful interests made many lawmakers wary of supporting a change in the law, even though many of them were keenly aware of the effects of substances on their constituents back home—and, in some cases, members of their own families. I remember the bolt of angry dismay I felt when a member of the House who had voted against an earlier version of the bill sought my help in getting her granddaughter into treatment.

"Treatment works!" became my mantra whenever I showed up to lobby Congress for change. I wasn't the only voice carrying this message. The sustained call for healthcare parity rallied thousands to put their faces and voices to the issue. Beyond Hazelden, this energized grassroots advocates in big cities and small towns across the nation.

Now, after years of pleading and pushing, there was movement building among Democrats and Republicans in Congress, and the Bush White House had signaled interest. Despite this growing support on the government side, competing agendas and petty jealousies among our brethren in the field continued to dog our ability to stick together long enough to get it done. As 2007 rolled into 2008, however, a small consortium of treatment providers led by Hazelden and directed by our lobbyist, Carol McDaid, brokered a détente that we hoped would last.

I was responsible for coordinating Hazelden's lobbying in DC and planning how to mobilize our board of trustees, employees, and alums to contact their members of Congress on the home front. Maybe it was sheer coincidence that the paperback edition of *Broken* hit bookstores in the fall of 2007, but at the time colleagues and fellow advocates suggested that the success of my story added muscle to these efforts and may have even gained us a few votes.

Once again, I found myself in a bright spotlight. Treatment centers invited me to speak to their alumni or fundraising galas. A national nonprofit we named Faces & Voices of Recovery (FAVOR) was born in 2001 after I helped to secure a half-million-dollar grant from the Robert Wood Johnson Foundation. I was on television again too—a regular talking head expert in the national media. As 2008 began, I was on a roll.

The Paul Wellstone and Pete Domenici Mental Health Parity and Addiction Equity Act finally passed the House and

Senate and made it to then-President Bush's desk, where he signed it into law on October 3, 2008. I wasn't in DC for the celebration, however. That day, I was happily in the stands at my sons' football game in St. Paul.

Between the book's success and the advocacy victory, I finally felt like I belonged—and that I deserved to belong. I had worked hard to do my part to smash stigma, expand access to treatment, and affirm Hazelden's leadership in the field. I even enjoyed the rare-for-me feeling that I had met my own expectations for success.

Without a doubt, getting the parity bill passed helped my career. It raised my profile at Hazelden and introduced me to many others in the recovery movement who shared my passion. No longer was I on the outside looking in or even on the inside trying to get to the middle. I was surrounded by people who affirmed that I deserved my seat at the table, and now I wanted to keep belonging. I wanted to keep being recognized and appreciated as a leader.

Given my private and personal failures during these years, being celebrated at work and in public felt like magic. I wanted to keep that feeling going, even if it killed me. When Mark Mishek took the helm as CEO of Hazelden in late 2008 and soon thereafter offered me the chance to direct the organization's fundraising efforts, I said yes immediately. Flush with success and fed by earned praise, I was ready to keep proving my worth to the new boss.

TODAY, I GRASP just how intense this period of my life was and see that I felt pulled in so many different directions. Many of my decisions were driven less by logic and more by a kind of hunger. It's not that I wanted *more, more, more*—I just wanted to stay in the club. I took on too much, trying to keep pace with my duties at Hazelden even as I filled and piled sandbag after sandbag against the rising waters that kept eroding my marriage. It never occurred to me to "just say no" because it was easier to "just say yes" to whatever was asked of me. *Yes, I'll make that speech in Tulsa. Yes, you can have the congressman call me at bedtime. Yes, I will do a book reading at your parents' association at school. Yes, it is all my fault our marriage is falling apart, so yes, I'll move out of the house. Again.*

For as long as I can remember, I have been afraid of letting down other people. To avoid this, I constantly strive to please them. When my efforts are successful, it works almost like a drug. Sometimes it eases a hurt. Sometimes it boosts a pleasure. Sometimes saying yes—even when I'd rather say no—keeps me feeling numb. During this period of my life, when it seemed I was under bombardment from every quarter, saying no would have required me to spend time getting to know myself and what I needed and wanted. And I wasn't ready or able to do that yet.

WHILE MY RECOVERY "stuck" during these tumultuous years—and by that I mean my ongoing abstinence from alcohol and other drugs remained intact—the "contented sobriety" that the Big Book promises, and that had once seemed to be within reach, kept eluding me. Whenever I slowed down, I found it hard to escape the uncomfortable sense that my life wasn't altogether truthful. My story inspired people because they wanted "what I had." But what did I really have?

Beyond the freedom from craving a drink or a line of coke, my recovery was also supposed to include benefits and blessings like peace of mind, equanimity, and happiness. These did not appear in my inventory. My home life was crumbling. I was exhausted and unable to say no. I was sober, and I was successful by some measures, but much of my life—the part people didn't see and I didn't share—was far from uplifting or inspiring. People sought and celebrated me as an example of the peace and joy that come with healthy sobriety, but in some ways, I felt like an imposter. My success was skin-deep, my happiness incomplete.

I couldn't accept the reality of my life. I wanted to change it somehow. I kept going back, back to the past, back to the affair and my shameful part in the wreckage of my once intact family. Even as I convincingly performed the role of recovery champion, signed books, and said the right things to the right people, inside I was trying to figure out what I should have done differently and how I had lost control of so much that had mattered to me.

Shame on me. Those three words became a mantra that connected present to past. *Shame on me.* All those times so many years ago when I was drunk or high and out of my mind, the nights I blacked out, the money I wasted, the time I squandered, the morals I violated, the laws I broke, the dishonesty and deceit, the lying and cheating, the utter selfishness. *Shame on me.* All those times I relapsed and went back to treatment, vowing to learn from my mistakes but every time doing the same thing over and over and over again, and in the process losing friends, disappointing colleagues, wounding my parents, my wife, my children. *Shame on me.*

The picture of my happy family in the magazine, real as it was, wasn't the whole truth. The character in the book, true as the story was, was incomplete. The advocate on stage, a model sober citizen, was flawed, even if he looked fine.

Shame became another drug. I didn't want it, but I couldn't avoid it. It hovered over everything—my emotions, my thoughts, my perspective. I couldn't escape it. If saying yes to everyone was an upper that drove me, shame was my downer. It kept finding me and I kept wallowing in it, feeling it seep into my pores and settle into my bones.

Shame on me. A knife that stuck when somebody who read *Broken* would ask about Allison.

Shame on me. A subtle flush of embarrassment every time an audience stood up to give me an ovation for inspiring them to action.

Shame on me. A bolt of impatience when yet another reporter asked how I had finally stopped drinking and drugging, when I wanted to scream, "There's more to my story than that!"

AFTER THREE-PLUS YEARS of professional highs and personal lows, I was tapped out. What energy I had left after delivering on my duties at work, I tried to commit to my kids. I was in a financial hole and an emotional abyss. While I wrote in my journal and read my meditation books and made it to meetings, these things brought me less joy and insight than they did a certain stability. Moving from a married life to that of a single dad produced lots of challenges and a busy schedule, but also a fair amount of loneliness. As the summer of 2009 began to fade, I was expecting a quieter fall and winter than we'd had in a while. What I didn't expect was what happened next.

I met Nell Hurley the same way I cross paths with a lot of people. Nell was facing a moment of crisis that involved a friend who was struggling with crack cocaine addiction. She found me on Facebook and sent me a message.

> William, hi. I'm not sure if you know me, but I live down the street from you (on the next block). Your name has come up a couple of times just recently and the other day my sponsor suggested that I read your book, Broken. I thought I would check with you to see if you have a copy I could borrow. If not, I'm happy to buy a copy on Amazon, but I thought I would check with you first since you're just down the street. Thanks, Nell Hurley P.S. I grew up with the sons of your sponsor, Bob B. (just to give you more context).

A few hours later I responded:

> Hello Nell, thanks for reaching out. I can help you. Why don't you drop by my house and I'll give you a copy? I've got a few on the shelf.

It still pleasantly surprised me when somebody mentioned or asked for my memoir. *Broken* had been in print for exactly three years that September—two years in paperback—and I was happy it remained relevant.

Nell stopped over the next day. It was a pristine evening,

so late in the summer that leaves on some of the trees on the boulevard were already hinting at the inevitable turn of the season. I was in the backyard grilling hamburgers for my kids' dinner. I had forgotten she was coming and didn't hear the doorbell ring, but she could smell the burgers and had the presence of mind to make her way around the side of the house. Her greeting startled me. I recognized her, vaguely, from Twelve Step meetings in the neighborhood, but I wouldn't have recalled her name.

"That's a lot of burgers," she noted, pointing to the grill. "Are you feeding an army or just a big family?" Her lighthearted question opened some floodgate in me.

"Well, that's six burgers for four of us," I explained, pointing at each sizzling patty. "One for me, one for my daughter, and two each for my two hungry teenage boys." I waved the spatula toward the house, where my kids were inside somewhere. From her face I could sense Nell was calculating a tally that was short one burger and one person. I didn't give her time to figure it out.

"I'm not married, at least not anymore," I said. "The kids live here with me full time—just us four." I continued, even as I realized this was already more information than she had likely bargained for, "I'm not a very good cook except in the warmer weather when I can use the grill. Burgers and brats, steak, chicken wings, sometimes fish. I'd offer you a burger except this evening we don't have one to spare. I've already been to the grocery store twice today, and I can't go back." As Nell would later discover, when I'm excited or nervous I tend to go overboard in answering a question, providing way too many details. This was one of those times. There would be many more with Nell and me.

I'd done all the talking. Now it was my turn to ask her a simple question that had nothing to do with my situation.

"What about you?" I asked.

"My little boy, Jasper, and I live in the duplex in the next block," she said. "I'm divorced."

To this day I don't know what I said in response. But I will always remember what I thought. More importantly, I remember how I felt—a sudden leap of excitement and possibility in the pit of my stomach.

I'm divorced, from a woman who was appealingly attractive in a healthy, wholesome way, lived up the block, was a foot shorter and appeared about ten years younger than me. I'd soon come to learn that Nell Hurley also possessed a sharp mind and kind heart. Added to that, she was a person who understood recovery. Like me, she had been working at it for most of her adult life.

I didn't know it then, despite the butterflies in my gut, but I had won the lottery, without planning to play the game or pick the numbers. Ever since Allison moved back to Bermuda, I had been solo parent to our two teenage sons and preteen daughter. I had a full-time job that included many weeks of travel every year and a long commute. When I wasn't up in the Center City office or out on the road for Hazelden, I was bone-tired at home or cycling through the countless chores that kept our home life running. Even if I had time to date, I had no idea how or where to start. I was halfway through my fiftieth year, and looked it. With two failed marriages in my past, I felt those years as well. My confidence was shaken. I had resigned myself to bachelorhood; living without romance—at least for the foreseeable future—seemed like a practical option.

But here was Nell, sitting on my porch smiling at me as I juggled a plate of burgers through the kitchen door and shouted to my kids that dinner was ready. I came back out with the book that had prompted her message. She was still smiling. So was I.

Although we agreed to carry on our conversation over a meal later, when neither of us was so rushed, it took ten more weeks before that date happened. We took up with each other as a couple shortly thereafter. By the time the snow came back to St. Paul—it stayed for good in December of that year—Nell and Jasper were regulars at our house; it helped that they lived a block away on the same street. My kids glommed on to them with remarkable ease. Jasper was only six years old when his world was suddenly filled with my three big kids. I loved having Nell around, and when Jasper was along, the lad's energy added to the hustle and bustle of our house. It felt good. Again.

■

4

Breaking Down

2009–2012

When you get older, your health
becomes important to you.
Things start breaking down; you've
always got a different ache or pain.

— TOM PETTY

"These two will have to come out first," the oral surgeon said, pointing to my stubby bottom front teeth. "And it looks like you'll need a root canal here and here," he said, turning back to look at the X-ray. The small mirror I held up to my wide-open mouth revealed the dentist's careful hands as they maneuvered a stainless-steel probe here, there, and everywhere, lightly touching my brittle teeth. Highlighting the plan of attack. "Then we'll insert an implant, maybe two, here on both sides of your jaw," he continued. "And in between we'll make a bridge, anchoring it to your canines on each side so everything stays in place." *So they don't fall out,* I thought, lying back in the chair, imagining random teeth tumbling past my lips in the middle of a keynote address or in front of my colleagues in a meeting.

It was February of 2012. The first months of the year in St. Paul seem to always give us either subzero temps and blue skies above bright white snow, or concrete-colored clouds and slushy drizzle. I don't remember what the weather was doing on the other side of the window over my dentist's shoulder that day, but I do recall that I wasn't yet concerned with how much the work he was describing might cause me pain. What I cared about was how much it would cost, how long it would take to get done, and when I'd fit it in. I had stuff to do.

The answers were alarming. The process to complete all of this work would involve many hours of me sitting in a chair with my mouth open and nothing else to do. In short, it was going to wreck my schedule.

At work or at home, I've long prided myself on my productivity—my ability to maximize time and effort and deliver on deadlines. Growing up I lived by the motto "When it's due it's done, and never before." I always managed to deliver, even if I had too much to do and waited until it was nearly too late to do it. Under the dental exam room's lights that winter, I had yet to really understand how this drive and my capacity for multitasking are defects of character as often as they are talents for me. Time spent in the dentist's chair was only going to get in my way.

And then there was the expense. My insurance plan classified virtually everything the dentist suggested as "elective, cosmetic procedures," which meant almost none of it was covered. I'd be paying many thousands of dollars out of pocket.

"From an insurance perspective, a good smile isn't good health," the dentist said. "But you'll feel good about yourself when you give one of your speeches in front of an audience." He had known about my work at Hazelden for years, and he knew that my mouth was a big part of my mission. "From start to finish we should get this done in six to eight months, and in the meantime when you do have a speaking engagement, we'll rig you up with a temporary prosthetic and nobody will know that anything is any different. You'll look just fine and sound the same too. Yes, it will feel inconvenient. But in front of an audience, in front of your boss or anyone, you'll be the only one who knows what's going on." His confidence reassured me. "Nothing will be much different, I promise."

GROWING UP AS the oldest of three siblings, I always liked my smile. Even after falling head over handlebars off my bike when I was seven, busting a lip and knocking out a front tooth, I never needed braces—unlike my younger siblings Suzanne and John, my first girlfriend, and most of my teenage classmates at school. In my family every trip to the dentist was, in my mind at least, a contest between me and my siblings. I never had a cavity, and they always seemed to have at least one. I was the winner, though I am pretty sure now that I was the only one keeping score.

"Metal mouth" and cavities or not, my mouth and my mind are constantly in motion. I seem to have been wired to keep score and worry and generate stress my whole life. It's part of what makes me the type A personality I am. Sound asleep or wide awake, I often unconsciously shift my jaws back and forth so that my teeth rub against each other until the grinding inside my head sounds like the dull roar of the sea in a conch shell. When I started to use cocaine in my twenties, the gnashing and scraping got much worse. Coke cranked my grinding into overdrive. Even the dealers or other addicts I spent time with were unsettled by it—sometimes begging me to calm down. I remember the day I was nearly tossed out of a crack house in New York City because of my hyperactivity. "Dude, you're making us all nervous. Get out!" the guy who rented the apartment yelled at me. "You're making *me* grind *my* teeth." It was one of the few times I remember being embarrassed in front of a group of other addicts.

In addition to the obnoxious grinding, my drug of choice had another effect on my mouth. Because it affects things like saliva production and the enamel of the teeth, cocaine can be as damaging to the mouth as it is to the nose or heart. Even long after I had stopped ingesting the drug, the damage remained—a long-term and irreversible consequence of my years of snorting powder and smoking rocks.

Even though I had been off drugs for more than twenty years, by the time I reached my mid-fifties, the combined effects of cocaine use and habitual grinding had stripped away most of my tooth enamel. My fragile molars were vulnerable to cracks and cavities. The two front teeth in the middle of the bottom row were pathetic nubs that had become so small that my lower lip managed to screen them even when I smiled broadly.

"Babyish teeth," my dentist explained. His diagnosis was "consistent dental erosion" that he could not halt, much less reverse. But he could repair the teeth, he assured me, and he had a plan. He had proposed this course of treatment several years earlier, but I had postponed it. I demurred not out of any fear—he had been my regular dentist for decades, and I trusted his abilities and his counsel—but because of my constantly grinding life. In the years since the divorce, I had been too busy to carve out the time needed for an undertaking that would involve several specialists as well as my own dentist. It felt like too many logistics to manage, too many competing demands and complicated schedules to coordinate, so I kept putting it off.

SINCE THE FALL of 2009, I had been home alone with my two teenage sons and preteen daughter. Every day felt exceptional for all of the experiences that make parenting adolescents so memorably endearing and utterly exhausting all at once. For me it was three times as endearing, three times as exhausting. All at once three times.

The first few years after the divorce were the most intense. The most rewarding. The hardest. To help me focus, I tried to separate my waking hours into three six-hour chunks. My day would start at about 5 a.m., when I would wake up and make coffee. Then I'd sit quietly in the living room—or the front porch in warm weather—and read a daily meditation while savoring those first two cups. I closed these early morning minutes by adding a few paragraphs or a page to my journal. Now grounded for the day ahead, I shifted into parent mode.

On school days, I'd do my best to prepare breakfast for the kids so it was ready when they came downstairs at 7 a.m. I rarely had to rouse them. In the spirit of my mother, I'd try to serve something nutritious and cooked. Eggs and bacon were standards. When my father was responsible for feeding my siblings and me breakfast as children, it was pigs in a blanket: Vienna sausages wrapped in Pillsbury crescent roll dough and baked in the oven for twelve minutes. My kids loved these as much as I did.

Our lives got a little easier as, one after another, the kids each earned their driver's license and could get themselves to school in the car they shared. The nervous angst I felt the first time I watched from the front porch as each of them drove away solo to go on a date or rendezvous with friends was worth the freedom they found. Their independence and mobility also freed me from having to take them everywhere. On weekday mornings, even these few extra minutes gave me more time to catch up on emails or get showered and dressed for the workday ahead without being so rushed.

The rest of the morning block, along with the next six to nine hours, was dedicated to my job. By 2008, I was a vice president at Hazelden and with the title came a raft of new responsibilities. I was on the road, giving a major speech somewhere in the country at least once a week. I had also taken on leading fundraising efforts, which required making a nearly ninety-mile round-trip commute to our corporate headquarters for in-person meetings and office hours three or four days a week. Cell phones made it easier to conduct some business from the car, but the commute was still a killer. On many days I was stressed out trying to get home in time to greet the kids and get something prepared for dinner.

It was the last chunk of the day that mattered the most in those early years. I was determined to make the dinner hour "family time." Though I am not a culinary whiz, I can cook steak or burgers or shrimp on the backyard grill. In the wintertime, the kids relished as much as I did my dad's go-to dinner recipe, a satisfying mixture of ground beef, egg noodles, and a can of English peas. When I got home later than planned, or if the mood struck us, we relied on plenty of takeout too.

The food kept us going, but it was the conversation that nourished us. When I was growing up, my parents had made our family dinner table a place to share and process what each of us had done during the day and also talk about world affairs. I recall this as a formative part of my childhood and youth and wanted to replicate the experience for my three children. The four of us invariably spent longer at the table than it took to eat what was on our plates.

I always felt blessed that my kids seemed to enjoy my company and our time together, especially in the months when Allison's absence was still raw. The dinner hour gave us a chance to talk about what had happened during the day—good or bad, hard or fun, exciting or boring—all of it was relevant, all welcome. Most of the time I just sat there and soaked it in, blessed to be a witness to the fine people my children were becoming.

During the final few hours of the day, the kids would retreat to their rooms to do homework or use their computers, and I would clean up the kitchen and handle the housework that has always been part of my routine. At bedtime I rarely had to track down the kids to say goodnight. They almost always came to my bedroom to sit for a few minutes and chat some more before we exchanged a kiss or hug and went to bed.

Of course, this semi-orderly routine only worked when I was home. For work events that involved travel, I usually managed to limit my time away to just one overnight, but sometimes I was gone for longer than I wanted to be. The kids felt it, and we all paid a price.

IN LATE 2009, Alaska's division of health and human services invited me to speak at its 2010 statewide conference, planned for the following spring. They sweetened the pot by offering to tack on an extra day's lodging and a guided salmon fishing trip. I don't often linger in any place long enough to appreciate it after my work is done, but this invitation seemed too good to pass up. Here was a chance to catch a fabled fish in a land famous for its wild salmon. I rarely turn down speaking opportunities if I can fit them in, and the Alaskans' hospitality was generous and welcome. I told them yes, happily marking out the May dates on my calendar. By the time the trip drew near, I had been looking forward to it for months.

Even before the divorce, my mother, Judith, had been our family's go-to backup kid-sitter. Being a grandmother is one of the roles that has delighted her since Henry was born. Stepping in and taking charge of my three children with nobody else around to tell her how to do it or help her get it done is the kind of challenge in which she and the kids thrive. After my solo parent era began, she had opportunities to assume this role even more frequently, traveling from New York to St. Paul to cover for me when I was away on the road for more than a night or two. Her steadfast presence and willingness to help us was critical to making our family life work in those years.

I had confirmed the dates with Mom shortly after accepting the Alaska invitation, and I arranged her flights so we'd have some overlap.

This time, however, my always-rock-solid home-front backup fell through. A few days before I was set to depart, my mom called to tell me she couldn't make it. Her reason was serious, but not an emergency. She was sorry to let us down. I told her not to worry about us, even as I began to strategize how we'd manage; Nell was unavailable as well.

Having had my childcare plan fall through would have been a valid reason to cancel the Alaska trip. Some might even suggest that not canceling the trip, given those circumstances, was irresponsible. Despite the disappointment I'd share with the sponsoring organization, the show would have gone on. Nobody would be crushed because they missed a chance to hear me speak. Everything would have been just fine.

But that May I didn't even consider saying no, and it wasn't just because of the fishing trip (which I had decided I would forgo). Over the course of my career as a traveling speaker—a career that has included thousands of speeches and public presentations all over the United States—I've rarely backed out on a commitment. Whether it's fear of missing out on an opportunity or concern about offending someone, this aversion to letting others down has sometimes come with costs and consequences, both for me and for people I care about.

I once flew to St. Louis and back to give a speech while suffering from what turned out to be strep throat. That return trip featured an unplanned and agonizing three-hour delay on the tarmac before we finally took off. Over the years I've sacrificed evenings and given away too many weekends all because the need to be needed elsewhere felt more urgent. Call it a defect of character or a sterling attribute of professional consistency, I simply cannot or will not allow myself to cancel on commitments like these.

So instead of communicating my regrets to my hosts, I devised a plan to make the Alaska trip work. If my mom couldn't come through this time, and my girlfriend was unavailable to help out, my kids could manage. Henry was seventeen years old now, and more responsible than I had ever been at his age. I'd leave my three at home alone. Big brother would be in charge, with the house rules well established ahead of time. To that end, I convened a family meeting the night before my flight.

"As you know, I'm going to Alaska for a conference. I leave tomorrow morning. Grandma can't come this time. I will be gone less than thirty hours or so and will be home in time for dinner the day after tomorrow," I explained. "You know my expectations: get yourselves up and to school; in the afternoon get home and do your homework; make dinner and go to bed at a decent hour." For a moment I paused, then added: "No people over—no parties either." I scanned their suddenly thoughtful faces. They hadn't even considered taking advantage of being home alone on a school night until I uttered that last sentence. I regretted saying it.

We all left the house together the next morning. "Don't worry, Dad. I'll make sure everything around here goes okay," Henry said. He gave me a thumbs-up and waved goodbye from behind the wheel of our car. The kids drove off to school as my taxi pulled up to the curb.

The cab had barely turned off our street when I began kicking myself for not trying harder to find a friend or neighbor to stand in for me at home. Foisting this kind of responsibility on Henry wasn't fair to him or to his siblings. It wouldn't be the last time I asked my kids to bend around my schedule or accommodate my absence, and it wouldn't be the last time I felt regret over it. As the car pulled into the departures lane at MSP, I patted my pockets and gathered up my overnight bag, trying not to imagine the worst-case scenarios. Instead, I silently uttered a selfish prayer, "Please God, watch over my children and my house."

The flight from Minnesota to Anchorage takes about six hours. Fortunately, Delta had a flight that departed just before nine in the morning. With the time change I gained three hours, so it was only midafternoon when the Boeing 757 touched down at ANC. Getting there was the easy part—the first step in a sequence of events that had to work exactly as planned.

My reason for coming all this way was to deliver the dinner keynote at a conference for counselors and other addiction treatment professionals. Following my speech, I'd make a quick visit to a local treatment center. When I entered the hotel ballroom, I was impressed and surprised by the turnout. Alaska is a huge state but sparsely populated compared to its land mass. The demand for treatment and recovery services requires an army of far-flung professionals, most of whom had apparently showed up for this annual conference to hear my speech.

The evening went well, and five hours after the emcee's welcome, my part in the conference was over. Although it was almost 11 p.m., the sun was still out. That far north in late May, daylight persists for more than eighteen hours. I had gotten my customary jolt of energy from the audience's response to my speech and from meeting the staff and clients at the center, but now I could feel myself fading. My body clock reminded me it was the middle of the night back home. I walked through the hotel lobby to my room feeling a hollow hangover-type ache behind my eyes.

All I wanted was to crawl into bed and sleep for hours, but I couldn't. To make my plan work and keep my promise to the kids, I had to be aboard a 6 a.m. flight. I struggled through the math: *Be at the airport two hours before takeoff. Thirty-minute drive to the airport if there was no traffic—is there much traffic in Anchorage at four in the morning? Twenty minutes to pull myself together and check out.* I figured I could afford maybe three hours of sleep.

Back in my room, I gazed at the bed with a combination of longing and worry. *What if I don't wake up on time?* Rather than getting between the sheets, I simply lay on top of the bedspread fully clothed. I was so tired I didn't even bother to take off my shoes or remove my tie. At last I closed my eyes and tried to relax, but the "what ifs" weren't finished with me.

What if I don't hear the alarm?

What if I miss the flight?

What if the kids get home from school and I'm not there?

What are the kids doing right now? Should I call?

The weird twilight seeping around the room's heavy curtains made me wonder if it was later than the time on the clock. Eventually, I jumped up, stripped off my clothes, and stepped into the shower. I made sure the water was only lukewarm—a hot shower would be enough to tempt me afterward to lie back down on the bed wrapped in a towel. But the tepid water didn't wash away my weariness as I had hoped. I dried off and got dressed: the same stale clothing I had been wearing since I left home fourteen hours earlier. Despite the shower, I smelled tired. My eyes felt as if they'd been salted. Catching sight of my pale face in the mirror, I had a flashback to the bleak mornings after a binge or bender, still wearing the clothes I had worn to work the day before. I looked and felt cheap and cheapened all at once.

"What am I doing here?" I asked myself in despair, tipping back over onto the rumpled bed, a damp pile of self-pity and regret. I looked up at the random pattern of the popcorn ceiling. *Who really cares that I was here? Who would have cared if I wasn't here to make that speech—what's the difference? Why do I do this to myself? Why can't I just say, "No, I won't honor my commitment because I can't this time," or "Yes, I must stay home with my kids," and "No, I can't leave them home alone, sorry, but you'll need to find a last-minute substitute because I am canceling on behalf of my sanity and my kids"?*

The ceiling of that hotel room, for all its texture, didn't offer any opinions about my mental state, or my self-care, or my priorities as a parent. Finally, I gave up and got up. I'd just go on to the airport now, where I knew I could find a stout cup of coffee. At least I wouldn't miss my flight.

I managed to get a few hours of sleep on the plane, but it was nowhere near enough. Some twelve hours after I left the hotel, dead on my feet, yet another car deposited me back where I had started. I was home for fewer than fifteen minutes before the kids showed up after school. As I watched them scramble out of the car, they spotted me on the porch and waved. Nothing had gone awry. Relief coursed through me, as well as an odd sense of accomplishment. I felt as though I had won a contest or proven something to someone. That night after we all went to bed, I once again found it impossible to sleep. Over and over in my head I kept thinking about a river I never got to see and huge silver-and-rainbow fish that that kept slipping just out of reach.

NELL AND I HAD become more than boyfriend and girlfriend. Even though she kept her apartment in the duplex a block away—that's where she and Jasper called home—she often stayed at my house when her son was with his father, who also lived in St. Paul. For two adults who had become accustomed to having our own spaces, the arrangement was ideal. It gave us, and our kids, time together as well as apart.

Nell brought a renewed vibrancy to my life that I hadn't known for a long time. She helped me discover an ability to loosen up, if only a little, the tight agenda I always kept. On weekends we biked together, usually stopping at a neighborhood café for a meal before riding home. She convinced me to try yoga with her. I wasn't very good at mastering the fundamentals of the moves or the art of holding the positions, but sharing the experience was the real benefit to me. Having been a dedicated solo runner since my youth, I had never before considered exercise part of any relationship. Suddenly I found myself eager to go to a museum or on a bike ride or to a lecture on spirituality, not so much because I really wanted to—often I was tired or felt like I had too much on my plate—but because Nell asked me to go with her. We had fun together. Ours felt like a good match.

BY THE TIME I was discussing dental reconstruction plans with my oral surgeon in 2012, Henry and Thomas were out the door to college, both far away from home. The void made by their absence was notable. Suddenly there were no more touch football games in the street on bucolic fall family afternoons. The routine of church followed by brunch did not feel quite so satisfying with just two of us, even though Nancy and I still went on occasion and sometimes Nell would join us. With the boys gone, there was also a palpable dip in the frenetic spirit of our house. I welcomed this lull, as I was relieved to have fewer mouths to feed, less laundry to fold, and not as many homework assignments to review, but I felt my sons' absence every day. Nancy and I both missed the tight dynamic that had sustained the four of us after the divorce.

Nancy turned fifteen in January of 2012. She was a sophomore by then and loved volleyball. Between playing for the high school team and a league with games on weekends, she and I found and shared a rhythm of father-daughter comradery that brought us even closer together. When I cheered too loudly from the bleachers, she often glanced my way from the court and rolled her eyes. But she put up with me and continued to play. Tall and athletic, she would go on to captain the team as a senior. Every spike or block lifted me off my seat in every game, getting me so worked up you'd think it was me in the game, instead of among the fans.

Alongside falling in love with Nell and parenting teenagers whose interests and lives were as much outside the house as they were at home, I had managed to write another book. *Now What? An Insider's Guide to Addiction and Recovery* was released by Hazelden's publishing division in 2012. In contrast to *Broken*'s personal stories, *Now What?* was a straightforward primer for how to get from problem to solution. The title came from the question I finally asked myself at the rocky start of my final stint in treatment, way back in 1994. In the years since, I've come to learn that it's also the question that inevitably confronts millions of other people who finally hit a brick wall or a bottom that brings them face-to-face with the futility of the path they're on. In some form or another, it's a question I get three or four times a day on most every day of the year from the people who approach me for advice or support.

In sales the book did okay, though nothing like *Broken*. But I will always remember how startled I felt the day I was on an airplane reading the *New York Times* and came across a reference to my new book. I had turned the page to renowned health journalist Jane Brody's column and saw that she had reviewed the book. "A helpful new book. For those who need a structured program, Mr. Moyers describes what to consider to maximize the chances of overcoming addiction to alcohol and other drugs."

In that moment I actually rose out of my seat, jolted with excitement, my head bumping into the console above me, which inadvertently rung the call button for the flight attendant. "Yes, how can I help—what do you need?" she asked, hurrying down the aisle to my row. "Nothing, really nothing, I'm just fine,"

I replied, an embarrassed grin beaming all the same. "I've never been finer." She looked puzzled but nodded her head and moved on. She'd surely seen a lot of peculiar behavior from passengers over her years in the sky, even from sober ones like me. I could barely sit still for the rest of the flight; I wanted to prance in the aisle. Jane Brody! I couldn't wait to get home and wave this paper like a flag.

IT WAS ALWAYS a joy whenever my kids came home from college on their breaks. The first year that Thomas was at school in Vermont, his flight home for Thanksgiving arrived quite late. I had stayed up past my bedtime, eager for him to arrive. When he did, near midnight, we grabbed each other in a bear hug. Feeling my arms around his body made me realize how much I missed him around the house.

I suspected he'd be hungry. "I've got turkey and fresh bread, how about I make you a sandwich?" I said. A moment later both of us were in the kitchen: him at his familiar spot at the island, me on the opposite side where I laid out the ingredients. Seeing him leaning against the counter, I was struck by how much my second son seemed to have grown up in the six weeks since I had seen him at parents' weekend. He looked more like a man than a college freshman, and though he was tired I was impressed by how mature he sounded.

For a little while we caught up on college life. He told me about his classes and the handful of new friends he'd met on campus. Then he leaned over the shiny stainless-steel counter. His eyes shifted downward, even as he seemed to be trying to get closer to me. When he spoke again, his voice was quieter.

"Dad, I've stopped drinking, but I can't stop smoking weed." There was sadness in his voice. He took a breath and looked me full in the face. "Dad, I need your help."

I don't know what shocked me more in that moment: Thomas's blunt admission that he had a problem with a drug or the fact that he had done exactly what Allison and I had always encouraged our kids to do if they got into trouble with substances. He had spoken up. He had said something to someone.

I didn't know whether to start shaking with worry or jumping for joy. This was serious, but it was also something I knew about—it was something I could handle. I kept my cool.

"Well Thomas, you've come to the right place," I said gently. "Tell me more." I tried to pretend that I was paying careful attention to how much mayo I was spreading on his sandwich bread, but I was actually focused with every fiber of my being on what he was sharing. For the next fifteen minutes, he poured out the details. He didn't hold back, but he didn't fall apart either. The more he talked, the more he seemed to relax. When he finished, it was with a palpable sigh of relief.

As I gazed at this young man, I suddenly saw him as the boy he was many years ago, standing in this same kitchen. I reached across the island and mopped his hair with my hand. As a young child, Thomas was the one who got scared by a neighbor's dog or feared touching the fish and baiting the hooks at the lake. I was flooded with a rush of pure love for my son.

I told him that I wasn't too surprised. It made sense, given the handful of incidents he and I had been forced to confront when he was in high school. I reminded him of the time I had discovered a small container of marijuana in the trunk of his car while he and I were loading bins of raked leaves to drop off at the compost center. A year or so earlier he had been ticketed by the police for holding an open container of alcohol in a car his friend was driving. Each of those incidents had resulted in consequences, but little more than a slap on the wrist. At the time, so soon after the divorce, I had been afraid to come down hard, not wanting to drive a wedge between us.

But this time he had asked for help.

"First, I think you need to tell Mom what's happened," I said. "Listen to what she has to say, then we'll figure out our next steps."

Thomas had started in on the sandwich. "Are you mad at me, Dad?" he asked between bites. His big brown eyes found mine. I looked back and sighed.

"How can I be mad at you, Thomas? I'm not even disappointed. I am worried—worried but also relieved. I'm pleased that you came to me now, before things get worse." I paused. "I was your age when I started to have problems at college. Things got worse for me precisely because I was afraid to say anything. I didn't get help." I reminded him that there was a copy of *Broken* on his bookshelf. He could read about that part of my life if he wanted to. One upside of having a few copies of one's memoir around the house is that there's a convenient resource guide at hand whenever the kids have questions about one's life.

"Do you think it would have made a difference if your parents had known, if you had gotten help earlier?" he asked, recalling troubles I'd encountered in college that went largely unaddressed by my parents, even though they were obvious and alarming. I was relieved he was willing to talk further about this. I sensed that he was trying to draw contrasts and parallels between his experiences and mine. "I don't know, Thomas. But the point is, I didn't. I wasted all of my college years. I don't want that to happen to you."

Our father-and-son talk lasted into the small hours. As it got later and later, and as I watched his eyelids start to droop, I asked what he wanted to do next. I knew what I wanted him to say, but he needed to answer for himself. "I guess I should talk to a counselor."

Thomas was the first of his siblings to reveal a challenge with substance use and ask me for help. The steps he took after our midnight conversation didn't solve his problem right away. But through trial and error and the gift of time, he eventually found the solution he needed.

Over the next few years, Nancy and Henry would both come to me with their own stories of struggle with substances. Their details were different, but the agony and confusion about being unable to stop were the same. It was all about a baffling inability to "just say no." Unlike my experience as a teenager, decades earlier, my kids knew they had a safe place to seek help, and people in their lives who wouldn't judge or condemn them for needing it. I was humbled by their stories and honored that they chose me to share them with.

AS THE DAY on the calendar marked "Dentist: Teeth Out" approached, I started to get nervous. I knew these appointments might leave me in pain for several days, and this worried me.

I've dealt with low-level discomfort in my teeth for most of my adult life. Even so, I was afraid that the procedures my dentist was proposing would hurt a lot before they helped. The thought of letting someone expose all those wildly sensitive roots to air, probing tools, and drilling machines was enough to make me question whether I really wanted to go through with the plan.

I don't do well with pain. I have a vivid recollection from my childhood of a time my parents took my sister and brother and me to a Civil War museum. In an exhibit that portrayed medical care on the battlefield, my father pointed out a lead bullet that had small, evenly spaced dents in it. He explained how those marks had been made by a wounded soldier's teeth when the man bit down on it to keep from screaming as an army surgeon amputated his leg. My dad went on to tell me how the phrase "bite the bullet" came from this era, when anesthetics hadn't yet been invented and patients had to endure pain by whatever means at hand, often biting against belts or pieces of wood—or musket balls and bullets like the one on display. I was too young for my father's linguistic lesson. All my young mind could imagine was that poor man, still wearing his blue uniform coat, twisting his body in helpless agony as the saw worked its way through his flesh and bone. From that moment on, the thought of unrelenting and real pain has made me physically shudder.

Since quitting drugs in 1994, I have stayed in fairly good shape, physically. This is fortunate, given my aversion to pain. I'm grateful for my health and work to maintain it with regular exercise. For me, this includes a three-mile run a few times a week and two days of light weightlifting in the gym I built in the basement. I am not exactly a healthy eater, but I try to stay away from junk food. When I've needed the care of a doctor or dentist, it's been for routine stuff like a cavity or a sore throat or the flu. Almost without exception, my experiences with healthcare providers over the years have been positive and helpful.

Before 2012, I had gone under the knife for minor surgical procedures only twice. In the year 2000, I was diagnosed with melanoma. The diagnosis—an aggressive and potentially lethal form of skin cancer—terrified me at first, but my dermatologist had noticed the dark, irregularly shaped mole on my upper left arm before it got too big, and the procedure for removing it was relatively simple and remarkably painless. With a local anesthetic to numb the area, the surgeon excised the threat with a slice of the scalpel, stitched me up, and sent me home, with Tylenol as needed. In a day or two I was fine. A few years later, I had some running-related bone spurs removed from both feet.

Thanks to the miracles of modern medicine, I will never have to bite the bullet. But I am no different from anyone else in that I hate to hurt. I was scared about the upcoming dental work. The surgeries I had undergone years before were uncomfortable and inconvenient, but they were one-and-done. They probably didn't compare to what I was now facing: an ongoing series of procedures on my teeth and inside my mouth—one of the most sensitive parts of the human body.

It was more than that, of course. *Babyish teeth. Dental erosion.* The observations the dentist had made about my teeth made me cringe. *I did this to myself.* I had a vivid memory of myself, crouched in the filthy corner of some derelict house, windows blacked out, eyes wide open despite days and nights of no sleep, my jaw clenching and grinding. The horror from those days was not over, it seemed. Consequences always seem to find their way home. Shame settled over me, an old and familiar blanket of despair. I had fucked up so much that was good and right about my life. My marriage. My kids' childhood years. I had even fucked up my teeth.

5

Breaking Point

2012

> When we are tired, we are attacked
> by ideas we conquered long ago.
>
> — FRIEDRICH NIETZSCHE

The dental technician slipped the clear mask over my nose.

"Breathe deeply, slowly, in and out, in and out," she instructed.

"I want you to count to ten," the dentist said. His voice was confident and soothing. "Count slowly, from one to ten."

"One, two, three . . ." I counted and breathed. "Four, five . . ."

"That's right," he said. "Good."

"Six . . . seven . . ." The air in the mask smelled sweet and felt cool in the back of my throat.

I didn't get to ten before bursting into tears.

In those first few moments of breathing in nitrous oxide gas in the dentist's chair, I was overwhelmed by a flood of emotions and sensations like nothing I had ever experienced. The gas was supposed to help me relax, but I suddenly felt swept up in a flash flood of terror and panic. My body stiffened. My eyes darted around the room, vainly seeking some familiar perspective for what was happening to me.

This was no orgasmic euphoria from a line of cocaine or hit of crack. I didn't feel the gentle burn of whiskey. It wasn't a flashback to a sad chapter of my life or a nightmare recycling bad times gone by. There were no demons born of hallucinations like the times I dropped acid or ate mushrooms in college.

I was completely conscious—acutely aware of the moment, in fact—neither too numb nor too high to care about what was happening to me as I reclined against the chair back. Emotions coursed through me, my initial shock expanding into a vivid whirlpool of awe and helplessness that pulled me deeper and deeper into a fear I thought would drown me.

I floated in a strange tide in a place I'd never been before. I couldn't stop the tears from flowing. I was terrified at what had just happened and equally afraid of what would come next.

I was in a room beneath a light, I reminded myself. I was in the dentist's office. I was here to have teeth pulled. I had planned this.

I knew that what was happening to me was real—not a mirage of my imagination or an out-of-body moment. Everything around me was tangible, but it was also changed. I was awestruck, incapable of understanding the intense flood of emotion that surged from some source within me, so deep that it had never been tapped before.

The fear dissolved into wonderment. With the euphoria came intense and unbidden memories: the first time I made love with my high school girlfriend; the bitter taste of that first can of lukewarm Budweiser my high school friend had filched from his parents' house; hearing the sizzle and watching the melting rock of cocaine dissolve into white fog and drift up the pipe into my lungs and drive me to my knees.

I cried with real grief and despair, and in the same moment I was mesmerized, sensing a perspective I'd never experienced and was incapable of understanding. I wanted to swim in it. I wanted to go deeper and deeper into it, explore its exquisite turquoise surface and its darker mysteries, but at the same time I was terrified of where it was taking me and what lurked below.

Wonderment and fear swirled into each other in a waking dream. I was living, existing, floating in a place that was different from anywhere I had ever been or imagined. I couldn't escape, and then I realized I didn't want to. Why would I? All I needed was to be left alone, immersed in the awareness of this moment that felt so profound.

I was weightless, free from any and all of my life's duties and challenges. In that immense emptiness, I was untroubled by any demands. My entire existence was right here.

Did a minute pass, an hour? And anyway, so what? I didn't care what the dentist was doing, even as I saw him hovering over me. The Novocaine I had been given earlier had done its work. I had a vague sense that my head was moving from side to side as he tugged at my jaw. At one point I heard a distant crack. I must have reacted in some way because he reassured me. "Don't worry," he said from some faraway place, "the tooth broke, but we're not saving that one anyway."

I didn't care. The tears were gone now, along with the fear. I drifted in a safe, secure wonderland. I began to scrutinize the holes in the square ceiling tiles above my head, searching to connect them into what I was sure would reveal a picture or a pattern or maybe a secret message to explain what this moment was all about.

I felt the air in the room caressing my skin, heard the distant back-and-forth between dentist and assistant echoing like they were in a cave. The noises around me modulated in and out and all at once, chased by bright pulsating colors of the rainbow, shades of gray, deep blacks, and bright whites. The peach aura around the lamp over my head looked so appealing I wanted to stick out my tongue and lick it. My brain switched gears to concentrate on solving the twisting and turning Rubik's Cube that seemed to be in constant motion around and within me—every second marked by interaction and sound and color.

I don't how long the procedure took. Time had no meaning.

"Fifty percent," the dentist told his assistant.

"Down to fifty percent," the assistant echoed.

Their voices were suddenly jarring, an unwelcome intrusion into my private, mystical space.

"Now forty percent," he said.

"Down to forty percent," she replied.

The real world was ready to assert itself again. The gas that had terrified me at first had created a lovely, colorful, peaceful place that I did not want to leave.

"Thirty percent."

She's making it go away.

Suddenly overcome with panic, I tried to fight back. I didn't want to emerge from where I was. I breathed in sharply, deeper and faster, in and out, over and over, desperate to inhale more of the gas even as the tech worked to pull me back to the real world.

The hiss of the tank's valve slowed, then stopped. I lay heavily in the reclined chair, barely able to move. That morning I had rushed off to the dentist to get two front lower teeth pulled and undergo a root canal—the appointment one more item on my week's list of things to get done. All that seemed like it happened a lifetime ago. Now I lay helpless and exhausted, like I had just come down from the holy mountain after standing before a burning bush.

"What just happened?" I mumbled through the fog. My jaw was heavy and unresponsive. "Why did I cry?"

The dentist pulled down his mask to reveal a half smile. "Many of my patients have the same reaction, William," he said. "Their emotions are unleashed. It isn't at all that unusual for them to cry. There doesn't have to be a reason. The gas does just that—it unlocks emotions. You're no different. Don't read too much into it. There's nothing profound here."

Really? Nothing profound? I had been under the influence many times in my life, but I just had my mind blown. It was like my first trip on LSD in college, an indelible moment that still feels real, even all these decades later. This experience with the gas had barely ended but already I knew I'd never forget it.

"Tell me, doc, what just happened to me?" I asked again. He seemed disinterested in a postmortem on the spectacle that had occurred inside my brain. This was a dental chair, not a couch in a therapist's office. Doctor and assistant circled around me, putting away equipment and cleaning up. I knew my time was finished. But I couldn't get out of the chair quite yet.

"Could it be I was afraid of being high after all these years sober?" I asked.

No answer.

"Maybe I loved it so much I wanted more and I couldn't have it."

No response.

"The gas must have unlocked something in my brain somewhere."

Silence. For a moment, I wondered if I was even speaking out loud.

The doctor came around from behind and stood at my feet, looking right at me.

"Now's not the time for you to think too much or too hard," he said. "The gas is done, and the local anesthetic will wear off in an hour or two. Then you're going to feel the results of what we did in your mouth, and it won't be pleasant. You're going to be sore, uncomfortable, and irritable. I want you to go home, lie down, and take it easy; avoid solid foods for dinner. In a few days you should be fine."

I heard what he was saying, but I wasn't ready to leave without some sense of what in the world had just happened to me. I was convinced there had to be an answer somewhere in that room. I wanted to stay and find it, but my time was up. The tech was now pulling off the paper bib that covered my shirt and handing me a stack of papers—aftercare instructions stapled together with two smaller forms. "Make sure you take your meds on time. This one," she said, tapping the paper, "is the antibiotic. The other one is for pain."

I nodded, repeating to myself, *Antibiotic for infection, other one for pain.* My synapses weren't working too well. I was shaky with nausea and my head had begun to feel like a bowling ball.

She gently patted my arm. "You'll be fine. Call us if you have any problems."

"JEEZ, WHAT HAPPENED to you?" The pharmacist at the CVS on Grand Avenue knew me by sight, having regularly filled prescriptions for my family over the years. "You look like you've been on the wrong end of a fight!" I tried to smile back but my lips couldn't make the right curves. My swollen face felt stony and tight.

"Dentist," was all I could get out, pointing to my mouth.

"Ouch," she said, nodding in sympathy. She glanced at the two prescriptions. "I know you want to get home, but this will take longer than usual. Sorry about that. We've got a backlog of orders ahead of you. Do you want to wait or come back later— probably in about an hour?"

I was in no mood to plead for the pharmacist to bump my prescription to the front of the long list of orders any more than I wanted to make another trip. "I'll wait in my car," I whispered.

I didn't even think to start the engine to keep myself warm. As the afternoon sunlight slanted through the windshield, I was a thick mound of clay. Physically, my entire body was exhausted by what had transpired in my mouth. Mentally, I was still reeling from the encounter with the gas. Behind my closed eyelids, echoes of the swirling colors continued to shift and turn. The only part of me that didn't feel numb was my jaw; the strange rubbery sensation in my face was fading as the Novocaine wore off. As the minutes passed, it began to hurt with a pulsating throb. I just wanted to feel better.

BY THE END of 2012, America was more than twenty years into what would come to be called "the first wave" of the opioid epidemic. The country was awash in opioid pain medication. That year, healthcare providers wrote 259 million prescriptions for drugs with brand names like Percocet and Vicodin and Oxy-Contin—all versions of the semi-synthetic opioids oxycodone and hydrocodone. The bottle of pills I sat in my cold car waiting for was one of those data points.

In the late 1990s and early 2000s, these medications were touted by pharmaceutical companies as a miracle solution to the problem of pain—which had begun to be described as "the fifth vital sign." It didn't matter who you were, where you lived, how you voted, or what ailed you; if you were hurting, these drugs would provide immediate relief—and do it safely, they said, with a much lower risk of addiction than with the more notorious narcotics like heroin or morphine. Opioids were promised to be—and aggressively marketed as—a panacea, and thousands of dentists and doctors who wanted to help their patients feel better accepted that promise at face value.

Between 1999 and 2010, sales of prescription opioids quadrupled. In the same span of years, deaths from opioid-related overdoses doubled. Only after the Centers for Disease Control and Prevention recognized and named the opioid overdose epidemic in 2011, and released prescribing guidelines in the following years, did the number of prescriptions begin to slowly decline. By then it was too late for a great many people. Besides the hundreds of thousands who had died of overdoses, many more had become dependent on these powerful drugs. During the year I received my first prescription for an opioid pain medication, the National Institute on Drug Abuse estimated that 2.6 million Americans were addicted to opioids. It wasn't until October of 2017 that this crisis was declared a public health emergency with a nationwide impact; that determination has been renewed twenty-five times between then and the time of this writing—every ninety days.

"ANY QUESTIONS?" the pharmacist asked, handing me the plastic bag with the prescriptions.

I shook my head. Even that little movement made everything above my shoulders hurt. All I wanted to do was go home and go to bed.

"Don't take the antibiotic on an empty stomach; it can be kind of harsh on the GI tract," she warned. "For the pain medication—that's the orange bottle—follow what it says on the label. You probably won't need it for more than a day, but there are plenty here. My hunch is you can switch over to Tylenol tomorrow, or you can use the Tylenol in between to reduce the frequency of the other ones."

I mumbled my thanks. "Feel better!" she said brightly as I walked away.

When I got home, Nancy was sitting at the table in the kitchen flipping the screen on her phone—her usual method of avoiding homework. Only when she looked up for a second did she greet me. She was shocked. "Oh Dad, you look like somebody's beaten you up," she said. "You look terrible."

I glanced at myself in the hallway mirror. She was right. My face and cheeks were pale and puffy. My jaw was swollen and hanging slack. It looked almost unhinged. Any little movement intensified the throbbing pain in my head. As I shuffled past my daughter, she laid a hand on my shoulder in sympathy. Without stopping to pet the cat who was sitting on the middle landing leading upstairs, I climbed one step at a time. All I wanted in the whole world was to be in my bed.

Passing the bathroom, I thought about the meds. I was still gripping the bag in my left hand. I stopped and washed down one of the antibiotics with water from the sink, then two Percocet pills—as directed on the bottle. Swallowing hurt enough to make me wince. I finished the trek to my bedroom, stepped out of my shoes, and somehow slid onto the bed, still dressed in my socks and jeans and sweater.

I lay there with my eyes closed for ten minutes or so, vivid scenes from the afternoon in the dentist's chair running through my mind. I didn't know how to make sense of them, all the colors and sounds and emotions I had experienced, the warm light, swirling sense of time, the hot tears. The way my initial fear had given way to that deep sense of peace. I was exhausted now, but I couldn't sleep.

After a few minutes, something changed. I felt as though someone had gently drawn a thin, warm blanket over me. I opened my eyes and looked around. Had somebody followed me up the stairs? Was Nancy or Nell in the room with me? *Guardian angels*, I thought. I closed my eyes again and smiled. Now it felt like waves of relief were lightly washing over my whole body. The throbbing from my swollen jaw, aching gums, sore muscles, and stiff neck faded. I could feel the pain evaporate, picturing tender wisps rising from my body to dissipate like smoke in the air of the dim room. I felt easy, warm, content, happy, complete. I was smiling again. I may even have whispered out loud, "Life is good."

I sat up. *Life is good. So damn good,* I thought, *that I can't lie here all by myself. I need to share the feeling of this moment with people I love.* I swung my legs over the edge of the bed. It didn't hurt. I stood up and walked toward the sound of Nell and Nancy talking quietly in the kitchen downstairs. They looked surprised to see me upright.

"I feel much better," I said.

It's kind of a miracle, I thought as I sat at the kitchen table listening to them chatting about their days and watching them move about the kitchen as dinner came together. The agony in my face and jaw—pain that had felt utterly debilitating an hour ago—had vanished. But there was something else too. Something extra. Everything in the world now seemed somehow softer, gentler, more meaningful. The spaghetti sauce simmering on the stove smelled more delicious than any food I had ever tasted. The soothing purr of the cat who had stealthily found my lap resonated an octave deeper than I remembered. Her body felt warm against my legs. Nell was beautiful and Nancy was brilliant. Jasper, who had just arrived home from school, was witty and charming. Everything was in its place and under control, just as it should be—just as I always wanted and needed it to be—but without any effort on my part. There was nothing clamoring for my attention. Nobody needed anything from me. I saw nothing that needed correction. I felt peaceful. In this golden moment, all I had to do was enjoy my life. Worries and responsibilities could wait. I could just sit here and let it happen, give in, and let go.

Later that evening the feeling faded. As I lay in bed, the warm aura receded, and the pain creeped back into my face and head. *Every four hours,* I thought, wishing the pills lasted longer. Maybe four hours was too long between doses for a tall guy like me with a low threshold of pain and a lot of it right now. I debated my options. *Take more? Don't take more?* It seemed like a waste to sleep through the effects of two more pills when there were so few in the container. On the other hand, I didn't want pain to keep me awake; I had a big day ahead. I kept the amber bottle closed, swallowing three extra-strength Tylenol as the pharmacist had suggested "to stay ahead of the pain."

I switched off the bedside lamp and began my nightly routine of prayer and gratitude for the gift of another day. What a day it had been.

I barely got past the words "Dear God" when another thought interrupted my focus.

I can't wait until tomorrow to take more.

I HAD FELT this way before. A few years after my skin cancer procedure back in 2000, I had surgery to remove bone spurs from both of my big toes. My years as a dedicated runner had finally taken a toll on my feet. The podiatrist sent me home after the procedure with orders to rest and limit my walking for a couple of days. He also wrote a prescription for Vicodin. Like other doctors I've seen over the decades, he noted that I had checked the "substance abuse" box on the form detailing my medical history and asked me about it. I explained that I had been clean and sober since 1994.

"Well then, you know to take these *exactly* as prescribed—*only* for pain," he warned. That's what I did for the first few days of napping and hobbling to the bathroom and back to my chair. At some point, maybe on day three or four, I became aware that I was thinking about the small bottle of Vicodin tablets almost all the time. I was checking my watch, counting out the minutes until "every four hours" was up and it was permissible to take another pill. Each time I took one, after a few moments, I'd feel a warm, liquid sensation coursing through my veins, washing over my whole body.

Realizing how much I looked forward to the medication spooked me. I knew that my addict's brain was being teased by what I was experiencing. Finally, one afternoon, I flushed the rest of the supply down the toilet—about a dozen large, white, oblong pills. My momentary feeling of fluttery regret was outweighed by a sense of relief. Proud that I had done the right thing, I waved goodbye to the pills, saluting what I saw as one of those moments of temptation people like me need to watch out for. Pills gone—check. No more temptation—check. Recovery intact—check.

That memory didn't help me in the final weeks of 2012.

ON THE MORNING after my day in the dentist's chair, I wasn't much in the mood to write in my journal. My mouth hurt so much that I sipped my coffee with a spoon. I was hungry, but opening my jaw wide enough to take a bite of the buttered toast with blueberry fruit spread that is part of my early-morning routine was impossible. My head and neck ached too. It was all I could do to jot down a few lines.

Rough night. In and out of sleep all night. Had to lie on my back with head propped on two pillows higher than my body. Uncomfortable. Still processing what the heck happened with the gas. Felt like it got between me and my subconscious. Threatening. Did like the pain pills though. They work. Today I'll have to take them again.

I liked the way the pills had erased the pain, but I was wary of them too—not because of the experience I had with Vicodin after my foot surgery, but because I had to get back to work. A busy day loomed, and I did not want the meds to dull my focus. Besides, the dentist and pharmacist were right. The extra-strength Tylenol seemed to do the trick. My mouth was sore, and I was uncomfortable, but I could suffer through it.

Still, later that afternoon I found myself with two of the round white pills in the palm of my hand. *I probably don't even need to take these,* I thought as I popped them into my mouth and swallowed. Within a few minutes the pain in my mouth and jaw faded to nothing, taking with it my anxiety about the day, the to-do list, and everything else. The sharp, hard edges of my life softened.

On the fourth morning after my dental procedure, I sensed that there was more to my pill-popping than pain relief. That day I wrote in my journal again.

These past three days I've bumped up against the tempting grip of the pain meds. Basked in the warm, euphoric glow of the buzz, sat at my desk listening to music, banging out emails, getting stuff done. Schemed the timing to do it again yesterday. And I did. Plus one.

I also saw the other side of being under the influence. Eventually it fades. I was keenly aware that as the sense of being "at ease" faded, I didn't like how I felt, both in my thinking and in the altered sensory state. Mainly because it goes away.

Plus one. I had taken an extra pill. The bottle said two; I took three. To most people that might not seem like a big deal. Perhaps a larger dose makes them feel woozy or slightly out of it, makes their bad day a bit better and their good day a bit more pleasant. Either way, they might like that feeling, but my guess is they don't need a pill to get there. Besides, not many people would take an extra pill—a plus one—because they trust that the instructions on the side of the bottle are there for a specific reason. *Take two every four to six hours* means exactly what it says. It doesn't mean one more pill or one less hour.

I can read directions, and I have my share of common sense. Most of what I've learned comes from the mistakes I've made and the successes I've achieved over the years. I also learn from others' accounts. I had heard the stories of people who suddenly found themselves spinning out of control and falling into trouble after being prescribed mood- or mind-altering medications—especially pain meds.

Those stories always seem to start the same way: "I broke my arm . . ." or "I needed a root canal . . ." or "I finally had the surgery to replace my knee . . ." The medical procedure is legitimate, and the medication prescribed is meant to provide relief from real pain. But somewhere along the way something changes. Some people describe it as a slow unfolding, like a seed pushing up from the soil. Others say it hits like a lightning bolt out of blue sky. Mostly it seems to happen somewhere in between slow motion and the blink of an eye. For too many people, what happens next is inevitable. The medication that started as a solution becomes a problem.

I don't know why I took that extra pill. Was it rebellion? Opportunism? My addicted mind awakened from its long slumber? I had a busy, satisfying, fulfilling life. I had reasons to get up in the morning. Most nights I went to bed content that I had met my purpose for the day. My life was hardly perfect, of course. The mistakes I'd made, the heartache and disappointment, loss and regret, hurt a lot but I'd made it through the ups and downs—and I had done it without taking a drink or returning to other drugs. In my head and in my heart, I believed my life was worthwhile. Even so, some part of me also believed that if two pills worked as well as they did, three would work even better.

After dinner the next evening I found myself locked in a tug-of-war over what to do with the pills that remained from the prescription I'd gotten nearly a week before. My mouth was healing. The Tylenol had done its job during the day; the pain meds had become a kind of interlude, slipping into my pre-bedtime routine for three straight nights. Now there were only a few pills left. *I don't need to take these, I feel fine,* I told myself as I sat in the den, half-heartedly watching a college football game on television.

My mind kept returning to and playing with the idea that one more shot of that melting sense of well-being wouldn't harm me. The soft, warm glow of *life is good* awareness was available to me—right there in that little bottle. Just one extra. Or two.

I was eager to feel the slow softening of the tense muscles in my head, neck, and shoulders. I needed the day's anxiety to melt away, to cast off my resentments toward the people or situations that had disappointed me or pissed me off over the past twenty-four hours. Besides, this was the last hurrah. Why not go for it one more time? One more ride up and then a soft landing and back to the routine that was my life.

Let's do it, I told myself. I swallowed the remaining pills. Then I walked upstairs to my home office and turned on my iTunes music on the desktop computer. My favorite playlist featured a mix of the Beatles, the Rolling Stones, and a couple of tracks by Jimi Hendrix, including his classic "Are You Experienced?"

I've always loved the way he plays the guitar, but that night, it was the lyrics that captured what I was feeling. As the effect of the pills slowly spread through my brain and coursed down my body to my toes, I imagined that I wasn't stoned so much as *beautiful.* For a little while, everything was. The peaceful, relaxing moment morphed into peaceful and relaxing hours. When I looked at the clock it was midnight, way past my bedtime.

The next morning, certain that my experience with the meds was behind me, I tried to summarize in my journal what had happened.

> *I don't dislike the feeling, but I don't need it. It came and went and when it went, it faded slowly. I again find myself today grateful that pursuing oblivion is not what it once was so long ago, when I did it all the time. I really do love my life the way it is. I am relieved I'm done with them. I am glad I don't need them.*

Reading that journal entry now, after the months and years that followed, I can see what was beginning to happen to me. At the time, I had to tell myself that nothing had changed—and that nothing would change. I didn't yet know how so much of what I believed about my addiction and took for granted about my recovery would be tested by the subtleties of a substance that was like none I had experienced before.

I consoled myself with the observation that, for the past week, I hadn't missed a day of work or disappeared from home. I had even felt more productive than usual. I enjoyed the buzz, but that small pleasure could be my secret. No one else—even those who knew me best—noticed or suspected I was altered at all. It was the cleanest, simplest experience with an addictive substance that I had ever known.

I didn't note in my journal that I had paid close attention to the number of remaining pills as the supply dwindled. As long as there were any left, I had been certain they would end up in my stomach. I did, however, feel a sense of relief when the prescription container was empty and I could stop keeping track. Deep within me I sensed that the pills threatened the essence of what made me the man I was, professionally and personally. That was the man I still needed to be, at work and at home and in the ecosphere of recovery that I had known for so long. I could not imagine any other way of life.

Only it wasn't that simple anymore.

"I'M WILLIAM; I'm an alcoholic," I said when the introductions went around the room at my regular AA meeting. After what had just happened with the pills, it felt good to be there with these people who knew and liked me. This had been my regular meeting for more than fifteen years, and what I appreciated most about it was how many "old-timers" attended. These were members who represented what it really means to walk the walk of recovery, not just talk the talk. They lived it inside and out, but still refused to let their hard-earned wisdom crowd out the experience or needs of others. The old-timers were especially attentive to the newcomers, who arrived still raw in their journey of learning how to stop using and start living.

The blend of old and new, tough and tender, created a healthy—and frequently exuberant—exchange of ideas that I enjoyed and participated in. In the past handful of years, my marital struggles and the challenges of life after the divorce had given me more to share with my fellow travelers. Their encouragement and advice had helped me feel less alone. I wasn't the only one with problems that had nothing to do with drinking or drugging but everything to do with living life on terms that were not always easy and sometimes downright brutal.

At that meeting I shared what nobody there expected to hear from me.

"I had a run-in with pain meds," I said when it was my turn, reminding the group of the dental work I had recently undergone. "I liked the feeling. But it scared me. It is such a relief to be here tonight. This is where I need to be, I know it."

This was the first time I used the phrase "run-in" to describe what had happened to me with the painkillers. I didn't use the word "relapse." I couldn't bear to utter it. In Twelve Step circles, the implications of that term are unambiguous: a sober person is suddenly drinking or taking other drugs again, and their recovery has stalled or stopped. Relapse equals failure. No matter how many months, years, or decades someone's been sober, a relapse returns them back to day one and Step One.

I couldn't bear the thought that this was what had happened to me. People who relapsed needed to get their shit together. "Get your head out of your ass" was how my old sponsor put it many years ago in Atlanta. Back then I knew, up close and personal, exactly what relapse looked and felt like. I was in and out of sobriety and in and out of treatment, constantly on the cusp of losing everything that mattered, including my own life. No matter how many times I vowed not to get high or drunk again, it wasn't long before I was knocking on the door of the crack house or hanging my head drunk on a bar stool. Each of my relapses filled me with stifling, suffocating shame—as toxic as the drug itself.

And now the implications of that terrifying, stigmatizing word seemed even graver. Everything I believed and stood for, the power of my personal story and my public advocacy for Hazelden, was anchored in my streak of not drinking or drugging. Earlier that fall I had marked my eighteenth year of sobriety. Eighteen years clean and sober was a long time, and the impressive duration of my streak was part of what made me a credible and powerful example for others.

My life showed that that addiction could be beaten *and* kept at bay. Hearing or reading about my success inspired people to seek help. By the thousands, so many of them wanted not what I had, but what it looked like I had, what I *represented*: the arc of hope, a pathway out of confusion and chaos to redemption. Healing. Wholeness. Why would anyone believe in me if suddenly that solid arc had been broken by a relapse? What good would my story be now? What good would *I* be now?

I simply decided that I didn't relapse. I had a "run-in." This term for what had occurred with the pills was gentler—not as jarring or alarming as the other one. "Run-in" fit the narrative I shared at my Twelve Step meeting—how my use of pain pills had been sanctioned by my dentist and had not sent me spiraling back to square one and its shame. "Relapse" was cause for concern and follow-ups. "Relapse" was a D or an F in a class I should have been acing. "Run-in" was a B-minus, perhaps, a scary moment in the rearview mirror—a near miss, nothing more.

While "run-in" was easier for me to accept and easier to admit to my fellow AA members, I did note, by the look on their faces, that some in the circle of chairs seemed perplexed or confused by what I had said. To me, my depiction of the experience meant all was not lost and I was back on track. No need for concern. No need for consequences.

I did not share with the group that night that there was more to the story. I had gone further than merely noticing the pleasant effects of the opioids that had been prescribed for my pain. I had wanted more. Seeking to increase the effects and enhance my experience, I had gone past what was allowed. I had strayed beyond the boundary set by my doctor and outside the standard set by my group. This circle of sober friends knew too much about addiction to ignore the implications of the extra pill. *Plus one* was my secret, and I kept it.

At the meeting the verdict was unanimous: "Close call, William. We're glad you made it back. It is a good thing you are grounded in this program. Keep coming back."

The next morning I wrote about the meeting.

AA last night. Felt really good. What a relief to be back at my home group! People so affirming, friendly as always. Told me I'm going to be okay. I was surprised others had similar stories. Wise, sweet E shared about going home with narcotic meds after surgery. Said she could "hardly wait" when it was time to take one again. (I know the feeling.) T says next time (if there is one) I should give the Rx to Nell—that's what he did. His wife kept his meds supply, doled them out as prescribed. Said he's glad he had them for pain but felt like they were sneaking up on his sobriety. Didn't need them after a few days so his wife threw out the rest. Good idea. But I knew that already. Tricky me. It was a good meeting. Except I kept the secret about that extra pill. Not healthy for my head to keep it inside. Need to tell somebody. Who?

I didn't tell anyone. Not even Nell. Usually when she stayed over, I wasn't in the mood for a buzz. Besides, I wasn't sure how I'd explain why I had taken an extra pill here and there— sometimes an extra two pills. I wasn't ready to admit how much I enjoyed the sensation—call it a guilty pleasure—of being under the influence of a medication that had been legitimately prescribed for me. What was the problem with this "bonus" feeling? It didn't seem to get in the way of the busy routine of my life. In fact, it seemed to help a little.

Why worry my girlfriend, my family, my friends in recovery, my colleagues at Hazelden? I had a pretty good idea of what would happen if I was more open. They would warn me.

Some would want to lecture me. Word would get around. People would call to make sure I was back on track. They'd scrutinize my every move or wonder where I was if I wasn't where they thought or expected me to be.

I didn't need any of that hassle. I kept reminding myself that a dentist who knew my history had prescribed the medication for pain caused by an invasive dental surgery. My pain was real, and the relief was legitimate. The fact that the pills had the added benefit of taking the edge off my life for a few hours was beside the point. That little bump was like the novelty prize in the box of Cracker Jacks.

Besides, it wasn't like I had gone back out. I hadn't rushed off to drink or find cocaine. *Those* were my drugs of "*no* choice." *Those* evil substances were the villains in my story—the things that had always triggered an avalanche of harsh consequences whenever I used them. This was totally different. I was done playing with those pills anyway. The bottle was empty. I was out. Now I could put the whole chapter behind me with lessons learned and a clear conscience. My mouth was healing up. It was better; I was fine.

THE REST OF 2012 passed fairly normally. The year-end fundraising push at Hazelden kept me busy. Holiday prep and the return of Thomas and Henry for winter break occupied our household. I kept going to meetings. Filled as they were with the tasks of day-to-day life, these weeks were also persistently shadowed by an odd sense of discomfort that I couldn't shake. It was like a slight fever or a nauseous stomach that emanated from my insides out. Rarely did it disrupt what I was doing—except by interrupting my thoughts. Usually this happened in the solitude of the evening, after the hubbub of the dinner hours. As whoever was home left the kitchen to retreat to their bedrooms or to the den to watch television, I went to my favorite place, the desk of my home office.

It was here that the vague queasiness gently blossomed alongside whatever it was I was focused on: an email, opening the mail and paying bills, writing a thank-you note, or organizing files. A peculiar presence—like a hazy memory—ebbed and flowed with just enough intensity that it vied with the task at hand. The sensation bugged me as much as it enticed me.

I wanted a pain pill. Even just one.

I'VE KNOWN WHAT it is like to crave a cold beer on a warm summer's evening at an outdoor baseball game or a frosty margarita on the rocks with a plate of Tex-Mex food. I remember how a few tokes of marijuana enhanced the sublime experience of listening to a Beatles album in my headphones. A glass of deep-red port with a New York strip. One more hit of crack as the hint of dawn brightened the New York City skyline after a night of bingeing.

The "phenomenon of craving" is a term in the Big Book that any alcoholic or addict can relate to. In all the years of my active use I had thousands of cravings. Some were so intense that they blotted out logic and derailed commitment. Some cravings were impossible to shut off, no matter what I was doing and regardless of what my head knew I shouldn't do and my heart ached to avoid. At these times, I was powerless—not just against taking that first drink or hit but also and inevitably against having one more and one more and one more—regardless of any consequence. And there were always consequences. This cycle inevitably ended in despair, regret, and shame.

I can still remember my last hit of crack in 1994, but I no longer crave it. After I finally gained sustainable recovery, this acute phenomenon dissolved like fog in the sunlight. There's a good reason so many of us describe the freedom from cravings as a miracle. Only rarely did I ever again want a drink or a drug, and even those early flashback feelings faded with time. I never questioned why or how this happened. All I knew was that the longer I stayed abstinent, the less I wanted to get drunk or high again. Those temptations were no longer part of my life.

IN DECEMBER OF 2012, I hadn't been taking the pain meds long enough to experience the physical withdrawal or the intensity of cravings that come with heavier or extended use. Those would come later. What I missed, as I sat at my desk tending to my mundane end-of-day tasks while another busy year came to a close, was the sweet break those first pills had offered me. I wanted—just for a little while—to become wrapped up again in the gentle cocoon of the pleasant world that I had tasted. A world without the invasive prodding and probing of life's incessant demands, relentless duties, and irksome distractions. I longed for that perfectly balanced, harmonic state when my mind, body, and spirit floated free and easy, uninhibited by outside forces. I simply wanted to go back to where I had been when I took the pain meds on those six or seven nights after my surgery.

I was due for my follow-up with the dentist. The appointment had been on my calendar for weeks, and I hadn't been anticipating it with anything other than a fear of more pain. Returning to the dental chair would mean more poking around in my mouth to check on the status of his handiwork and making plans for the next phase of treatment. There would be no actual procedure involved in this visit—no invasive cutting or anything that might cause discomfort—but on the eve of the scheduled appointment, after I got into bed and turned out the light, I did not fall right to sleep.

Instead, out of nowhere, a new thought flared across my consciousness. It was a simple idea, and it gave me a chill. At the same time, I could feel an uptick in palpitations in my chest. A combo of thoughts and feelings blossomed in my mind, so topsy-turvy that I had to turn the light back on, get out of bed, go downstairs, and quickly scribble in my journal.

> I will complain about my mouth, tell him it still hurts, even though it doesn't, not really. Ask him for more meds. If he does, great. Maybe he won't. That's okay too. It's not like I'm desperate. I can do without them. I don't need them.

■

6

In Pieces

2012–2014

I know what to do. What not to do. I do both.

—PERSONAL JOURNAL, NOVEMBER 9, 2013

DECEMBER 19, 2012

*Back to the dentist yesterday. Yes, I did as I feared.
Had a hunch I would the moment I walked into the
office and sat in the exam chair. The whole time I was
there I felt that low-grade, out-of-nowhere flutter in
my stomach, like a euphoric recall of the old days, only
much softer. The doc says things look good; healing is
on schedule. He asked me how I was doing. I told him
I don't like not having two teeth and the temporary
is uncomfortable—it hurts when I eat and when I lay
my head on the pillow. He didn't seem to bite (no pun
intended—funny though) so I asked what I should
do for the pain. He suggested Advil or Tylenol. For
a moment I was nervous, the seconds of silence felt
awkward. Then I went for it. "I think I need something
stronger please. For the nights," I told him. "Plus, with
the holidays coming . . ." It worked. Got an Rx for ten.*

Couldn't wait to get home and after dinner took the two
and one more and had a little "pop" for a few hours.
A productive night at my desk and putzing around
the house until bedtime. Back to the real world today.
I feel good this morning. I feel a bit guilty too. The
Tylenol would have been enough; I probably didn't need
anything stronger. But I like knowing I have a few more
for later in the week.

I wouldn't have admitted it at the time, but I had scored, and I was happy.

Merry Christmas.

TODAY I READ these words, and the entries that followed in the weeks and months to come, with a sense of awe and horror. How did I not see or understand what was happening? All the signs and symptoms are there—the justifications, rationalizations, denial, cravings, and the creeping sense of losing control. Stealthily, relentlessly, the addiction took over my life. I wonder now why I did not, how I could not, see it in all its familiar adornments, its bells and whistles, its shiny promises, its hands outstretched, its whispers and enticements. The reality is that I knew it was there. I thought I could beat it.

In the hundreds of pages of my journals from 2012 to 2015, and in the memories those entries recall to mind, stories of light and hope share space with mounting evidence of creeping disaster. For every positive mention of a pill or admitted hunger for another, there are stretches when these things seemed to recede into the background. For every painful return to the dental chair or shamefaced trip to the pharmacy, there are mundane accounts of daily living. For every heartfelt vow to stop the insanity once and for all, there are also details of memorable good times and deeply important moments.

Henry graduated from college, followed a year or so later by Thomas. I spoke from the pulpit at the National Cathedral. In 2014 Hazelden and the Betty Ford Center merged into a powerful new nonprofit, called the Hazelden Betty Ford Foundation, with an ambitious nationwide mission (this development also added the airport in Palm Springs, California, to my list of regular travel destinations). My mom and dad celebrated sixty years of marriage. I taught Nancy to drive and watched her pass her road test. I proposed to Nell—and she said yes.

Along with accounts of these milestone events and experiences, there are scores of entries about the difference I made in others' lives as well, memories of seemingly small interactions that became part of larger stories of frailty and strength, darkness and light, hopelessness and faith. Without knowing at all what I was experiencing, people kept reaching out to me for a lifeline to hope and I continued to answer. I held on tight for my own sake too.

Hopeful notes like these have a place in the three-year story of my increasingly fierce addiction to painkillers, not because I want to dilute the significance of my return to use or gloss over the turmoil of this hard chapter of my life but because these are the experiences that left me confused about what was happening to me. I couldn't make sense of the way I used to be under the influence of crack cocaine and alcohol compared with the way I was able to keep living my life now even as the grip of opioids tightened.

Before, with cocaine and alcohol, my relapses made me drop out. I disappeared into the dark recesses of crack houses, I hid in closets, I ghosted my employers and cut off contact with my family. Within days—within hours sometimes—of using again, I was stealing and lying, spiritually bereft, slowly going mad as I chased one more high. Using those substances made me unrecognizable to myself and others. Under their influence I broke every promise I had ever made.

This was different. If alcohol and crack took me out of the game, pulling me from my life and plunging me into chaos, these painkillers seemed to have the opposite effect. At first, opioids gave me a full-body release from trying so hard. They freed me, not just from the pain produced by all that dental work, but also from the emotional discomfort that had colored my days for years. The pain pills helped me keep pace with the demands of my peripatetic routine while cushioning the stressors that were part of my life.

At work I showed up on time for meetings. I kept commitments, met deadlines, and delivered results. Together with my talented colleagues, we raised millions of dollars to strengthen the organization and expand the mission. Even as my need for the painkillers sent me in search of dentists and doctors to beg for more (my begging always couched in calm, reasonable, and *stable* requests), I had no jump in sick days. I never disappeared. At the time, and for a long while after, I believed I was meeting my commitments at home too. I provided for my family and showed up for celebrations as well as crises. I was functioning. I loved and was loved back.

In November of 2014—nearly two full years after my first attempt to convince a dentist to prescribe drugs I didn't need—I wrote: "What is most baffling about this entire experience is how I continue to function, produce, love, and live despite the pills. What kind of addict am I? Certainly not the addict I was a long time ago." If there is one theme that runs through all my journal entries of these years, through the good and the bad moments, the flashes of clarity and the floods of self-deception, it is the painful paradox of knowing I wasn't abstinent even as I continued to count the mileposts of a recovery journey that made me who and what I was. And that confounding question I scribbled in my journal—"What kind of addict am I?"—got tangled and twisted into another that was almost like it: "What kind of recovering person am I?"

JANUARY 29, 2013

I am not sure what happened within me yesterday. But I lived the day in quiet desperation, low-grade fear, a sense of isolation, and unsteady malaise all probably rooted in the pain meds again. Tired physically, drained emotionally over these things. I hated the notion that I was caught up in their effect. Obsessed with the knowledge they were there waiting for me. Acutely sensing the craving unlocked by their presence inside me over the past few days. I planned my entire day around taking a handful after dinner. And I did, even missing my AA meeting under the guise of needing to be home with Nancy so we could have an early night. I didn't get the buzz I anticipated. When I went to bed I was glad the meds had come up short. I don't like this.

FEBRUARY 21, 2013

Dentist again. Four more teeth pulled and twenty stitches put in, and I've been down and out ever since. Down and out and once again under the influence of narcotics. A more powerful pain med this time. At first it was a gentle, pleasant sensation. But yesterday in eager anticipation of justified use because I do have legitimate pain, I took too many. The effect was heavy and eventually unpleasant, even burdensome. And I had the mental anguish of knowing I shouldn't misuse these meds but doing it anyway. I think about how good I felt at church last Sunday, my resolve to stand firm against them. I am keenly aware of the conflict between the meds and the sober life I relish and need.

MARCH 1, 2013

On Monday I took too many meds. At my desk and knocked out tasks all the while energized by the music on my computer. Then downstairs and back into the routine of responsibility that is part of every day. Went to bed that night aware of the meds' effects but fascinated that they don't derail my focus or the importance I place on staying focused on what matters. Except that I missed my Monday night AA group.

MARCH 9, 2013

I am hung over from the pain meds of the night before. Depressed and tired. Not happy. Not satisfied with a life well lived. And then the moment of clarity— meeting at 7 p.m.

Today I am back on track.

APRIL 7, 2013

*Just before the church service on Friday night a man
I did not recognize asked me: "Do you know who I
am, do you remember me?" I didn't. And I have scant
recollection of the story he relayed about our chance
encounter on an airplane to Vegas a long time ago. He
wanted to drink. But I told him not to as we both stood
in the aisle in first class. And he didn't that day on the
plane or in the years since. A remarkable interaction
that fills my cups. Again.*

APRIL 11, 2013

*Took pain meds two days in a row, after the doctor
reached out to me unexpectedly. The spark ignited the
train of thought and bingo, I had a fifteen-count supply.
Same effect, feeling relaxed and pleasant and particularly
focused, so I got a lot done Tue/Wed without feeling
disconnected or out of it. I actually felt more present
w/o feeling tired. Almost like the meds are a stimulant,
even though they are not at all. What an unusual
paradox. I love my sobriety, the program, and helping
other people. But I take the meds that I don't think I
really require. I like what they do to me for a few hours.*

APRIL 29, 2013

*I was up late unable to fall asleep, my head was filled
with all kinds of odd awarenesses that made for fitful
rest. . . . Was it the dessert I ate at bedtime or the pain
meds? I didn't need them but I took them anyway. Not
too much. But too many, and for what? Except for that
violation of all that is dear to me, I would be content
with everything that is my life today. The meds intrude.*

Get in the way. Disrupt my journey. Compromise my values. I shall be content when all this dental work is done, and I don't have the opportunity or the excuse to get and take them.

MAY 12, 2013
This morning I read the recovery literature for the day. It just doesn't resonate with me. Seems syrupy and optimistically juvenile, not realistic at this juncture of my journey.

MAY 19, 2013
Today I am in a space with much light, fresh air, freedom of movement and flexibility of time. Yesterday I did chores around the house, not office work but tasks to keep this house running clean and neat. Thomas planted flowers. I supervised. We went to an art show, Nancy then came home and we ate dinner. A movie with Nell in the den. Today Henry comes home. Time. My time.

JUNE 19, 2013
Yesterday I spent a wicked two and a half hours in the dentist's chair. More work on my teeth. The worst yet, especially because the anesthesia started to wear off toward the end. Afterward I felt punch-drunk in pain and exhaustion. Got home and took a handful of pain meds "legitimately" and did not feel guilty or cause for alarm. Odd that the dividing line is physical pain vs. pain/stress of life's demands.

JUNE 20, 2013

I must get through the next round of dental work. Painful. Frustrating. And seemingly never-ending. Last evening all of my temporaries fell out!

JULY 13, 2013

A plate of brownies and thank-you notes from a family I've helped are at the front door. I am proud of the work I do.

AUGUST 4, 2013

My father told me how much he admired my staying power over adversity. That despite my many mistakes I had owned them honestly and responsibly. Got through it with dignity. With steadfastness. And as a result had helped many people too. I told him he'd played a big role in all of it, too. "I love you" was how we each signed off. We've come a long, long way.

AUGUST 14, 2013

I took some pain meds I didn't need yesterday afternoon. There was a short peak of euphoria and a burst of energy that allowed me to get through the mail at my desk. It's like the meds help me to overcome the fear-molded procrastination of getting stuff done. But they really only detract from the foundation essential to my strength.

SEPTEMBER 2, 2013

I took five pain meds on the plane yesterday. In a confined, comfortable environment, where I sat in one spot listening to the Beatles, playing with my iPhone, and updating my calendar. The two-hour flight passed in twenty minutes.

SEPTEMBER 10, 2013

My dentist rejected my request for a refill of my prescription. In that moment I was hit with the clarity that it was time to stop this nonsense, this dance along the narrow precipice, the scheming and obsession with easing the stresses and enhancing life. For a moment there was a sense of release from this pursuit. But then I became fixated on "one more round." And by the late afternoon I had managed to pull off a convincing appeal to the dentist. By 7 p.m., just after my AA meeting, I was again under the influence for the evening. And I enjoyed it.

The power of the substance over mind, body, and spirit. It compromises everything that matters to me. Everything I am! I like and need my life in recovery. I don't want anything more, less, or different. I know too that the run is just about over (four left). I'm ready to move on from this.

SEPTEMBER 22, 2013

I did nothing but little stuff here and there around the house. Tiny chores with big satisfaction.

I also gave myself "permission" to take some pain meds for no reason other than to relax and enjoy the experience. Took 'em twice too—the second time justified by wanting to finish them off once and for all. Put them behind me. Done. We'll see. I've been at this juncture before. Only now I sense I'm out of options. Really out of options.

SEPTEMBER 24, 2013

Today's meditation captures this moment for me: "I pray I may follow the dictates of my conscience. I pray that I may follow the inner urging of my soul."

I know how to live and why I must live within the context of the Steps, the solid framework of recovery that has sustained me for nearly nineteen years now. Yesterday I went to a noontime meeting at Uptown and shared my struggle with pain meds. I know inside that honesty is a cornerstone of my life. Why when I'm not honest nobody needs to tell me so. I can feel it as much as I can think it. My actions of the past few months have not achieved this benchmark.

The obsessing of the mind and the phenomenon of craving jumped in and out of my day. At times I even considered online pharmacies and finding another doctor. I felt the urge to get high but I went to the meeting. I pondered the alternative to my life today. I moved through the feelings. Today I start fresh again.

SEPTEMBER 27, 2013
At the volleyball game last night, I could not contain my enthusiasm. Nancy was the star in a gymnasium filled with parents, teachers, and players marking another homecoming weekend. I felt like a kid again, cheering, jumping up, and generally making a fool of myself to the other adults. But afterwards, when we got home, Nancy said all the other players say she's got "the best dad" because I'm always present with cheering and whatever else they need. That makes me feel so good.

OCTOBER 10, 2013
After a hiatus I'm dabbling again with the pain meds. I know the truth so fully that I prefer not to put it down on paper.

OCTOBER 12, 2013

Today I have nineteen years of recovery since walking out of a crack house. For the first year I cannot stand up and say that I haven't had a drink or a drug, nor the desire for one, since 10/12/94. Because I've struggled this past year against the temptation of pain meds.

OCTOBER 21, 2013

My satisfying weekend was propped up and nearly torn down by my use of pain meds beyond what was necessary for my sore mouth. I've been all but unable to turn off the spigot since the dentist sent me home last Wednesday with forty Percocet. I used them daily, only four a day but four at once instead of as prescribed. The high was satisfying and seemed to enhance my productivity. But then yesterday I took too many in the afternoon and last night when it was time for bed I was flooded with anxiety. Much of it driven by my dismay over what I had done, drug-seeking behavior at a time I must be strong for Nancy, honest with Nell, and sharp on my feet with everything. I like the effect but I hate the cause. I lean on God but don't let go to God's will. Lying in bed last night, all of these emotions pulled me down into the memories of years ago. I disdain it. I loathe who I am when I do what I know I shouldn't.

NOVEMBER 12, 2013

In the afternoon a yearning to get high. I became depressed, and only by doing little tasks around the house did I move through the hours, though the craving still hovered right behind my ears. A phone call from a young man in Utah suddenly was the answer. One

addict talking to another and most of the craving
passed. He even asked how I was doing. And it worked.
One alcoholic talking to another. How it works. Yester-
day it seemed impossible to put one day between the
last high. Now it's happened, and this morning I feel
better. I can again see between the space of what I had
become and what I want/need to be.

NOVEMBER 17, 2013
For twenty-four hours I staved off the thirst. But by the
afternoon the new plan was hatched and at 5 p.m. I
was at the emergency dental clinic nearby alternately
bashing myself over the waste of time even as I craved
another pill. Then I was in the chair. The dentist identi-
fied a root canal as the solution. Five hours later I was
"fixed." Hard to fathom how addiction works and how
the addict's brain works harder to keep pace.

DECEMBER 6, 2013
Another 'script for pain meds, this time for my back.
But I've built up a tolerance now, and so the kick is
only a firm tap. The pursuit and score are fading away.
Life continues to unfold in front of me. I keep walking.

DECEMBER 10, 2013
I've still taken pain meds. But I don't seem to struggle
with them now. They are what they are. An influence.
Not a monster.

Dr. Jim Giefer's nurse had always greeted me pleasantly. On the eve of the 2013 winter solstice, however, she did not seem interested in bantering about the weather or kids or plans for the upcoming holidays. Instead, she led me down a long hallway to the exam room where she took my vitals without comment. "The doctor will be in shortly," she said.

I had called the clinic the previous day, during one of those desperate stretches when the ache in my jaw was matched by the craving in the rest of me. The dental office was closed for the week leading up to Christmas, so I had reached out to my longtime internist with a vague complaint about pain.

Dr. Giefer entered the room. He wore his white coat and stethoscope. In his hand he carried a partially rolled-up sheaf of papers. Usually jovial, my doctor was not smiling today.

"William, I don't know what to say," he began, waving the printout. "This is not at all acceptable. At all."

I didn't know exactly what he was talking about, but my stomach lurched anyway.

"This is a list of prescriptions you've had filled this year," my doctor said, pushing the pages toward me. "The docs you've seen, the pharmacies, every date, and every amount."

I pretended to scan down the first page before flipping it to the second, then the third, then the fourth. In the silence I could hear heavy breathing; I don't recall if it was mine or his. Both of us had reason to be upset in that moment. Me, because I had been called out and discovered. Him, because the facts on the printout did not align with what he knew about his clean-cut, friendly patient who worked for a drug treatment organization.

I felt exposed. I wanted to run. Jim was my personal physician. He was the expert I had trusted for years, and for all this time he had been a benevolent presence. Whether it was for a sore throat or skin cancer or the flu, Gief had always taken care of me or steered me to the person who could. More than that, Jim knew about recovery. He knew me *from* recovery. He hadn't seen this coming. I could tell he was angry.

"Dr. Giefer," I began, choosing my words carefully, "I've had a lot of dental work done since last December." I pointed to some of the names on the sheets in my hand. "I know this looks bad, but these were all legitimately prescribed." I turned the pages. "It gets worse when I fly," I continued. "And you know how much I have to travel for work—"

The doctor cut me off. He wasn't interested in hearing my explanation. "You need to go and see your sponsor right away—this afternoon," he said. "Then I want you to get your butt to a meeting." His voice was getting louder. "This needs to stop!"

I was too embarrassed to respond so I began to gather my coat. As I got up to leave the room, I paused just long enough to ask if I could keep the printout. Dr. Giefer nodded, though he seemed to be waiting for me to say more. I walked out of the exam room without another word.

By the time I got home the tension and embarrassment of the entire interaction had morphed into an overwhelming sensation of exhaustion. I was also hurt and angry. My doctor hadn't even heard me out. Instead of medical care, I got a lecture and a spanking. In my bones, I knew Gief wanted to help me, but his solution—the prescription he had made—felt worthless. I was too tired to go to a meeting and I didn't feel like calling my sponsor. I decided to try and manage the craving with a big meal and the throbbing in my jaw with four extra-strength Advil. Before I went to bed, I wrote in my journal.

The shortest day of the year is long with the truth.
I've been on the run for too long fueled by the pursuit,
acquisition, and effect of pain meds. Today Dr. Giefer
laid it out plain and simple, in a four-page printout of
my prescriptions since 2012. A pattern. I can justify
or internalize the whole thing by saying/arguing that
the meds were legitimately prescribed, never illegally
procured. True. But I'm a convincingly conniving fellow
who cuts a clean image. Until I'm up against a four-
page printout with a doc who knows the truth.

So it is done. It is a relief. I like the way I was and
am. Not what I had become.

Thank God. Thank the doc.

RUN-IN. SKIRMISH. DANCE. The words I use in my journals from 2014 are euphemisms, attempts to diminish the seriousness of my life-and-death struggle. I claim that honesty is my bedrock principle and yet I tell my AA group only a version of the truth, leaving out a few "jagged details." My words about "respectable, legitimate" use of painkillers are the self-justifying and deceptive tools of an addict.

My 2014 journal begins with a prescient sentence: "I am still battling the sea serpent of my disease." Toward the end of the year, it has become a "poisonous snake." In the final pages, I face the truth: "The beast inside me consumes my spirit." The monster was not outside me; it was deep inside, entangled and encircling the coils of my gut, choking off the lifeblood of my truth and integrity.

The flashes of insight into my craving and addictive behaviors are undermined by ongoing scheming, scoring, and counting (pills, hours, days) that I describe in my efforts to find more drugs and use them—not as prescribed, but as needed. I *needed* them—at first for the pain, then for the relief, then to avoid the agony of withdrawal. My take-it-or-leave-it use of painkillers morphed into addiction, and yet I continued to deny it. I continued to delude myself into thinking that I would be able to stop on my own.

We shall see. These three words make their way into the year's journals as well. It's a phrase and a stance familiar to anyone who has ever been addicted to anything. Spoken or unspoken, consigned to a diary or whispered to oneself in a moment of half-resolve, we believe all we need is just a little more time. *Give it another day. Let's see what happens tomorrow. Maybe things will turn around. Tomorrow. I can beat this thing. Tomorrow.*

JANUARY 12, 2014

The longer I stay away from the pain meds, the more days I put between that last run of meds and now— all days of full-blown sobriety—the clearer the picture becomes. I was tight in the grip of opioids, the obsession for more, the skewed perspective that everything was okay. The junkie behavior. More than anything, the lack of appreciation for my sobriety. I was glad that my reservoir of recovery was deeper than what I drained out of it, only as I've now refilled it these past few weeks have I once again experienced what it means to live sober on a daily basis. Fully sober. Because I like being honest. I like helping others. I feel the complete connection to God. To the program. To myself.

JANUARY 15, 2014

Had surgery on my back yesterday. Basal cell cancer.
Convinced the doc I needed pain meds. Took a few.
Pleasant. But no big deal. I prefer a sober life.

THE FIRST TIME I was diagnosed with malignant melanoma,
back in 2000, I was scared. The surgeon dug out the cancer with
what he said were "acceptable margins," meaning he got it all. I
can recall no prescription for pain meds, though I still have an
impressive scar from the surgery. I was in the clear until peculiar spots and patches began to show up on my skin in early 2014.

"Basal lesions, squamous cell carcinoma, and a scattering
of pre-cancerous anomalies on your face," a new dermatologist
said. "We'll burn them off by freezing them with gas."

"That's a paradox," I said.

She laughed. "I know. Burn and freeze."

In follow-up appointments, she was not so lighthearted.
At my next exam she informed me that several of the cells
they scanned from samples on my back had mutated into more
dangerous melanomas. This would require a few more procedures over the next three months. The cuts were deep and
required stitches. I experienced enough discomfort to convince
the surgeon and nurses that I needed painkillers.

After those first few surgeries I walked out of the day clinic
thinking, *Gosh, this is too easy,* as I held a prescription in
my hand for a dozen Percocet or OxyContin. When the nurse
practitioner called to follow up, I complained of pain, even
though I felt good enough to return to work and my daily
exercise routine. Refills were ordered without question.

After surgery to remove a large but not particularly deep spot on my shoulder, the doctor and her nurse reviewed the post-op instructions.

"What about pain?" I asked innocently.

"Take Advil or Tylenol every four hours, if necessary," she said.

"Doc, I'm going to need something stronger, you know how I hate pain," I pitched. "I'm a patsy when it comes to suffering."

For a moment I felt as if she could see through my words into my sneaky, conniving, craving brain. It spooked me. "We don't want to get you addicted," she said, looking me straight in the eye to let me know she was dead serious. Like most of my doctors, she knew my history because I never kept it a secret. But I had counted on leaving the office with a resupply. It had been days since my last boost. I felt defiant, and for the first time I pushed back.

"Well, yes, I know that, but I've been around a long time. You know I can manage these meds."

"I'll give you half the number I did last time," she said, reluctantly. "But this is it." After a tense moment, I thanked her and left the office without stopping at the reception desk to make another appointment. As I crossed the parking lot to my car, I felt like a dog with its tail between its legs.

FEBRUARY 1, 2014

It doesn't take much in the way of manipulation or misinformation to score. Scary. Yet the thrill has gone out of it all.

FEBRUARY 15, 2014

My op-ed appeared in the Star Tribune. *Pegged to the overdose death of Philip Seymour Hoffman, from heroin—another opioid tragedy. There are more and more of these deaths every month now it seems. The op-ed got rave reviews, a big impact, and in the past day a rush of queries from people who saw it and need help. Five yesterday. All in Minnesota.*

FEBRUARY 16, 2014

This dance with pain medication has really got to end. I get a temporary buzz thinking about the upcoming buzz. But it isn't really fun or satisfying or worth anything. And I find myself wondering how I could want to go through a day with a few hours of a buzz, when for so many years I went through these days without ever desiring to feel an altered state. It's easy to acquire the meds. I'm convincing to doctors because I'm more than they see. But the deceptive gaze, the frank dishonesty and scheming isn't who I should be anymore.

APRIL 29, 2014

Yesterday I exhausted what was going to be my final supply of pain meds. Had a nice glow for an hour or so, which made for a pleasantly productive time at my desk. And for a moment, I convinced myself I was done, that it was fun while it lasted but time to move on. Until thoughts of more poked into and out of my head, not in desperation but in the need to nurture the fleeting feelings the meds provide. By the afternoon I was scheming again, made a call to the doctor, was certain I had convinced the staff, didn't hear back for hours, and then called as 4:30 approached only to hear an Rx had been called in, but not what I wanted! Frustrating, then acceptance, and I went to bed knowing that today is the day to start again and resume recovery as I need, want, and like it. I went to bed having made peace with this. Only today I am up and still sick with a bad cold and here are the cravings in the form of thoughts about how to get more meds.

MAY 7, 2014

On the plane home I took a few pain meds. They worked, for all the right and wrong reasons. I take them when I have them. I leave them when I don't.

JUNE 6, 2014

Quick trip to NY to celebrate Dad's 80th. Low-key affair despite the big number. He wanted it that way. We had dinner at their favorite place, Scaletta's, around the corner from the apartment. He is really getting old now. But looks damn good and seems in good shape, all things considered. Mom too, though she is much slower on her feet. They each told me separately how much they admire what I'm doing at Hazelden Betty Ford. Said they've had numerous people remind them how I had helped somebody here or there who reached out at their suggestion.

JUNE 8, 2014

Knowing what I know about priorities, mine are not in proper order. Especially as I continue to be taunted and pampered by pain meds. Which never seem to run out, thanks to trusting dentists and my old junkie tricks of the trade. Notably too, the meds don't seem to *hijack my abilities outside of my insides. But their grip of my insides is disquieting as is illustrated by my lack of initiative to do things like write, pray properly, and recover.*

JUNE 9, 2014
Spent most of the afternoon under the effects of meds and then tried to amp it up again in the evening. The effect loosens me and seems to erase my procrastination. But the euphoric effect is long gone. So I don't know why I do it. I mean really. The effect isn't worth the result. And the result is so counter to everything I've lived for so long now. This afternoon I see the dentist for the crown, which once in, should once and for all close the gap and resolve the problem that I've parlayed into this destructive opening to pursue a toned-down chance to get high. It's just not worth it.

JULY 21, 2014
I'm engaged to Nell. It feels good and feels right. I have only a wisp of trepidation, based solely on my past failures at marriage. But no reluctance about Nell. None at all.

I asked Nell to marry me on a beautiful July evening. The prospect of our engagement had been on the table for a long time—we had been dating since 2010 and had discussed it on and off for years. Still, I managed to surprise her with the place I picked to pop the question.

We decided to walk up to Grand Avenue for dinner that night—not an uncommon summer choice. As we exited the house, I pretended to fumble for the key to lock the front door.

A step ahead of me, Nell began to walk off the porch. "Oh my gosh, look at this," I said. "I can't believe it!" She turned around wide-eyed, alarmed but not sure what she was on the lookout for. As her attention focused, I thrust out my open hand, revealing a ring set with a glittering diamond. Nell's mouth dropped open, but no sound emerged. "Well . . . here we are," I said. "Right where it all began." I smiled. "Will you marry me?"

Her answer was twice as long as "yes" or "no."

"Of course!" she cried.

We hugged and kissed each other on the front porch of the house on Fairmount Avenue, a block away from the house where she was brought home as a baby in 1969. This was the neighborhood of indelible memories and enduring hope, and it was home to both of us. I was marrying a hometown girl in the city and the state that figured so prominently in my journey, beginning in 1989 when I arrived in Minnesota for treatment at Hazelden. My first sober home—a room at Fellowship Club—was a mile away from that front porch.

"It feels good and it feels right," I wrote in my journal. "She is the loving symbol of my life in St. Paul, for she is the love of my life today in the city I love forever."

The photo taken of Nell and me on the night we became engaged is a favorite. We are sitting in the restaurant on Grand Avenue. She has one arm around me and the other on my shoulder, holding on tight. I sit relaxed, my arms casually folded on the table. Both of us are smiling. The image represents the paradox of my existence in those mixed-up years. How could I love my life and hate what was happening to me all at once?

JULY 23, 2014

*Today I embrace who I am, all these things that make
my life worthy even when it is hard, even when
I struggle. Even when I fall short. My life is worth it.
I am fortunate beyond my own abilities.*

AUGUST 17, 2014

*I'm going to try to get back to the basics with my recov-
ery. Meditations every morning. Regular AA meetings.
Prayer. And no plotting to get pain meds. The cause
isn't worth the effect. My tolerance is very high. It's not
fun. I feel the wisps of release. But that quickly fades.
Besides, life's good as it was. Meds don't make it any
better.*

AUGUST 19, 2014

*So much for the commitment to get back in the groove.
I was back at the dentist yesterday to relieve the ob-
session. And I found it, again. I feel guilty and fearful.
Though there is nothing illegal about what I do. Still,
I wake up in the night feeling shame and guilt and angst.*

AUGUST 22, 2014

*When I was on the road this spring I used trips to
Indiana and Texas to feed my streak with the meds.
Now I've done the same in Siren, WI, of all places.
Stopped at a dentist with my broken crown as a tool
to ask for more. And got fifteen! The dentist explained
that a combo of Ibu with something else non-narcotic
is just as effective and has reduced his treatment of
narcotics by 90%. And then he filled my request.*

AUGUST 31, 2014

My run-in with pain meds has been unrelenting. I've developed a tolerance, so more are required and even then, the effect isn't the same. I've managed to secure a supply that defies all safeguards. That I've done it "legitimately" is obscene. It even took the extraction of an impacted tooth to keep the run going. Today the run ends. Again. We shall see.

SEPTEMBER 7, 2014

Sunday morning on the porch. The pain meds "routine" continues. Somehow I manage to keep the pipeline moving. But the effect now is unspectacular, almost rote to the point of being boring and not worth it really. But I note the power of craving when I stop.

Sometimes I feel guilty and ashamed of it all. Yet I see it in the context of what all of us experience in life's journey—stuff happens. Fallibility reigns. Imperfection textures the good times and pinpricks the bad.

SEPTEMBER 10, 2014

In Center City on my way from lunch to meet staff, I encounter a man who stops in mid-stride when he sees me. "You're Mr. Moyers, aren't you?" he asks. We talk. He tells me he's a "retread," on his second go-around in treatment here. Says he heard me speak at a conference for counselors and clinicians in NY years ago and that's why he ended up in treatment the first time around, at Hazelden NYC. Says he's back now after reading Now What? *and was spurred by the chapter about relapse—that it's not a dirty word. Says he was filled with shame "because I couldn't stay sober even though I work in this field." I feel the urge to update him on my story! But I don't. Not the time or place. Not sure how I would explain it all. I give him my card. Maybe someday.*

ON A FRIDAY afternoon in mid-September, a new problem developed in my jaw. I was in the car after a long week, driving home along I-35 south from Center City. Suddenly, the entire right side of my face seemed weighted down, as though it were packed with wet sand. It was as if a switch had been flipped from off to on. My head felt crooked on my neck. I actually looked in the rearview mirror to check, but I appeared fine. My head was straight on my shoulders. Apart from my wide eyes, my face seemed normal.

I didn't know what was happening. I hadn't been on a plane for at least a week—the changes in pressure that come with flying were the usual culprits when it came to the pain in my jaw—so where was this coming from? Was it a figment of my imagination? But how can something that felt so real be imagined? I didn't know the answer, and I didn't care. All I knew was that I had to have relief.

I pulled over to the side of the freeway and called a dental office where I had been treated when a crown had cracked in the spring. "It's an emergency," I told the receptionist.

Twenty minutes later I was in the chair with a dentist who tapped my teeth gently, each time asking "Here? Or here? How about now?" I flinched with each tap, even as the pain was constant.

"It looks like a construction zone in there," the dentist said. "Exactly how long have you been having this problem?"

I recounted the surgeries and repairs I had endured since the first procedure back in 2012—almost two years earlier. I described the heaviness in my jaw that had just exploded in the car, feeling as if the bone were unhinged from its socket. I explained how it was similar to what happened on the flights I made for work. I told him that I couldn't afford to be slowed down. I had too much work to do, too many places to be, and I was desperate for a solution.

What I didn't say was that this was the same story I told all the other dentists I had seen for years now, month after month and in cities around the country. I didn't tell him that they, too, had been baffled about what might be wrong. I wasn't willing to admit how what I really wanted from him that day was fewer questions and more pills.

When I asked for a prescription for painkillers, the dentist disappeared from the exam room. The minutes that ticked by seemed to last for hours. I squirmed in the chair, literally itching in anticipation. *What if I don't get what I want? What if the dentists are consulting or calling other dentists? What if, what if?* For a minute I considered leaping out of the chair and hurriedly leaving the office, but I was anchored there by that light flashing in my brain. *MORE, MORE, MORE.* I closed my eyes and tried to calm down.

"Here you go, William."

The dentist handed me a piece of paper. I didn't dare look at it but made eye contact with the dentist as he described how the meds were to be used. I had to show that I was a person who listened carefully to directions for taking pills. I nodded my head at the right intervals. I was a good patient.

"I want you to see a specialist next week," the dentist said. "He's only here on Tuesdays and Thursdays, but he knows neuralgic pain issues better than the rest of us. I am pretty sure this is the problem we need to address."

I nodded obediently. "Okay, that's a plan. Thank you."

I left the office and headed back to St. Paul. It was always the same:

Relief. *I pulled it off.*

Shame. *I did it again. What kind of a person am I?*

Urgency. *I gotta get to CVS quick.*

Shame. *This is dishonest. It's not who I am.*

Excitement. *I'm going to have a good night.*

Shame. *I don't know how to stop.*

> **SEPTEMBER 16, 2014**
> *What a waste of time, even with money, for all the long anticipation of the short effect that five or six pills brings. I marvel at how long I've managed to stretch this out. But am weary of stretching it further. It should be easy to let it go. It isn't.*

> **OCTOBER 12, 2014**
> *Twenty years today. Twenty years of what?*

> **OCTOBER 29, 2014**
> *Two nights back-to-back of mental anguish, physical discomfort, and the restless, irritable, and discontent evidence of the addict that I am. I'm not as I want to be and as I've lived my life for so many years until this thing with the meds. Hard to believe, too, that I've even been on a run this long now. Amazing I've kept the furnace fed for this long.*

Couldn't sleep last night again. Tired physically. But my mind races with thoughts, plays tricks with my emotions, or maybe it is the other way around. I don't know anymore! I do know this—I'm playing with fire. I ponder what is illegal about what I'm doing. Nothing that I can figure out, and for moments I feel "better." But that's not the point at all. I'm conniving and decep- tive. Dishonest and obsessive. Wrong. Not living my life as I want, as I need to be. I think I've got a grip on the situation, but I've got a rattlesnake by the rattles. I may not hear the warning. But I sense it, feel it. And it is still a snake. A poisonous snake.

On Monday night I got a feel for what's good. Went to my AA meeting. Shared the essence of my struggle, sans the dirty details. Walked out of the meeting feeling good again in a healthy, holistic way. Then promptly got high on the meds again. Why can't I simply go back to who and where I was for all those years?

NOVEMBER 1, 2014

Prayer for the morning: Oh God, help me to stick to the path that is well-worn. And proven.

The pain meds won't go away. By the afternoon I'm scheming again to garner a refill. Which happens by the late afternoon. Doctor pushes back but not hard enough. A few more, though the effect is negligible, and in the night I am up and down with guilt and shame. Not right thinking or living.

NOVEMBER 3, 2014

Right now I am connected to a rope being pulled in two directions. One direction is the substances of addiction,

and all the thoughts and behaviors that are a force
against which God and my faith and my program all
combined into one pulls in the opposite direction. It is a
tension like nothing I have known for a long time. And
though I know which way I want to go, I know which
way is winning right now. This is far more serious than
I'd like to admit.

Yesterday I ran out of meds after one short pop-up
that felt really good and then was gone. As the day
unfolded I got the craving for more, and I schemed a
solution that did not bear fruit no matter how hard I tried.
Last night I was practically desperate, yet in between I
was relieved, almost to the point of joy, that I was "free"
again. I took a long, hot bath and went to bed early. But
all night I was physically uncomfortable—sweats with
stomachache and churning, tortuous thoughts. Withdrawal? Maybe. We will see what this day brings.

NOVEMBER 15, 2014

The dentists find something wrong every time. Yesterday the doc noticed I work at Hazelden and said, "Your
organization is fully aware of the dangers of addiction
to opioids." He said he sees young kids all the time with
the problem. They buy their pills and their heroin "down
on Lake Street." Then he wrote me a script for twelve
Vicodin and told me to get a root canal.

DECEMBER 15, 2014

An up-and-down two days since my last entry. I don't
feel well. My hunch is that withdrawal is the main
instigator, as I felt uncomfortable like never before.
Nauseous, restless on the skin, and hot and cold every

hour. And anxious, too. A tug-of-war between more and the desire to put days in between the last pill. It was a hard Saturday night. And Sunday (yesterday) was a mix of feeling better for chunks of the day but feeling overwhelmed as I walked through the tasks at hand. Got them done. By 8 p.m., I've hit a wall. Weary and feeling old. Too old. Physically uncomfortable in my belly and my back and legs. Worn out. Depressed. I'm asleep by 9. But wide awake this morning at 3:15. Long day ahead. I can't seem to catch up or slow down.

DECEMBER 16, 2014

I get on my knees and make a promise to Jesus, Lord God. I turn over my will and my life. A promise is a commitment I must keep. To God. For me. How I've lived my life is not how I want to live my life. The beast inside me consumes my spirit and robs from me and Nell and the kids all that I am. All that I should be. How was I so imperfectly whole all those years? And now I can barely string together a few days. I must return to the way of life that is the only way to live my life. I pick up the 24-hour book for the first time in months and read: "The way of AA is the way of faith."

Amen.

DECEMBER 27, 2014

Yesterday I convinced my dermatologist to give me a few more.

DECEMBER 29, 2014

I'm getting married today. Nell, me, and the four kids. In our living room.

BY THE CLOSE OF 2014, I was worn out inside and out. I was traveling nearly every week, and each notification about an upcoming flight spawned a visceral fear whenever it appeared on my calendar or phone. I dreaded the aching pain in my jaw that occurred every time the plane gained or lost altitude. The travel, speaking, and far-flung meetings that had energized me for so much of my career now felt like cruel cosmic punishment for my closely kept secret.

I could not imagine an alternative to the way I did my job. I was the "outside" guy, not the inside strategist, the accountant, or the counselor who worked with patients. I made my contribution to my company's mission away from the office, down in the trenches, carrying the message and meeting people. I needed to be out there. If I couldn't fly, I couldn't tell my story to people all over the country, spreading the word about the value of treatment and the reality of recovery. If I couldn't fly, I couldn't meet with alumni and donors where they lived—in small towns and big cities in nearly every state—seeking support for our mission. What good was I, then, to the organization? I feared becoming invisible or irrelevant.

I hid my pain and fear during these years in the same way I hid my drug use: by moving. Masked by my always-on public persona, a full calendar, and my breakneck pace, I avoided moments of intimacy where self-reflection or honesty might be expected of me. Insulated by my reputation and role—not to mention my gender, age, and the color of my skin—I escaped scrutiny from the people who prescribed the meds and filled the bottles. Immersing myself in the lives and stories of people who reached out to me for help, I avoided facing my own reality.

I lied by omitting details and practicing vagueness. I cloaked my desire for relief in the obvious wreckage of my ongoing dental problems, excusing the discomforts of withdrawal by attributing them to the pain in my mouth and jaw.

The moments of my life during these years came and went, and after each moment—be it good or bad, painful or promising—another followed.

7

Broken Apart

2014–2015

As the gap between what we experience and
what we can express grows, we get sicker.

— OMAR MANEJWALA, MD

The pills were beginning to take a toll. I hated them as much
as I needed them. And as 2015 ramped up, I relied on them
more and more to stave off the ache in my jaw and smooth out
the other discomforts of my life so I could keep up the pace
on the road and everywhere else. With few exceptions, doctors
and dentists gave me what I wanted—all I had to do was open
my mouth, put up with a few questions, and complain. But
the carnival had stopped being worth the price of admission.
The tolerance I had developed now required I take an extra
pill on top of an extra pill until I began to realize each bottle
of the prescription meds emptied a lot faster than the last.
This meant more trips and contortions and more time and
more angst, and in between, even the slightest kink in this
process meant the first signs of withdrawal tapped me on the
shoulder and whispered in my ear, *Oh no, William, here it*

comes. Between that subtle but relentless taunt and a jaw that complained nearly all the time, the painkiller merry-go-round was spinning faster and faster. I wasn't sure how to hold on, but I was too scared to let go and jump off.

I needed help as much as I was desperate for hope. Yet fear got in the way of pursuing either. I was afraid to reveal too much, to experience the shame of having hidden my problem for so long, and afraid to expose myself as who and what I had become. At times I convinced myself I could stop on my own and pull it together, only to wring my hands and excoriate myself when I couldn't. This sad cycle recurred again and again.

Sometimes I'd imagine I was an inch away from finally giving in and admitting defeat—knowing that then I could get better. But then I'd pull back, scared of how others would respond, and put on my brave, convincing face and push onward. I was taunted by the echo of my sponsor's admonition from years earlier, "Your problem, William, is that you're honest by omission—you'll willingly tell me ninety percent of what you want me to know, but not the ten percent I need to know." I didn't dare show up at Bob's door now. I hadn't even been able to tell Nell the full truth.

Like every other important person in my life, Nell was in the dark about my struggle with opioids. Yes, she knew all about the mess in my mouth. She had been there at the start, when I shuffled through the front door after that first big surgery. She knew I had been sent home with pain pills then, and she was aware that I got occasional refills after the procedures or setbacks in the years that followed.

More than once, after she and Jasper moved in, Nell suggested that she take charge of dispensing the pills I brought home. I put her off, assuring her it wasn't necessary. I told her I had it under control. I wanted to believe my own words. She relented, and I responded by being more careful about hiding the prescriptions I acquired.

As the grip of the opioids tightened, Nell didn't know my truth because I kept it from her. Nobody knew that I required at least a few pills every couple of days to quiet the cravings and the relentless consequences of withdrawal. I hated the restless legs, the itching sensation, the jittery spine. I was embarrassed by my short temper, which occasionally flared as a sharp retort to an irksome comment or a surprised irritation with a colleague or even a stranger in the aisle at the grocery store. Dis-ease and discontent seemed to stalk me like my shadow.

But there was an added twist as well. Despite what my need for these drugs made me do, I still longed for the way they made me feel. For a few hours, they removed me from the anxiety of real life. Also, paradoxically, they focused me so that I was able to concentrate for long evenings in front of the computer or on long flights home. Alone and afloat on the soft tide of peace the pills provided, I could turn toward the texts and emails that kept coming, further blunting my own despair and confusion by immersing myself in the anguish of others. *I can help these people,* I assured myself, *because I had been there and done that.* Because I was still there and still doing it.

I found relief through responding to the needs and pleas of

others—and I recognized it as key to keeping me from sinking entirely into the pull of the painkillers. I also took comfort in believing in the "legitimacy" of my use. I clung to the idea that this thing with the pills wasn't at all like those years when I emerged from the crack house, hollow-eyed and shaking. I was hurting and grouchy as I tried to contain and control my opioid use in 2014, but I sold myself on the idea that this experience was completely different from my relapses in the late 1980s and early 1990s. Back then, my return to drug use transformed me into a pathetic zombie—hating the light that burned right through me after hours spent in the dark, scared to look up at the concerned faces of the people I loved best in the world, both relieved and angry that they had found me, tortured and ripped apart inside.

Every day presented a version of my continual dilemma: tell all and face the truth that I would have to give up the pain pills for good or keep being "honest by omission," revealing just enough of my predicament to avoid having to face the full reality of my problem. I loathed what the pills did to me even as I loved what they did for me. But the more I loathed and the more I loved, the harder it was for me to deny that I was chasing my tail. This had to stop. I had to get help. I just didn't know how to say it. Or who was ready to hear me.

THE HALLWAY WAS crowded with employees and patients coming and going to lunch at the cafeteria on the main Hazelden Betty Ford campus in Center City. I was making my way to rendezvous with Dr. Marvin Seppala. As well as being the chief medical officer of the organization, Marv was and continues to be my dear friend and fellow traveler, whose inspiring journey in recovery began on September 4, 1975, when he was nineteen years old.

A Mayo Clinic–trained physician with an impeccable reputation, Marv had gained international renown and that had recently been enhanced by his efforts to revise our organization's approach to treating patients who are addicted to opioids. The program he started, officially named Comprehensive Opioid Response with Twelve Steps but quickly dubbed COR-12, was a significant innovation for our organization.

In the first decade of the 2000s, Marv and the others who developed the COR-12 program were alarmed by the increase in admissions for people addicted to opioids—especially among youth and young adults. They recognized that opioids posed unique challenges to the way we had always thought about and provided treatment. The doctors also found that people with opioid use disorders tended to experience more complex obstacles than those seeking treatment for other addictions. In part because of the intensity of cravings and the difficulty of withdrawal and in part because they arrived with co-occurring mental health disorders, many opioid users had a harder time sticking with treatment. Feeling stigmatized by other patients and misunderstood by care providers, many left early. Some ended up overdosing.

COR-12 was a new way for Hazelden Betty Ford to apply the insights of our biopsychosocial model of addiction treatment. It combined Twelve Step facilitation with other therapies and supports, including the use of stabilizing medications like buprenorphine and naltrexone. These medications helped patients deal with the physiologic instability, cravings, and mood dysregulation that often accompany withdrawal from opioids. The goal was to keep people engaged in treatment so they could stay alive. Only the living get a shot at long-term recovery.

When it went public in 2013, the program provoked some fierce objections—especially from AA and NA groups. Many wondered whether, by using medications in this way, our organization was abandoning or compromising the commitment to abstinence-based treatment that had guided Hazelden since its founding. Marv was at the center of this activity, taking the heat from all sides of the debate—including from some of his own colleagues.

You wouldn't know any of this from talking to him. A humbler man would be hard to find. Unfailingly kind and empathic regardless of the crisis or circumstance, Marv Seppala embodies the values that ground and guide the Hazelden Betty Ford Foundation. He's a truly gentle and beautiful soul, with a voice and a demeanor to match. I felt better as soon as I spotted him, even though I was certain he could see my heart practically pounding out of my chest.

With coffee in hand, Marv and I sat down together at the "Bill and Bob" table in a corner of the cafeteria's foyer. On the wall above the small table were photos of AA's cofounders, Bill Wilson and Dr. Bob Smith. A few books—the Big Book and some meditation books—lay on the surrounding tables, along with a couple of blue ceramic coffee cups. This spot represents the "gathering place" and is intended to be emblematic of the fellowship in which alcoholics and addicts meet to share their "experience, strength, and hope." The table sits by a window overlooking the bucolic 500-acre campus.

When I had emailed Marv a few days earlier asking him to meet with me, I didn't tell him why, and he hadn't asked. We often got together when he flew in from his home base in Oregon. Now that we finally sat face-to-face, I felt relieved. Still, I was nervous. I had plenty of "experience" I could share with him. It was the "strength and hope" that seemed in short supply for me in those days.

"Marv, I've had this run-in with the pain meds I've been prescribed for my dental work and the ongoing problem in my jaw," I said. "It's been going on for a while." I paused.

"I can't beat these damn things and I don't really know what to do." The last few words came too fast.

Marv listened with his characteristic calm intensity. Nearly sixty at the time, the man still somehow looked like a teenager, even with his glasses and thinning blond hair. This is partly due to his genes—he comes from a long line of healthy Finns—but it's also a testament to the strength of his recovery. Sitting across from him, I felt like a lesser man: old, weathered by addiction, body parts aching, weakened from struggling with the pills, ashamed of my need to ask for help from someone I admired so much.

Even as I spoke, I regretted taking his time. I knew how busy he was and how many work-related projects and problems he was asked to consult on.

"I'm sorry to pull you into my personal stuff—I know I really shouldn't—but I don't know what to do," I said. "Or who else to talk to."

As I finally released these words, I felt a warmth in my chest. A weak smile shone on my face. I was carefully pulling one corner of the veil away, no longer hiding but instead admitting to a great friend, and an esteemed doctor, that I was struggling. Marv was a person I had worked with and—more importantly—shared recovery with for so many years.

As passionate as Marv is about recovery and as knowledgeable as he is about addiction and treatment, he's not one for chit-chatting or idle talk. Many people assume he's introverted, but I know him well enough to know that his demeanor is part of a quiet confidence that comes from peace of mind and a balanced soul grounded in humility. Despite my faith in his kindness, trying to read his thoughts that day suddenly made me anxious again. Surprise? Concern? Alarm? I was suddenly afraid that maybe he was thinking less of me for getting into trouble with what we both knew were dangerously addictive drugs.

"Well, this isn't good," Marv said evenly. I was careful to suppress it, but I had a foolish urge to laugh out loud. Given the reality of my situation, I couldn't imagine a more profound understatement. Of course, Marv knew only what I had just told him. He had no idea how serious my "run-in" had become.

I was losing my tug-of-war with pain meds. While, with a great deal of effort, I could go days and even a week or more without pills, without fail the hour would arrive when the craving gripped and overpowered me with that itch that I couldn't scratch. And the withdrawal symptoms were fierce—heavy sweats, restlessness, fixation, desperation. My body and mind ached and burned for just one more, or maybe two or three more. I always gave in.

"It's not the end of the world if you hang in there and slowly taper off the pills," Marv said.

A part of me wanted to tell him I'd tried that already, not exactly a slow taper, but stopping for days and even weeks at a time—usually when I ran out of pills, or when I escaped to the cabin, or when I was finally filled with so much shame and self-loathing that I vowed to be done forever. That resolve always faltered when I found another opportunity to get a refill or acquire a new prescription.

Another part of me didn't want to tell Marv the whole story because it had gone on for so long and because I was in such deep trouble. It felt good to pretend—even for a few minutes—that the inability to stop was a common problem, that lots of people went through it, that it wasn't, as Marv put it, "the end of the world."

Still, I didn't leave it at that. "Well, the cravings are pretty intense, and it's darn near impossible to slowly cut back. I count down the number of pills," I admitted. "I count the hours between the pills. Sometimes I take two at a time."

That was a lie. I didn't count the hours and watch the clock. I wasn't taking the pills as directed. I took two, or three, or four pills to get the hit I needed. I wasn't only taking the pills for the pain in my mouth—except when I was on a plane when things were the worst, that pain was more like a steady background ache. I was taking them for the other pain, for the bigger, harder, sharper pains that came with not taking them. I was taking them for the pain that came from taking them when I knew I shouldn't be. I was taking them for the pain that came from not knowing who I was anymore. I was taking them for the way they made me feel and not feel.

In the end, I didn't tell Marv any of this. I was ashamed and afraid. I worried that he might judge me or warn me that I might lose my job or some other truly terrifying response. The shame burned inside me. Here I was, lying to my friend, hiding behind the ever-helpful curtain of selective omission and minimal sharing, downplaying the severity of my problem. I had asked Marv to meet with me, hoping for help, but now I refused to tell him the whole truth. Instead, I backpedaled.

"I read a thing about Epsom salts and Benadryl for withdrawal symptoms," I said. "What do you think?"

Marv tilted his head as he considered these tactics.

"Well," he said, "Benadryl might help with the itching." His voice was calm and thoughtful. "Hot baths can ease aches and pains and muscle tension . . ." Marv kept talking as my thoughts continued to spin. My itching for a pill went deeper than the skin, deeper than the muscles and tendons, deeper even than the liver, lungs, and heart, reaching into my brain and disrupting the synapses, lighting me up with the demand: *MORE, MORE, MORE, NOW, NOW, NOW.*

"It might take seven to ten days to completely wean your way off the meds," he counseled

Marv sipped his coffee.

"And meetings," he added. "You need to go to meetings."

I know that! I know all of that, I wanted to shout at Marv, *and it's not working!*

Instead, I nodded and said, "Ah, yes. Meetings."

I wanted to tell Marv how, when I had admitted to using painkillers at AA meetings after my dental surgeries, some people, especially the old-timers, looked at me sideways as if to say, "You need to get your act together, William," or "That's a slippery slope you're on, son." I wanted to shout at them, too. *I know that!* "One is too many and a thousand too few." *I know that!* But I wanted to take those slogans and platitudes in my hands and crush them. *For God's sake, I know all that, but I still can't stop.*

How was I going to wean myself off these drugs when, if I took one less than I took the day before, I'd fall one pill short of the same buzz—and it was that buzz I wanted as much as the buzz I needed to keep the withdrawal symptoms at bay and give my craving brain some peace? What would I do for the pain—the real and increasingly unbearable pain in my jaw and head—when I flew to Atlanta or DC or Seattle or Palm Springs, or all the other cities and towns in between where my first responsibility was to show up smiling?

I had need. I had reason for hope. I even had enough self-awareness to know how dangerous a road I was on. What I lacked was courage. As well as being unwilling to reveal the extent of my problem with the pills, I also didn't have the guts to tell Marv that I was frustrated with the meetings and the readings and the Steps. I felt like the Twelve Steps had failed me. They felt like an old friend that had helped me out of a jam years ago, but somehow failed to show up when I needed them now. I was convinced that these drugs were too powerful for this remedy. Prayers and platitudes were like Epsom salts against the urges I was experiencing. Meetings had become just another place for me to feel like a failure and a fraud. I had tried to stay on that path, the same path that had worked for me for nearly two decades, but it simply didn't do the job for me anymore.

How could I tell Marv any of this? The Twelve Steps were such a critical part of his recovery. They were a cornerstone of the Hazelden approach to care—and central to the COR-12 opioid treatment program he had developed.

I still wanted to trust in the power of the program of Steps and fellowship and service. Commitment to its principles had seen me through days, weeks, and years of steady recovery. My service to others in need had been a lifeline for me in the past years—a thread of connection I clung to even after I had stopped going to meetings. The Twelve Steps contained so much practical wisdom and spiritual truth. They pointed me to the essential elements of character that make our lives worth living: gratitude, forgiveness, humility, honesty. But they were failing against this drug and what it did to me.

I had never experienced craving like I did with opioids—not with alcohol, not with cocaine, not with crack. I had returned to those substances repeatedly. My first attempts at sobriety were marked by one relapse after another, but that wasn't because I liked the drugs or what they did to me. My addicted brain needed them in order to feel normal.

The painkillers gave me more than that—so much more than normal. With the other drugs, it was all about hell. With the pills, it was as if heaven itself opened up to me. Maybe the need was similar but the result—oh my god—the result wasn't the same at all. It wasn't even on the same planet. There are a few moments of ecstasy on crack or cocaine, and alcohol always gave me a burst of calming release, but these effects lasted for only a few minutes before the brain went numb or the need fired up again. With opioids I got *hours.*

The painkillers offered more than ecstasy or anesthesia. They gave me an experience of life writ large. That sensation of being detached and suspended from anxiety and fear—that's what I wanted out of life. It's what I have always wanted—that sensation of being right where I want to be, of being exactly who I want to be, of being content, of being myself, but more than myself, better than myself, bigger and even more real than any self I had ever been.

How could I explain this to Marv? It's not that he wouldn't understand; Marv understood everything about recovery. He probably knew more about painkillers and opioid addiction than just about anyone. I was afraid that he would understand all too well.

If I confessed everything that day at that table, would he urge me to go back into treatment? That would mean admitting to everyone at Hazelden that I was addicted to painkillers and that I had been hiding the fact for years. I might lose my job. I most certainly would lose respect. I had no doubt that some people would regard me with scorn—not just my close colleagues either, but the office staff, the people who ran the bookstore, the people who published my books. That scenario was too humiliating to even contemplate. And I feared the ramifications would extend beyond Hazelden Betty Ford. Alumni, donors, supporters, fellow advocates, people whom I had helped into treatment and guided through recovery—all these people would judge me for preaching what I wasn't practicing. I was talking the talk without walking the walk.

Would the donors ask for their money back? Would they think I was a liar and a hypocrite? Would they abandon Hazelden because of me? For sure they would wonder why I was the organization's recovery ambassador. Why should I be out on the road week after week speaking passionately about the reality of recovery when it wasn't my reality?

I imagined the inevitable questions and sidelong glances, the raft of emails and texts. Some would be concerns about my health and well-being, and others would be angry calls for Hazelden to cut me loose. All the good work I had accomplished would be down the drain. All the people I had helped might wonder if they, too, were headed for a downward slide.

And what about my mother and my father? For decades I had worked to restore and rebuild my parents' approval after those hideous and shameful years that had roiled their lives along with mine. They didn't have many years left on this earth, and this news would fill their final days with fear and concern for me. They'd have a multitude of questions about how it happened and how I had managed to hide it from everyone for so long.

I could not face the shame. So I chose to keep hiding instead.

I could handle the questions that arose periodically and that I wrestled with in my journal. I could deal with the occasional disapproving gazes from pharmacists. I could keep convincing prescribers of my pain. I could continue to take these hits internally, but externally—to have people I love and people I work with daily think less of me, to imagine what was going on in their minds, to wonder whether they believed that all the years of my recovery were false and fraudulent—I just couldn't face that.

"I can't tell you how much I appreciate your counsel, Marv," I said. "You are a great friend and a wise man. I'm going to CVS right now to buy some Benadryl and Epsom salts; then I'll go home and fill up the bathtub. And after that, I'll go to a meeting."

I don't know if Marv was taken in by my gratitude and effusive thanks or if he suspected the problem was worse than what I had presented to him. We shook hands, gave each other a hug, and went back to work.

When I got home that day, I sat in the driveway with my head in my hands. I pictured my life, a weak and rotted-out structure of half-truths and scrabbling survival. I saw it collapsing to the ground. I thought about how everything would cave in upon itself if I admitted to Marv—and thus to my entire world—that I needed treatment for an opioid addiction. I could not do it.

Besides, I had pills in the house. I wasn't ready to give up heaven yet. The only hell from these drugs was the scrounging and scrambling, the bouts of self-doubt and self-loathing, the dishonesty and denial, but all of that wasn't really so bad, was it? At least not when I considered the prize. I believed I had no choice now but to beat this thing on my own. I could. I knew I could. When it was time. When I was ready.

Tomorrow maybe.

Or the day after tomorrow.

Or the day after that.

DAYS WENT BY. Then weeks. Then months. As my conversation with Marv receded into the past, I began to recall it less as a failure of nerve on my part and more as a time I got some tips about how to handle cravings. I told myself that I was okay even as I continued to take the pills. I kept assuring myself that that I needed these breaks—even deserved them—because of the pace of my life, the nonstop travel, the endless commitments, meetings, phone calls, and emails.

The long Minnesota winter of 2014–2015 finally came to an end. The muddy season, with its steady and often torrential rains, extended into June before clearing. With great anticipation I packed a few bags and drove two hours to our family cabin on a small lake in northern Wisconsin. There is no finer time of the year in the Upper Midwest than summers, with their hot days and long evenings when the glow in the western sky keeps the night at bay until well after ten.

I regularly retreated to the lake to get away from the stress of work and the demands of never-ending chores at home. But that summer I had another reason to escape. I was out of pain medication and was hoping to put the pills behind me at last. I thought a change of scenery could help ease the craving I felt whenever I tried to taper off or quit before. It wasn't just the physical itching—that insatiable sensation of needing to scratch, which extended beneath my skin. The discomfort went deeper than that. Beyond the twitching and burning muscles, deeper still into my frazzled neurons (I imagined them emitting sudden, hot sparks of craving), the ache was in my soul.

I continued to torture myself. I felt guilt for what I was hiding from everyone, even Nell and my children, and I was ashamed of the kind of person I must have become to hide away with my stashes of pills and schemes for getting more. Despite my conversation with Marv, despite my knowledge that this game I was playing was dangerous, I still played it. The shame felt worse than the guilt because I could make amends for what I had done. But how could I atone for who and what I had become?

I swam in the lake, built fires, and watched the flames eat away at the burning oak logs. I listened to the loons calling back and forth across the water and ran along the country roads through the sunflower fields. As the days passed, the cravings eased. Slightly and slowly, a different kind of peace began to make its way into my mind and heart. This was the serenity of engaging instead of disengaging with life and it lasted not for hours, but for days. Instead of worrying about where my next pill might come from, I looked forward to another starlit swim, another gravel-road run, another smoky fire.

It happened in the early afternoon. I was answering emails on the porch, sipping a lemonade and munching on pistachios, when I heard a "crack." It sounded like a kernel of popcorn suddenly bursting. It felt sharp—a jolt along the line of my lower jaw. The pistachio shell had shattered a crown in the same place that had caused both acute and chronic pain over the years. I picked the fragments of the crown out of my mouth and laid them carefully on a napkin. As I examined the broken pieces, I felt that slow, inexorable surge of heaviness seep back into my jaw, along with a deep panic. The fear of pain, along with the knowledge that I would have to see yet another dentist, brought tears to my eyes.

Yet a moment later I felt a surge of excitement. My heart beat faster and the sparks in my brain lit up as if on cue. I now had a new and absolutely legitimate opportunity to score. Here, on the napkin in front of me, was evidence I could use to convince a dentist that I was in serious pain. But where was I going to find a dentist in the backwoods of Wisconsin?

Less than two hours later I was sitting in the chair at Dr. Del Bakkum's office in Spooner, Wisconsin, a town with fewer than 3,000 residents. I found his online listing and called the emergency number, convincing the receptionist that I required the dentist's immediate attention. From the very first moment I met him, I felt at ease talking to this country dentist. Dr. Bakkum had a pleasant, open face and a gentle voice. As I recounted my years of relentlessly frustrating and painful interventions to fix my teeth and jaw problems, he listened attentively. I didn't mention how these years had also included a relentless, increasingly desperate, and usually successful hunt for pain medications.

"I can see from the X-rays and my exam that you've had an impressive amount of work done," Dr. Bakkum said. His voice was soothing and his manner sympathetic. I felt that I had arrived at the right place.

"This crown is new and shouldn't have broken like this," he continued. "It seems your bad luck with your mouth simply doesn't quit."

Bad luck? Dr. Bakkum's assessment gave me a perverse sense of relief. Sometimes I wondered if all these problems were more in my head than in my mouth. Like I had willed the failed implant, the repeated root canals, the shattered crown, the neuralgia in my jaw—all to score more pills.

"You mean this isn't my fault?" I sheepishly asked.

"Hardly," Dr. Bakkum replied.

I jumped at the door he had just invited me to open.

"No wonder this really hurts," I said, suspecting that this confirmed innocence would be enough to get me on track for acquiring a new source of pills. My mouth *did* hurt, but then again I wasn't sure precisely where any of my pain was coming from at that point.

It worked. Dr. Bakkum wrote a prescription, but when he handed me the slip, I noticed it was for a pain medication I hadn't heard of, called tramadol. What if I had screwed up this unique opportunity to score more oxycodone? Maybe I should have made a bigger deal of the pain. When would I get another chance like this?

"I usually take oxycodone," I told him. "What should I do if this doesn't work for my pain?"

"As long as you take it as prescribed, it will work," he said, spending a few minutes to explain that studies had found that, for most patients, tramadol provided a similar level of pain relief as oxycodone—even though oxycodone is twice as potent as morphine and tramadol has only a fraction of morphine's potency. Plus, tramadol was less addictive than oxycodone.

On the way back to the cabin I tried to figure out what tramadol's potency was and if I'd have to take extra pills to get the buzz I now craved. If oxycodone was more than double the potency of morphine but tramadol was only a fraction—one quarter, one half?—of morphine's potency, it seemed I might have to take a whole handful at once. My rustic self-administered nature retreat from the pills was over. I couldn't wait to get back to the cabin to sample this new drug.

Minutes later I gulped down three tramadol tablets and within half an hour I felt a slow, creeping sensation of ease in my muscles as the pain in my mouth faded to almost nothing. But something was missing, so the next day I took two more and then two more and, yes—*finally*—there was the feeling I missed, the sensation of drifting and floating, being alive with all my senses dulled but somehow more alive, more attuned to the beauty of life than ever. I lay down on the dock and spent the afternoon watching the clouds go by. Puffy white, gray-bottomed clouds interrupted the sunshine, hinting at a summer storm to come. *This is life,* I thought. *Life as good as it gets.*

Two days after my visit with Dr. Bakkum, I drove back to St. Paul for a few weeks, comforted by the knowledge that I had a new, if somewhat irregular and inconvenient, source for more pills the next time I came up to the cabin.

THE SUN WAS RISING bright in a cloudless sky as I drove west along the interstate from St. Paul to Hazelden Betty Ford's adolescent facility in suburban Minneapolis. I was on my way to meet with the parents and siblings of our young patients in treatment. The family group met once a month, and my brief lecture was a standing agenda item.

"Family week" is often gut-wrenching for moms and dads. Many who attend harbor intense feelings of shame and guilt. They wonder if there was something they should have or could have done differently that would have prevented their kids from starting with substances. They're afraid they might have caused addiction to blossom in their household or somehow failed to stop it from growing. My story reassures them that they are not at fault. Just as my parents were not to blame for my drug use and rapid descent into addiction, their choices and influences did not determine their child's path. As we say to families, "You didn't *cause* it, you can't *control* it, and you can't *cure* it." I also deliver the encouraging news that, as terrifying as their situation feels, for the most part, their children are starting down the road of recovery at a much earlier age than I had.

"I wasted half my teens, all of my twenties, and half of my thirties before I got on the pathway to recovery," I said. "Your kids have their whole lives ahead of them." I heard a collective sigh as listeners leaned back into their seats. There were even a few hopeful smiles around the circle. As bad as things were, maybe the worst was behind them.

I repeated a key message—one that appears in every speech I gave to parents: "Let your children know you are there for them. Let them know that if they need help, they must ask for it. Let them know that you will not judge them, because you love them and you are there to help them. Repeat those words over and over and over so they sink in, and then do your part. Listen. Empathize. Stay connected. Do not judge. Set boundaries. Take care of yourself."

After my talk, there were questions. The parents were hungry for certainty—for some hope that their children weren't lost forever. I strolled across the parking lot feeling good about myself and my role. I knew that by sharing the details of my story—both as an addicted teenager and as a parent of kids who were on their own recovery journeys—I had become part of the community that walked alongside these hurting families with compassion and optimism.

My good feeling lasted about as long as it took to get to the car. *Stay connected. Do not judge. Set boundaries. Take care of yourself. Listen to yourself, Moyers.* In my speech I hadn't mentioned, of course, the most recent chapter in my story.

SHORTLY AFTER MY family week lecture, I drove back to the lake. I was by myself again, the last of my pills gone, the withdrawal symptoms steadily building inside me. I wanted to recapture the drug-free peace I had tasted earlier in the summer. I vowed to stick it out this time—swim in the lake, eat a lot of nourishing food, and go for long runs to ease the cravings. It worked for a day or two. But the itching and aching irritability just grew. Soon I was beginning to feel a deep panic once again, just like all those other times when I went without pills for several days.

I gave up and called Dr. Bakkum's office. "I am really hurting," I told the receptionist. It was the truth—I *was* hurting—but the pain was in my head, in my brain, in my muscles, and not in my mouth.

"Dr. Bakkum is out," she said, at which point my heart dropped to my feet. Maybe I moaned or said something, because she quickly promised to ask him to call me back. In less than an hour the dentist returned my call.

"How are you, William?"

"Ahh, not so great," I said. "The temporary is causing a lot of discomfort in my jaw."

I was stunned when this simple complaint earned me another prescription for a handful of tramadol. "This will take care of your needs for a day or so," Dr. Bakkum said, "I'd like to see you in my office within the next few days so I can examine you more closely."

I was supposed to go back to St. Paul the next day but, shoot, the pain pills were calling. For six tramadol, I agreed to the follow-up appointment, delayed my return, and immediately drove to the pharmacy. I also wanted to fulfill my part of the deal with Dr. Bakkum and show up for my appointment. He was someone I liked a lot, and I wanted to show him I was a good patient. I was also confident that I would walk out of the next exam with a refill for even more pills. Maybe ten, maybe twenty, who knows?

WHEN I SAT DOWN in his chair, Dr. Bakkum was his usual self. He inquired affably about the state of my jaw and teeth, but he also seemed clearly interested in me and my overall well-being. We swapped our latest fishing stories and talked about our plans for what was left of the summer. He asked me a couple of general questions about goings-on at Hazelden Betty Ford. Then we got down to business as he probed around inside my mouth. I reminded him how much it hurt and the specific places that caused me the greatest discomfort.

"This temporary crown shouldn't be causing you this kind of pain," he said as he moved the probe across my gums and tapped lightly on the top of the crown. "Are you sure this is where you're feeling the pain?" I winced and assured him I was suffering. Because I was. Did I somehow make myself hurt on purpose, to secure his empathy and convince him I needed more pain meds, or was I really suffering like I told him I was? I didn't know anymore. But I didn't dare tell him that I needed relief for what ailed me, imagined or not. He seemed to anticipate what I was after.

"Okay," he said.

It was such a simple word, spoken in a kind and unhurried tone. I imagined him sitting down in a comfortable chair by a fireplace with a cup of hot tea. He gently placed his tools on the small table beside my chair. "There are a couple of ways to go here, William. As you've explained to me already, you've seen a lot of dentists and had a lot of work done these past few years. I know you hurt," he said, his smile turning upside down in a show of sympathy.

"What worries me, though," he continued, "is that medical care has become so compartmentalized and territorial that sometimes I think almost all dentists and doctors have a kind of tunnel vision. If we see something that looks like a nail, we pull out our version of a hammer and start pounding. And if we stare at something long enough, almost anything can look like a nail. I have dentist acquaintances who have convinced themselves that they can cure almost any ailment with a bite adjustment and an occlusal splint." He chuckled softly. "If one is going to think like that, it helps to have a large dose of hubris."

Listening to Dr. Bakkum talk, I forgot about the itch and the pain and the pills. For a moment, I felt less like a patient and more like a struggling student when the light comes on—when the professor finally offers a cogent explanation of the complex formula chalked on the blackboard. Every time I had complained of pain, every time I had a root canal, a tooth pulled, or a broken crown, the dentist of the moment had simply seen another nail to pound. And when the hammering was done, I was sent on my way with yet another prescription for pain medication.

He continued, "More often than not in this field, there is some specific and identifiable problem that can be addressed with a procedure," he said, then paused for a moment. "And dentists like me are paid to do procedures. This can create a subtle bias in the dentist. Sometimes, though, the symptoms don't match the clinical presentation. And sometimes doing a procedure that should have resolved the symptom doesn't resolve the symptom or even creates new ones that just don't make sense when viewed through the usual 'see a problem, fix a problem' lens.

"You've had a lot of procedures," he continued, gesturing at my mouth. "And I know enough about your history that I suspect this is the case for you."

Unexpected tears sprang to my eyes. "You mean there is nothing you can do for me?"

"No, no, that's not at all what I'm saying," he assured me. "I'm very focused on helping you. I want you to feel better— you shouldn't suffer. It's just that I've come to the conclusion that there is no specific dental procedure I can offer that will help you."

I felt my heart sink. No more procedures meant no more meds. Even as I reeled at the thought, I knew that Dr. Bakkum was right. This insanity had been going around and around for too long. Something had to change. Starting with me. I had pain, yes. But the pain wasn't going to kill me. The meds might. My reliance on the pills was the real threat; the fear I had of the pain, though it felt as wicked as the pain, was the monster I had to face.

Yet my fear was about more than experiencing pain. I was afraid of falling short. I was fearful of who I had become. Fearful of getting off the pain meds. Fearful of how I would explain all of this to everyone who thought they knew me.

Never before had a doctor or dentist told me they couldn't help me. But I also understood that Dr. Bakkum wasn't giving up on me.

"Remember what I said about dentists and 'tunnel vision'?" he asked. "Well, I believe you need more than just my expertise and another procedure. You need a team that looks at your situation from many angles and comes up with a solution that takes everything into account and doesn't simply put a bandage on it with another procedure and more pain meds."

Dr. Bakkum paused. "You know by now that more pain meds don't work. Eventually they'll actually make the pain worse."

He looked me in the eye then before saying, "To you they're nothing but trouble."

For the first time in years, a dentist had shined a light into my wrecked mouth and admitted that the problems I was experiencing were beyond his ability to understand or solve.

"I'd like to refer you to the pain clinic at the University of Minnesota," said my country dentist. "I went to dental school there, so I'm familiar with the clinic and I've sent a few others there—people like you who suffer from chronic head and neck pain. You'll get the attention of an entire team who will look at your situation from a 360-degree perspective and come up with a plan. A plan," he added, "that includes how to manage your pain with and without narcotic medication. This is the right move. I'm convinced of it."

In that moment I was too.

Hubris. Yes, my mouth was causing me big problems—but so had the procedures meant to fix those problems. And so were the pain meds that, far from being a solution, had become the biggest problem of all.

Unfailingly friendly, intensely compassionate, perceptive, and disarmingly humble, Dr. Del Bakkum made it clear to me: He wasn't going to throw up his hands. He also wasn't going to give me a prescription for more pills. Dr. Bakkum didn't want to just clear me off his chart that day. He wanted to help me discover what was wrong with my teeth and jaw and neck—and he knew that would require a different approach. He wanted me to recover not just from the pain in my mouth but from what was tearing apart the rest of me as well.

I called the pain clinic the next day.

■

8

Busted

2015

Fall down seven times, get up eight.

— JAPANESE PROVERB

"It has to stop."

Dr. Donald Nixdorf frowned at the document on the desk in front of him and then looked up at me as he pushed the pages across the table. I didn't sense a lot of warmth coming from him, but I'm a likeable guy and I harbored the hope that we could at least have a meaningful discussion about the complex issues that brought me to his office at the University of Minnesota dental school. When I glanced down at the document in front of me, my heart sank. It looked just like the printout Dr. Giefer had waved at me back at the end of 2013. Dr. Nixdorf had accessed our state's prescription monitoring program database.

He folded his hands on the table in front of him and courteously but coolly repeated his statement. "It's too many. It's time to stop."

I nodded my head. Dr. Nixdorf had me figured out. I had come to the clinic seeking his expertise for the chronic pain in my jaw, but that was only part of my problem. Here, on the table in front of me, was the undeniable black-and-white proof that I had been using too many pain pills, prescribed by too many doctors from too many clinics for way too long. Of course, "using" didn't quite cover it.

I don't know if Dr. Nixdorf did his research ahead of time or if, in his referral conversations and notes, Dr. Bakkum told him about my addiction and recovery history and my work at Hazelden. Maybe Bakkum had even sent him the long list of medications that I was staring at now. I felt my face flush.

"You of all people," he said, neither raising nor lowering his voice, "have to know the dangers of opioid drugs, particularly with your personal history with substances. Then of course there's your professional life. It is not just your physical and mental health but your credibility, Mr. Moyers, that is at stake here."

There was a long pause. He stared straight at me, neither smiling nor frowning. Only when he lifted his thick, blond eyebrows did I understand that he expected me to respond.

"Can you call me William?" I asked. Honestly, I didn't know what else to say. I hoped he would understand that I meant the question as a somewhat lighthearted acknowledgment that we were in this together and had a lot of work to do.

"I prefer to keep our relationship professional, like I do with all my patients, Mr. Moyers," he said with a tight smile. "So, let me lay out the routine ahead of you. You will come to the pain clinic twice a week for acupuncture and physical therapy appointments. You'll attend psychotherapy sessions once a week. You will be given instructions for stress-reduction techniques to do at home. It is important that you do these exercises every day, multiple times a day, without fail. You will see me once a week for the next few months. Then we'll review your pain level and the management of it and determine a longer-term plan. Maybe up to a year."

Dr. Nixdorf let that information sink in for a moment. A year? I was taken aback by the detailed plan that had he suggested, which seemed way beyond what was necessary. It certainly wasn't what I had expected. Growing up, pain had always been a brief, unpleasant experience, like a bee sting or a broken bone playing sports. It came, it hurt, it dissipated in a few minutes or a few days. Granted, this time the pain in my jaw had been relentless, debilitating at times, with wave after wave of throbbing, aching, and tenderness that depressed me to no end. I knew pain meds were the lure that had snagged me because they worked almost instantly, at least in the beginning, but over time they worked against me. *Plus one* was what it took. Or *plus two*. Or *plus three*. Still, I couldn't quite figure out why I would need up to a year of appointments to get rid of the pain and get off the pills. Did it really have to be this complicated and time-consuming?

"If you're going to work with us to control and resolve your pain, then I need you to sign this," Dr. Nixdorf said, sliding a two-page document across the desk toward me. Even reading it upside down, I could make out the words in boldface at the top: "Medication Management Contract." This was something serious and binding. I picked up the pages and sat back in my chair. I put on my reading glasses to scan the finer print. Dr. Nixdorf seemed impatient.

"You will have to sign this document if I am going to work with you," he said. "It requires your agreement that you will, under no circumstances, seek opiate pain medication from any other prescriber. I will manage your use of pain meds—I alone. No ifs, ands, or buts." He paused. "Do you understand?"

Well, of course I understood; there it was in black and white. I hadn't felt this threatened by a piece of paper since December 23, 1980, when I had to sign a similar agreement to be released from jail into my father's custody after a drunken night that ended in my arrest for burglary. That "contract" had threatened to return me to a cell if I proved unable or unwilling to stay away from alcohol and other drugs. Sitting in this doctor's office now, I felt my face burning with shame as I pretended to read the document in my hands.

"If you agree to that—and I hope you do—then all you have to do is sign on the bottom line," Dr. Nixdorf said. "It is really quite simple."

Simple for you, I thought. *Was it really necessary for me to sign away my freedom of choice? I mean, come on,* Donald, *I'm a grown man with a hell of a lot of experience staying clean and sober. I know what to do and what not to do because I've been doing it for a long time, except for this stretch where I stalled, spun out, slipped up, whatever you want to call it, and my options narrowed, the pill supply dried up. I came to you for your expertise with chronic pain. All I really want is your help getting back on track and in the race to prove that I can manage my pain and my life on my own.*

At that point in my inner discourse, I mentally slapped myself across the face. *Come on,* William, *he wants you to sign this contract precisely because you can't be trusted to manage your pain on your own—or your life, for that matter. You completely screwed up any flexibility and freedom of choice. The pain meds and your craving for more, more, more are in control right now. They've dictated your thoughts and behavior for years now—and trampled your values and your integrity along the way. If that wasn't true, you wouldn't be sitting here at all.*

For the briefest moment, I considered drawing Dr. Nixdorf into a deeper discussion to see if there were some exceptions to this plan—maybe a few other options. I had a busy schedule, with all those exhausting days on the road. I had no time for so many appointments. Surely there was a way to do this differently. Could I maybe negotiate the Busy Executive plan?

Did I read a scowl on his face?

"Sign the paper," he said, "and let's get going."

It dawned on me in that moment that this man—this grump of a doctor—was willing and ready to take me and what I was suffering seriously, even as I was scheming for a shortcut. Like Dr. Bakkum before him—and like the dozens and dozens of counselors and sponsors and doctors and recovery peers before either of them—Dr. Nixdorf saw that I was hurting. He was offering me a lifeline. The contract and the plan were pathways to freedom from my jaw pain *and* my pill problem. I would be a fool to walk away from this opportunity.

I didn't bother to read any more. I found my name and the blank line next to it, signed and dated the paper, and pushed it back across the desk. The scratch of the pen on the page brought back another memory. On a stifling day in 1989 I lied about my name and address to the admissions counselor at St. Vincent's Hospital. This time, I wrote out my whole name. It felt like I was making a confession. *Drug seeker. Needs supervision.* Guilty as charged.

It also felt good. Weird as it sounds, as I signed and dated that sheet of paper, it seemed as though the weight of a thousand pills lifted off my body. I didn't have much of a clue about exactly how this next chapter in my saga would go, but I knew that I didn't have to navigate it all by myself anymore. Relief slowly flooded over me. The past few years had been the loneliest of my life in recovery—a self-imposed and confusing exile from connection and compassion that was rooted in shame and stubbornness and driven by my need for relief and escape. Starting today, I was no longer alone, no matter how gruff my companion was.

"I'm all yours, Dr. Nixdorf," I said, waiting for a handshake or a smile, hoping for some kind of acknowledgment that I was a flawed but decent man who was serious about getting better. I wanted him to know that William Cope Moyers was attempting to loosen his grip on his long-standing and pigheaded belief that he could solve every problem on his own.

"Let's get down to business," he replied.

LEAVING DR. NIXDORF and his clinic that day, I didn't even wait for the elevator. Instead, I hustled down six flights of stairs to the university pharmacy where I filled the prescription he had provided. I'm embarrassed to say there was a flutter of excitement in me as the pharmacist handed me the bag with its small bottle of tramadol. That night I took the meds as prescribed, my feelings of guilt moderated by a glimmer of hope. The doctor and I had a plan to manage my pain—one that would eventually eliminate my need to take painkillers at all. I reminded myself that the pills I took now were not simply a placeholder until the next time I could scheme and score. Now they were a bridge to healing. As long as I buckled down and lived up to my side of the bargain—as long as I followed the rules—I could be free.

THE UNIVERSITY OF MINNESOTA boasts many beautiful and architecturally fascinating buildings, but Moos Tower isn't one of them. Walking up the pathway, past a modern fountain and sleek row of planted trees, one sees a multilevel building with narrow, slit-like, windows peeking out of drab concrete. It looks like one of the old flak towers built by the Nazis to defend Berlin from Allied bombers in World War II. Or maybe a kid's haphazard Lego creation.

This brutal exterior, thank goodness, belies the elegance and industry that happens inside the building. Moos Tower is a beehive of activity: students coming and going to dentistry classes, dentists and doctors in white lab coats or smocks consulting files as they emerge from one consultation room to enter another, and hundreds of patients in at least that many offices waiting for appointments for specialists in structural speech disorders, cleft and craniofacial services, and chronic dental pain. My visits brought me to the sixth floor and the TMD and Orofacial Pain Clinic. As I learned, temporomandibular disorders (TMDs) are conditions that cause pain and dysfunction in the jaw joint and the muscles that control the jaw and face.

"Part of your problem is in your jaw," the clinic psychologist said in our first session. "The rest is more complicated . . . it is in your head. You depend on those meds for the pain, yes, but you also depend on them to take care of the issues that led you to like them in the first place."

That matter-of-fact, no-argument-accepted assessment caught me by surprise.

"I certainly didn't start taking pain pills to make myself happy or less anxious," I said. "I took them for pain."

She nodded diplomatically. "Perhaps. But as someone who understands addiction from the inside out, you know that for people like you, drugs affect not just your pain but the emotions that come with it, how they can make you feel better or seem to affirm your sense of place in the world. Opioids have a profound effect on the brain's reward system. They can expose emotions and feelings even when they've been locked up and dormant for years."

She was right, of course—about the effects of opioids and about how they had unlocked something inside me. I remembered the first night, days after that initial dental procedure, when something deep inside whispered, *Plus one.* If two worked on my brain and my emotions, then why not take one more? Soon I discovered that when it came to these pain meds, an extra pill or two eased *whatever* ailed me, from a bad day at work to the daily stresses of my life to the discomfort in my mouth. Sometimes I wanted nothing more than to feel better. Or feel less bad. Or feel less of anything.

Exercise, prayer, sitting quietly for an hour in church on Sundays, making a good speech, and going to AA meetings also made me feel better, but those things took a lot of effort and a lot of time. Taking a pill was so much easier. The pills let me off the hook and gave me a way out—until they turned on me.

Physical therapy was eye-opening in a similar way. The repeated dental surgeries had altered me. Somewhere along the way the nerves that connected my teeth to my jaw had been damaged, causing relentless aches and pains. I hurt. I did not like to hurt. I did not deserve to hurt. I wanted not to hurt. I wanted to feel better. Pills made me feel better but, as Dr. Bakkum had pointed out, they were a temporary fix, not a long-term solution.

"You of all people already know what I tell my patients about the exercises I assign: 'It works if you work it—but you've got to work it,'" the physical therapist told me the first time we met.

I have to admit I was growing a little bit tired of hearing the phrase "you of all people."

"These stretches are designed to improve the normal functioning of your jaw and mouth, which should also help heal your jaw," he explained. "You'll also start to feel more empowered. The routine will help you realize that you don't have to rely on pain medication, especially when you feel the symptoms coming on."

What he said made sense and charged me with hope. I wouldn't have to wait in dreaded anticipation for that awful heavy sensation in my jaw. Maybe I would also lose that automatic urge to reach for a pill to knock out the pain I knew was coming. Maybe I could gain some control over this merry-go-round once and for all.

Good patient that I am, I stuck to the daily routine the physical therapist assigned. I rolled my head like I was a wiggly-jiggly bobblehead doll. I rotated my shoulders up and down for thirty seconds, four times an hour for a minimum of five times a day. Another exercise had me sticking out my tongue and moving it from side to side, then trying to touch my tongue to the tip of my nose and the bottom of my chin while looking in my bathroom mirror. Staring back at myself made me laugh. I looked like a cartoon character or one of those actors in Monty Python whose facial expressions were key to the comic schtick. Within a week, though, I could tell that the routine was working. Bit by bit, my pain began to fade.

MORE WEEKS PASSED. By now, Nell was aware that my occasional dental pain had become a chronic problem and that the pills had become part of that complicated problem. She was glad I had found my way to the pain clinic, with its structured approach. For my part, I was glad to be able to start sharing more of my experience with her, even as I continued to hold back the true extent of my struggle over the past years.

Abiding by the contract turned out to be surprisingly easy. I took one or two pills—exactly as prescribed—before I boarded a plane and dutifully wrote down when and if I experienced pain in the hours that followed.

"No pain!" became my two-word assessment, logged into my journal or via text to Nell following trips to places like Dallas, Portland, Atlanta, Palm Springs, Los Angeles, or DC.

The anticipatory dread I had come to expect when I stepped onto a plane was gone too. I wasn't tortured by pain—real or imagined.

Real or imagined. I was beginning to understand what Dr. Nixdorf meant when he explained that our basic human fear of pain can have a profound effect on how we perceive and experience it. Having been through the agony of withdrawal more than a few times in my life, I knew how the first signs of sweating and shaking often lead to a sense of panic—an overpowering need for relief from the anticipated physical and mental anguish that would undoubtedly follow.

Anticipation of pain intensifies its effect. For people addicted to painkilling drugs in particular, there's the added and deeply ironic agony of remembering how easily and quickly the drugs we crave once made the pain go away. We know what works and how it feels as it blankets us in relief, even as we know it has the power to kill us.

On top of that, ongoing use of these painkillers can literally change the way we perceive and experience pain. Opioids activate specific receptors that interrupt pain signals as they try to reach the brain. When we use these drugs regularly, our bodies sometimes try to reroute these blocked signals through other pathways, which can end up making heavy opioid users even more sensitive to pain than they were before starting the meds. The poison is the antidote is the poison is the antidote.

ON A MISTY Sunday night in October 2015, about a month after meeting Dr. Nixdorf and his team in Minnesota, I stood in front of a much different crowd. Approximately forty thousand people were gathered on the National Mall in Washington, DC, to celebrate the reality of recovery. This unprecedented event, called Unite to Face Addiction, was the result of years of dreaming and planning and organizing. The addiction and recovery field had been talking about a "march on Washington" since before I came to work at Hazelden in 1996. Now it was actually happening. We had gathered for a daylong rally to prove, with our many faces and gathered voices, that addiction to alcohol, cocaine, marijuana, opioids, barbiturates, and other substances does not discriminate. We were showing the world that people—hundreds of thousands of us—can and do overcome it.

Somebody once referred to me as a "recovery rock star," and it stuck. It's a label that usually makes me feel uncomfortable, but that evening, I did feel like one. At least I was rock-star adjacent. I shared the stage with legit musical stars, including Steven Tyler of Aerosmith, singer and songwriter Sheryl Crow, and Joe Walsh of the Eagles. If I was a rock star in recovery, I must admit that the title felt good, like it fit, like I could own it—and I tried to.

As the amazing sound of tens of thousands of voices joined in singing the Beatles song "Come Together" dissolved into thunderous applause and cheers, I stepped to the microphone. The rally's organizers had given me exactly two minutes to offer my message of hope. I was the final speaker; after me Aerosmith would take the stage. Seeing me projected onto the forty-foot-high screens at the back of the stage, the crowd quieted in anticipation.

"For too long, addiction has been an illness of isolation," I began. "For too long, addiction has been cloaked in the stigma of private shame, the stigma of public intolerance, the stigma of discriminatory public policy. For too long, too many people have known addiction as nothing more than a lonely, lost condition of hopelessness and helplessness."

I paused to let the realities I was describing echo across the mall.

"But today," I paused again and gestured toward the gigantic crowd. "Today, too long is no longer. Because today . . . HERE WE ARE!"

I shouted those last three words, and the audience roared its approval. *This is it,* I thought, *this is really it.* A moment I have chased after for nearly twenty years as a public advocate in the movement. I paused again for a few seconds and opened my arms as if to gather the crowd together, even as I stole a few quick glances at my prepared remarks on the teleprompter positioned near the edge of the stage.

"Today on the nation's mall we stand together as the antidote to addiction, the power of WE. Today in our nation's capital we stand up together, for those across this nation who cannot yet stand, we stand for the power of WE.

"Today WE speak out on behalf of those who have no voice. And yes, today WE sing aloud in celebration of the promise and possibility of recovery. WE stand for hope. WE stand for help. WE stand for healing. WE stand together. WE stand UNITED!"

As I came to the end of my two minutes, I glanced at the screens where my face was projected, huge and pale beneath the bright lights. I felt the gravity of the moment and the importance of the message the day carried. I took a deep breath.

"No longer do we simply *dream on* about the promise and possibility of recovery. Today, in our reality that recovery is real, we *live on!*"

I stepped away from the microphone and paused for a few seconds to absorb the rolling waves of applause and shouts of support. I lifted my fist above my head in unity with others on stage. We were one.

Towering behind the roaring crowd, now animated by the music pouring from the enormous speakers, the Washington Monument gleamed in its monolithic splendor against the night's misty sky. It reminded me just how far I had come. Half a century earlier, I stood near this spot on a Sunday outing with my parents. For most of the 1960s Washington was my dad's axis of influence, and it became my playground.

Other memories crowded in, darker than my childhood adventures in the nation's capital. In my late twenties I nearly met my end on the sordid backstreets of this city. One night, trying to score crack cocaine, I was robbed by a young man with a knife. He demanded the sixty dollars I was ready to hand over, but he refused to give me the plastic baggie of drugs. No deal, and I ran away. I shuddered at the memories. Holed up in hotel rooms and back alleys with strangers who held me hostage to my needs and theirs. United by the preeminent, overpowering need to get high and stay high, we engaged in a sick, parasitic relationship. My money and their connections kept the train running.

But that was a long time ago, I reminded myself, standing

up straighter, my focus on the crowd. Stories can change, can't they? I knew that my story had changed. I did not die in DC back when I so easily might have. My life had been spared in New York and St. Paul and in Atlanta. I had been given chance after chance. It took some time, but I got well. I worked hard. Now, today, my presence in this advocacy movement told a new story—another chapter. Now, along with these thousands of friends and colleagues and fellow travelers, I was part of a movement, I told myself. We embodied a powerful truth. Not only is there a solution to addiction, but the silence, secrecy, shame, and stigma can be overcome and smashed once and for all—when we come together. We can stand up to speak about addiction. We can celebrate recovery. We can reclaim the stories of our lives.

As I gazed out at the vast crowd of people who, at least tonight, were united in their commitment to life over death, I thought about my own story and how strange it had become to me. I thought about how hard it is to keep choosing life, and how hard these years of pain and pills had been for me. I also felt in my weary bones how hard it was to keep living so split and divided as I had become.

I could confidently share my passionate rhetoric in front of a huge crowd in America's capital, but I wasn't whole. I could rub shoulders with rock stars and even take the stage alongside them, but inside I was still missing pieces of myself. I could feel my soul gripped by uncertainty and shame because nobody knew my secret. The triumphs we celebrated that day were real—of course they were. But so was the fact, undeniable in the era of opioid epidemic, that many of our stories had changed.

OCTOBER DRIZZLED its way into November. The bright lights and excitement of the march on Washington faded into memory. My visits to the pain clinic began to feel less revelatory and more routine. Slowly, at first barely perceptibly, I began to feel subtle pings—reminders of what life was like in the more unfettered days when I enjoyed the influence of stronger stuff than tramadol. It was as if the synapses in my brain were on a dimmer switch and something was turning that switch up, just a click at a time. Those *more, more, more* reminders were growing brighter and stronger. Sometimes I felt irritable. Sometimes I was just bored.

The Big Book describes the disease of addiction as "cunning, baffling, powerful." I've learned over the years that it is also patient. In the regular routines of my life that fall, it was keeping pace with me. I began to think that maybe, just maybe, I could have one more round with the pills. This would be a different experience, I told myself, because it would be a *tramadol plus one*. I didn't need extra pills for my pain, but maybe they could be a sort of reward for sticking to the contract, for driving to the clinic in the middle of an insanely busy day at work, for sitting in therapy sessions. I was cranky and restless. I wanted to be free of "doing" anything, and I knew the pills would give me that.

This "squirrely thinking" coincided with an especially arduous period of business travel. In-person visits and presentations are where I seem to do my best work. I'm pretty good at traveling, but the constant movement often drains me dry. Added to the general wear and tear of travel, simply being in an airplane had begun to trigger cravings. Even though my jaw and head no longer hurt constantly, I still associated the ups and downs and pressure changes of flying with pain—and with pain pills. That week's itinerary included trips from Minnesota to Kentucky to Minnesota to Georgia to North Carolina and back home again to Minnesota.

I had grown weary of the physical therapy exercises and excused myself from doing them when I was on the road. I missed how easy it was to erase discomfort and melt my angst all at once with a couple of those little white pills. But I gutted it out and stuck to the limited allocation of one pill per day when I was on the road—mostly because I feared emptying the bottle too early and having to go without.

When I finally got home, with no trips scheduled for the upcoming week, I took my prescribed dose of tramadol: one pill at dinnertime. A few hours later, because I decided it was an extraordinary situation, I took another pill. I waited for the effect I wanted and the relief I needed, but it didn't come. Maybe I didn't want it to come because I had a better, more instantaneous solution.

I took another pill. And then another.

I woke up the next morning alarmed by what I had done and terrified by what it meant. I did not want to fail at this clinic effort. I didn't want to let Dr. Nixdorf down. It would be a disaster if I was kicked out of the pain management program. Dr. Nixdorf's regimen was the anchor for the only hope I had. I didn't see any other way to get through this. It was critical that I escape the grip of the pain pills. The thought of going back to the incessant round-and-round and up-and-down scheming and hiding made me shudder. It would be intolerable to start over again with craving and counting, plotting the next score while taking my last pill—I was tired of it all, and I knew it was a dead end. Without his help, I was doomed to fail. I needed his team. Nothing else had worked. But my actions had put all that in jeopardy.

I came clean with Dr. Nixdorf at my next appointment.

"Dr. Nixdorf, my pain is nearly gone," I said. We were sitting in his office again. "You and your team are amazing," I began, hating what I had to say next.

"I broke our contract. I couldn't keep it. I'm sorry." I paused for a deep breath, then hurriedly continued. "It had nothing to do with my jaw. It's the pills."

I wasn't sure what he thought of me.

"Everything we've done is important," I went on, "and I'm grateful to every member of your team here at the U—and most of all to you." I hesitated. "But honestly, doc, I'm stuck." I looked down at my folded hands on the table. "I'm craving, impatient, tired. I don't know what to do."

How could I explain that the tramadol taunted me? It eased the physical discomfort in my head and neck, so I knew it was working as it was intended to, but it wasn't working the way I needed it to. My brain was not satisfied with what this drug seemed capable of delivering. Still, it seemed to occupy my every thought. I was either obsessing about something stronger or obsessing about how the hell I could be done with these damn pills forever. I felt like I was out of time.

"I've got to get back to my life," I said. "I can't keep going this way. I'm tired of fighting it but I am terrified of giving in or, even worse, giving up. Honestly, this is harder than anything

I've ever done. It's worse than crack cocaine and the booze. I just want my life again. Restored. Resumed. That's all I need. I just don't know how to get there like this, with you."

Deflated and oddly relieved with this admission, I slumped in my chair. It felt as if somewhere deep inside me a dam had burst and the jagged flotsam and tangled jetsam of all those months of confused struggle were in motion now. There was no more hiding, no more pretending. I hadn't been this honest in years—not with Marv, not with Dr. Bakkum. It felt like we were in a Twelve Step meeting, and I had blurted out what I needed to share, instead of what I thought he wanted to hear.

Nixdorf scribbled something on a piece of paper on his desk. His face revealed nothing. The silence between us frightened me. Had I failed him and his team of counselors and therapists, who had worked so hard to help me understand and fix what was going on with my pain? Was he disappointed? Was he going to kick me out of the program? Had I doomed myself to suffer?

I swear the doctor read my thoughts. He also seemed to sense the anguish in my soul, for his eyes softened. And for the first time since I met him, his expression and his demeanor changed. Suddenly he seemed less like a clinician and more like a confidant, even a friend. He leaned forward with a sigh, his brow furrowed.

"When you first came to me as a patient, I had no reason to assume you were different than any other patient who seeks help for chronic pain," he said. "Our goal with you—as with anyone who comes to us—was to get the medications under control while treating and managing your pain. We use the contract to let patients know what to expect while in our care. It can also help keep people focused and honest." He paused, then said more gently, "We don't want anyone to suffer, William."

It was the first time Dr. Nixdorf called me by my first name.

"The more time I spend with you, the more I understand that you are not a 'typical' pain patient." He smiled, the lines around his eyes deepening. "I'm glad you feel we've helped you," he said, "and we'll continue to help you learn how to manage your pain." I was relieved that he wasn't kicking me out. "But the help you need now, to address the ongoing cravings, is beyond my expertise.

"You've had so many years of sobriety—of stable recovery," he said. "In some ways you need less than what we offer patients who don't have that experience, but in other ways, you require more than we're equipped to offer."

We spent the rest of the hour discussing my options. When I described my internist as a person with his own recovery experience, he suggested I make an appointment with Dr. Giefer.

AS I PASSED the pharmacy on my way out of the building, I felt the cravings whisper just beneath my ears. Without a prescription to fill there was no reason to stop. I picked up my pace. So did the craving. It followed me all the way to the parking garage. A light streak of perspiration moistened my upper lip and forehead. I tried to convince myself I was okay. Nearly two years earlier, Gief had confronted me with my prescription history. I ran away. Now my pain doctor was sending me back to him for the help and insight he was uniquely able to give.

I knew I had to call, but first I had to do what Dr. Giefer had ordered me to do years ago.

I had to go to a meeting.

I got in my car and drove toward the entrance ramp to eastbound I-94. The clock on the dashboard showed that I had time to spare before lunch. *The AA meeting at Uptown starts at noon.* It was on my way home.

It had been months since I had attended a Twelve Step meeting. How could I share with other people what I didn't yet understand about myself? The dissonance between my love-hate relationship with the pain pills and what I had always assumed to be acceptable content to share at an AA meeting kept me away. I no longer knew how I fit or how I related to the Steps and the assumptions and expectations they entailed. What would I do if the group went around the room sharing their sobriety dates? Shit, what was mine now?

Located in a century-old mansion on St. Paul's Summit Avenue, the Uptown Group hosts dozens of Twelve Step meetings every week. For nearly two decades, the lunchtime meeting had been a semi-regular stop for me. In all those years, I had never experienced even a hint of trepidation about walking through the familiar front door. Now I did. I felt like an uncertain newcomer—*or worse,* I thought, *like a burglar about to commit a crime.*

"Well, look who it is! Welcome, my friend—it has been a while." It was D, a fellow traveler I had met right here at this meeting years earlier. I liked him a lot. Next to him was K, a real estate agent on her third marriage. She waved at me with a smile. K was such a fixture at the Uptown House that she often joked she'd list the place for sale one day—if only she owned it. Two or three other people I recognized but didn't know by name also stood in the foyer. The boisterous banter and laughter coming from the adjacent room were as reassuringly familiar as the smells in my mother's kitchen.

"Hi, I'm William. I am an alcoholic and a drug addict." We went around the room welcoming each other. Somebody volunteered to read "How It Works" from the Big Book, followed by a few housekeeping announcements. The basket was passed to collect a few bucks in donations and then, for the next fifty minutes, it was time to share. At the close, we stood to hold hands and recite the Serenity Prayer.

There was nothing remarkable about the meeting, except for what I did—or rather what I didn't do. For once, I did not raise my hand to share. I didn't offer any particular inspiration, nor did I ask for it. I didn't try to prove anything to anybody. I just sat there and paid attention. Mouth closed, eyes open, I listened to what others shared. Some of what I heard that day resonated deeply; other stories just made me glad I didn't share the problem described.

Beyond the details, what touched me was the deep familiarity of the struggle we had in common. It's a struggle that often has more to do with living than it does with drinking or taking other drugs. All these people were there to deal with the "shit happens" stuff that gives texture and weight to AA truisms like "Life on life's terms" and "One day at a time." The meeting reminded me that I wasn't unique—not in my suffering and not in my joy. It's a truth that I continue to carry, even as I'm frequently tempted to assume my troubles are without compare. We all face or are burdened with some challenge. We all have problems. I am not the only one. None of us has to be alone.

I left the Uptown House feeling the opposite of when I arrived an hour earlier. I had landed at the Twelve Step meeting disconnected and afraid of what kind of welcome awaited me. But gathered again into the circle, accepted without question, I had seen my struggle in the context of what others were going through. As I walked back to my car, I felt the power of connection. I felt better. I felt how I have almost always felt after a meeting.

But I was still craving. I needed to somehow turn it off. Not even a meeting had quieted that.

Once in the car, I pulled out my phone. After scanning the messages that had arrived during the previous hour, I found Dr. Giefer's contact card. For the first time ever, rather than dialing his office or the nurse line, I called his personal number. To my surprise and relief, he answered. He agreed to see me the next day.

I TOLD DR. GIEFER my story. I explained not just why I had ended up at the pain clinic, but that I had been sent there by Dr. Bakkum—the country dentist who saw more clearly than anyone else what I needed. I described how, even when my jaw pain had subsided, I hadn't been able to abide by Dr. Nixdorf's medication management contract. Then I recounted how Nixdorf had sent me back to Gief's care because he didn't completely understand the addict's craving brain—my brain. I told Gief that I was suffering badly enough right then that if

I had one wish, I'd ask him to write me a prescription for the cravings and send me on my way.

Dr. Giefer took off his glasses and leaned back in his chair. "Tramadol is a less potent opioid than oxycodone, but it is still an addictive drug and dangerous for people like us," he said. "If you are continuing to experience cravings despite all you are doing to reduce your pain, it's clear that tramadol isn't the answer."

We sat in silence for a moment.

I was ready to hear him take me to task again, to counsel prayer and fellowship and a fearless moral inventory. I was ready to explain how yesterday's meeting, good as it was for my soul, hadn't even touched the desperate need in my gut.

Finally, Gief sighed. "You need to go see Frenz," he said.

I had no idea what he was saying. What friends did he know that I had who could help me figure this out?

"Friends?" I asked. "Who do you mean?"

"*Frenz*," he said, "with a *zee*. Dr. David Frenz."

I still didn't understand. Gief went on.

"You've got AA, you've got Nixdorf at the pain clinic, you've got a lot of recovery under your belt, decades of it. But right now, none of that is enough. The cravings will win in the end unless we devise a new strategy." He rummaged around his desk for a pen.

"For years I worked here in this health system with Dr. Frenz. He's an addiction doc. He moved on to his own practice. He knows more than me when it comes to helping opioid patients. I think you should see him as soon as possible. And you know I am always here for you too, day or night, in this office or out in the community."

I did know this. Dr. Giefer's expert care and kindness had sustained me for years. He had always steered me right. His medical skill was bolstered by his practical experiences as a man and fellow traveler in recovery. Gief's understanding and empathy filled my heart and soul with something infinitely more potent than the temptation of a bottle full of white pills. He gave me hope.

He also sent me on my way with a referral to yet another doctor, and a prescription for ten tramadol—just enough to carry me to what happened next.

■

9

Breakthrough

2016

What's right is what's left if you
do everything else wrong.

— ROBIN WILLIAMS

The day my sobriety story changed forever I was wearing a dark blue Patagonia vest and fur-lined Crocs. It was an oppressively gray yet surprisingly mild morning in early January 2016, not long after my face-to-face with Dr. Giefer. I sat in a waiting room somewhere within North Memorial Health Hospital, just north of Minneapolis. I was freshly showered and shaved, dressed in clean jeans and that bougie vest. The shoes were a size too large, and the faux fur was grayed by winter's grit, but still—fur-lined Crocs?

It's safe to say I stood out. Most of the other people in the room were wearing stained sweatshirts or worn-out lumberjack flannels. Along with duck-brown Carhartts, there were jackets and hats in the familiar purple-and-gold hometown colors of the Minnesota Vikings. A few of my seatmates coughed quietly into their fists or coughed without bothering to cover their mouths; two or three leaned back in their chairs and appeared to be dozing. An air of worn-out desperation pervaded the area, and a stale odor made me wonder if someone close by hadn't showered in a few days. Fluorescent tubes buzzed quietly above us all. It felt more like a bus terminal than a hospital.

A young couple arrived and sat down in the chairs across from mine. One of the woman's arms was tattooed with a dancing skeleton that featured butterflies circling its skull; her other arm was lined with what I was pretty sure were track marks. As I watched them settle into their seats, they looked me up and down as if to ask, *What are you doing here?* Maybe it was the Crocs. Or maybe it was more like what happens in AA sometimes, when somebody you recognize from another part of your life walks into the room—maybe a doctor, waiter, minister, or teacher—and you had no idea that they were struggling, much less with what. *You too?*

My first appointment with Dr. David Frenz lasted less than forty minutes. He took my vitals and reviewed my family history as well as the medical questionnaire I had filled out in the waiting room. I was eager to dump all the details of my dental-pain-and-pill story on him, but he didn't need to hear it to know what was wrong. Like Dr. Nixdorf, he had downloaded my history of opioid acquisition from the Minnesota Prescription Monitoring Program database before our appointment. I saw the printout on his desk. Unlike the clinicians at the pain clinic and my dear Dr. Giefer, however, Dr. Frenz didn't wave the pages at me. He didn't frown; he didn't yell.

"You meet five of the eleven *DSM-5* criteria for opioid use disorder—that's moderate," he said. Then we sat in silence. I wondered if he could hear my pounding heart.

"Well, at least my glass is still more than half full," I offered, trying to lighten the mood. I needed him to reassure me. Since five was less than half of the total, maybe "moderate" suggested I wasn't so bad after all. I wanted the doctor to tell me that even if I had a problem, I didn't have a PROBLEM. I wasn't like all those lost souls in the waiting room. I was in much better shape than all of them. Wasn't I?

Dr. Frenz gazed thoughtfully at me over his wire-rimmed eyeglasses. "Certainly it could be worse. But here's the thing. Your personal and professional stakes are very, very high. You have a long history of remission, a stellar track record of recovery, and your public persona is all about your journey from addiction to hope and healing. Of course, we both know that your employer needs your story to continue to be one that inspires others. Your 'brand' as a man in long-term recovery espousing the reality of recovery and promoting Hazelden Betty Ford's brand as a place where people can get well are intimately wrapped around each other."

He was right—there was no way to spin my particular situation—not with a weak attempt at humor nor with crafty language about legitimate use or the completely legal way these pills kept rolling in. My "run-in" with pain meds was more like a head-on collision.

UNDERSTANDING THIS was a major leap for me, one that would, as it turned out, finally bring alignment into my life—allowing the actions in my personal life to match the words I uttered so often in my professional life. An event only five months earlier demonstrated just how far I was from walking the walk that I spoke about so freely and confidently. My boss had asked me to facilitate a nine-hour opioid summit that Hazelden was hosting. Titled "Pain. Pill. Problem—Use and Overuse of Prescription Painkillers in Minnesota," the event was part of the Minnesota Moving Forward Together conference. It was sponsored by, among others, the US Department of Justice, the Minnesota Department of Human Services, the US Drug Enforcement Administration, and the Mayo Clinic. The event drew a thousand people, all of us crammed into an auditorium on the University of Minnesota campus. The governor spoke, as well as others who had deep personal and professional experience working with the issue. Over the day I moderated panel after panel with dozens of experts. The conference also included testimonials from people in recovery from opioids and parents whose children had died from an overdose.

I sat on the same stage as practitioners and patients and policymakers—all of whom were sounding alarms and speaking clearly and persuasively about the problematic power of these drugs. Information about opioids wasn't my problem. Ignorance of these facts wasn't what kept the pain pill train moving in my life. I listened and nodded along, even as a part of my mind knew exactly how many tramadol tablets I had left from my last refill prescribed by Dr. Bakkum and how long it would be until I could dip into them.

I even "outed" myself that day. In my opening remarks, I admitted to having had a problem—always couched safely in the past and described deceptively as a "run-in"—with painkillers. I compared opioids to the Trojan horse in Greek mythology—the weapon with which the ancient Greeks deceived and defeated the heavily fortified city of Troy. Presented as a parting gift from the Greeks after a long and failed siege, the huge wooden horse statue they left on the doorstep held a deadly hidden secret. It was hollow inside, filled with armed Greek soldiers. After the citizens of Troy hauled the thing through the gates and went to bed, the hidden warriors burst from their hiding place, opened the gates to their full army, and proceeded to defeat the city and win the war.

It was a good analogy. Unfortunately, back then I couldn't accept or admit how it applied to me. But so much had happened in the intervening months. My eyes had finally been opened, and I could see it now—I could see myself now. Sitting across from the doctor who so clearly perceived my problem and pointed out the stakes, I knew how much I had been like the overconfident defenders of Troy when it came to opioids. I understood, now, what the people had been describing at the conference—the parents of kids who overdosed after knee surgery, the Olympic runner who never smoked or drank but still became addicted to the meds he received to treat scores of sports injuries, even the doctors who prescribed these pills to their patients, trusting that the medication's benefit outweighed its risks.

None of us wants this to happen.

We take the gift of pain relief inside the gates as willingly as the Trojans accepted the huge wooden horse. We're overjoyed that our long battle with pain might actually be over. We start out hoping the drugs will help us—and we're amazed when they do. But we end up surprised by the stealth and speed of the enemy that was hidden inside. We watch in horror as this enemy dismantles our defense before we even have time to put one together. And too often we are soundly defeated by the drug's power.

On that August day, my outer walls appeared firm. At no point during that conference or after, as crowds of people gathered to talk and process the information, did anybody come up to me and ask if I was okay. My boss didn't pull me aside and say, "Hey William, what exactly do you mean by 'run-in'?" In a room of eleven hundred people, not one person asked me to explain myself. Why would they? I was wearing a suit; my hair was combed and my teeth were brushed. I was engaging and funny and serious and responsible. To everyone watching, I appeared put together and polished, a professional performing at the top of his game.

But like the Trojans, whose ramparts remained standing even as their soldiers were slaughtered in the streets, I had already lost the war. I was as overwhelmed and overcome as that doomed city in the story. It didn't matter what I was wearing or what I did for a living. It didn't matter if I could wash my face and get to work on time. It didn't matter how many people stood to applaud my speeches. It didn't even matter how many struggling souls I had helped find treatment or take their first steps in recovery. Opioid pain medication had hollowed me out as powerfully and painfully as alcohol and coke had all those years ago. The fact that the pills had done it with so much less visible damage or drama was both ironic and terrifying.

NOW I SAT ACROSS the table from someone who saw me clearly. The more he talked, the more I felt my mind quieting and the breath coming into and out of my body. His matter-of-fact assessment of my condition pushed gently past my euphemisms and excuses. His words flowed beneath the facade I had built to keep reality at arm's length and touched bone. Five criteria or five hundred, it didn't matter. I was not in control of my need for opioids. If ever I was calling the shots when it came to these pills, those days were long past. Alcohol had consumed me when I was a kid in college. Cocaine had eaten away my teeth and ruined my relationships as a naive young man. And in these past years—when I was older and should have been wiser—painkillers had invaded my life and eroded my integrity. Once again, I was dancing at the edge of an abyss that threatened to destroy me and everything I believed in, everyone I loved. At some point in the future, near or far, I would end up looking like all those people in that waiting room who just moments before I thought looked nothing like me. It was an intolerable moment.

"It's been three days since your last pain pill. I suspect you are in mild opioid withdrawal," Dr. Frenz said, suddenly sounding less threatening to me, even as what he was saying cut like a knife.

"We don't want it to get worse, so let's start by putting you on a daily dose of Suboxone." He paused, though barely. "I assume you are okay with this."

WAS I "OKAY" with this?

I had been a passionate spokesperson for abstinence-based recovery for decades. Even while I was flailing through and failing at treatment in the early nineties, I trusted the professionals and the people in recovery when they said there was only one way for someone like me to get well. My counselors and sponsors assured me there was no drug I could take to end the insanity that had overtaken my life. Before I was even sober, I knew that my substance-taking days were numbered. They'd only add up to a one-way trip to destruction and death. There was no middle-of-the-road solution. The Big Book said as much.

I was on record as a person who had long been skeptical about the idea of using any medication to treat drug addicts. When Marv Seppala had explained the COR-12 program's parameters and potential to a roomful of Hazelden's leaders back in 2012, I dismissed it as a thing that had nothing to do with me. Suboxone and medications like it were for treatment patients who were desperately hooked on things like heroin, I thought. It was for people who were so far gone they couldn't otherwise focus on treatment. I wasn't alone in my assumptions. Upon hearing that Hazelden was adding Suboxone to its toolbox for treating opioid addiction, some longtime friends and supporters of our organization had called me, alarmed and irate. They told me how betrayed they felt. As they saw it, the institution they had loved and respected was now spreading "a poison" into the recovery community with COR-12.

Many others raised an eyebrow or balked at the suggestion of using Suboxone as well. Sober living houses in my community and in communities all over the country are often deeply suspicious of medication use as part of recovery. Some even reject applicants for housing, refusing to offer a bed and a place to live if the person is using prescribed medicines like Suboxone or methadone to quiet cravings and get well.

The voices of some of my fellow travelers echoed in my mind:

You're only replacing one drug for another.
A drug is a drug is a drug.
You aren't really clean and sober if you're taking it.
It's a crutch.
It's the easy way out.
Medications like this one block people from finding their Higher Power.

For years, I had agreed with these voices. I had even said some of those things myself. Back in 2010, I wrote a nationally syndicated column aggressively championing the success of Twelve Step–based, abstinence-only addiction treatment and decrying those who questioned or criticized it. I even went so far as to attack a practitioner who was pioneering medication-assisted treatment with his patients. In that article (which went on to be reprinted in my book *Now What?*), I accused him of "ignoring the reality that addiction is not only an illness affecting the mind but also the body and the spirit."

Now here I was with egg on my face, sorrow in my heart, and three days' worth of "mild opioid withdrawal" crawling through my belly. It had already captured my mind and broken my spirit.

Dr. Frenz was regarding me coolly but not unkindly over his glasses. "I know about the arguments against medication-assisted treatment," he said, noting my hesitation. "But aggressive, definitive treatment with Suboxone will end the mischief quickly."

I cracked a small smile at his choice of words. "Mischief" was an understatement. "Deep shit" was more like it.

Was I *okay* with this?

I hadn't been okay with much of anything for a long time. I had been afraid of so many different things for years. Fear of scandal and reputational ruin had infected the years before my divorce from Allison. From childhood, fear of rejection had saddled me with what I call *can't-say-no-ism*. Fear of not measuring up had kept my nose to the grindstone at work for decades. It kept me up late at night, compulsively responding to texts and emails from people who had reached out to me for a word of comfort or advice about what to do and where to go. Fear of being exposed as a failure and a fraud had kept me hiding my problem with these pills for nearly three solid years, even after I realized how compromised I was by their power.

And now, faced with the invitation to accept Suboxone, I was afraid of judgment. I feared that I'd be condemned as a heretic—a man who fell away from the true faith. I feared some of my friends and colleagues would think I was on my way to a drunken or stoned bottom, or worse. I feared losing or tarnishing what I had achieved and what I had represented in all those years of shouting from the mountaintop and showing with my very public life that treatment works and recovery is real.

If I said yes to Suboxone, I worried that people would disagree with my choice—especially those who had recovered with me or worked with me. I was afraid that all the people who depended on me to be the Twelve Step stalwart, the guy whose shiny life reflected the values of the Hazelden Betty Ford

Foundation, the man who had figured out how to carry the message so far and so well, would think I was a cheat and a liar.

I was also tired.

I was tired of letting my fear about what other people thought of me keep me stuck and sick. I was tired of the ways I allowed others' opinions to damage my health and break me into pieces. Fear hadn't served me well so far—not in marriage or parenting, not in my career, and not in the way I managed my recovery. I was ready to stop letting it direct my days and limit my life. I was ready to be whole again—maybe for the first time ever. I was unwilling to allow fear to keep winning.

"Okay," I said.

I WALKED THROUGH the waiting room on my way to the elevator, passing the men and women whom, just an hour earlier, I had considered completely different from me. In that brief appointment, I felt as if I had gained new lenses to look through. Now I saw them just as I saw myself—more clearly than I had for a while. Every person in that room suffered and struggled. We all had a lot at stake; our very lives were on the line. We were all the same, and each also different, our hearts broken and souls scarred along lines that were unique to every individual. Our hopes were personal and particular as well, and each person's resolve likely ebbed and flowed under the influence of all kinds of forces. But today we were here. We were taking steps to get better, to feel better, to be better. And if the simple act of getting ourselves to this clinic was any indication, we were coming to realize and accept that we couldn't do these things by ourselves.

I was also willing to bet that, despite our similar struggles with substances, most of the other people in that waiting room didn't have what I had going for me. My visit to Dr. Frenz was covered by health insurance. As desperate as I was, my privilege had shielded me from consequences for years. I enjoyed a good-paying job with benefits and a car to get me through the Minnesota winter. I lived in a quiet, safe neighborhood in a house I owned. I had a spouse in recovery and a family who was proud of me. I didn't smoke, drink, or suffer from serious mental health issues. I had money in the bank.

Along with all that, I also had the benefit of what I had lived and learned over decades of life in recovery from crack cocaine addiction and alcoholism. I had been lost in the woods these past years, but I still knew where I could look for direction and inspiration. Recovery was still possible. Honesty, humility, forgiveness, compassion, and gratitude were still real, and they were waiting for me to take hold of them. With help, I was confident that I could rebuild my integrity. The principles I knew by heart glittered like guiding stars overhead, no longer hidden by clouds. I didn't want to do anything ever again that would jeopardize all the gifts I had been given.

SUBOXONE IS THE brand name of a medication that combines two others: buprenorphine and naloxone. Buprenorphine, an opioid itself, is one of the most common medicines used to treat opioid addiction. Naloxone is a medication that prevents or reverses opioid overdose, and in Suboxone it serves to prevent misuse of the medication. The combination medicine works in the brain by attaching itself to the same neural receptors as other drugs like morphine and oxycodone. As it does, it interrupts or blocks those other chemicals from causing the same levels of intoxication, preventing users from getting high. As a "partial opioid agonist," this medication puts a limit or "ceiling" on the euphoric effect. The primary purpose of Suboxone treatment is to prevent the intense craving and painful withdrawal that would come with abruptly stopping opioid pain medications, reduce the risk of relapse, and improve the likelihood that patients will stay in treatment and engage in long-term recovery. For many people it begins to work almost immediately.

I picked up my prescription for a thirty-day supply of Suboxone one day after I met Dr. Frenz. I got it from the same pharmacy—the CVS near my house—that had regularly supplied me with painkillers since 2012. Since it was a new medication, the familiar pharmacist asked if I had any questions. I fought the urge to ask her the same. I couldn't help but wonder what she might want to ask, given all the bottles she had passed across that counter to me over the preceding years.

I took my first dose that day, a wafer-thin square that dissolved beneath my tongue in seconds. I did so hoping against hope that it would make a difference.

A few days later I wrote in my journal.

> Third day on the Subx. I just go about my day and take care of my business—without the distraction of the pain meds. Miracle drug? Time will tell. Need to contact Dr. Giefer and tell him what's transpired. There's no doubt he saved me.

On the same page, I wrote about what else I needed.

This morning's meditation reminds me to get back to my meetings. It's a big part of what's been missing for me. Especially the people. The fellowship is what really matters to me. The meditations are good. They resonate. But nothing like being with others in recovery.

I was back in Frenz's Minneapolis office the next week, gushing about how amazing the medicine was. "I don't have to think about the pain meds anymore!" Dr. Frenz seemed pleased.

"Because you have so many other tools in place," he said, "meetings, your community of people in recovery, your daily meditations and other readings, the work you do, and the satisfaction you get from helping others—I don't believe you need additional psychosocial supports."

Is it really that easy? I wondered. *Is it really possible to get over that final impossible hump with the painkillers?* It seemed unbelievable. Even though I had a diagnosable opioid use disorder—those pills had exerted such power over me for so long—I didn't have to make regular treks to the pain clinic or join a specialized therapy group or put my entire life on hold by entering a treatment program. The solution offered by Suboxone was shockingly straightforward. I took that first dose and it worked. Maybe I was a quick convert, but only because Dr. Frenz made it so easy for me to get better—and so fast.

IN THE WEEKS that followed, I went about my life. I went to work. I played with my cat. I shopped for groceries. I made love to my wife. I paid my bills and read books. I traveled to visit my parents and called to catch up with my own children. I did these things with a freedom and lightness I hadn't known for years. I was suddenly and surprisingly no longer craving a pain pill or fearing what I would do if I ran out. It felt like a gift. My obsession with preventing the withdrawal symptoms that had twisted me up for so long seemed like a memory from another life. My secret, frustrating, and tangled struggle with opioids was suddenly over.

My life wasn't perfect, of course, but my problems with the pills—along with the last vestiges of pain in my jaw—vanished. The slight bitterness under my tongue after taking the Suboxone reminded me that this amazing gift of clarity and freedom depended on my commitment to take my medicine on time, three times a day.

Magic bullet? This was a scientific marvel!

This was a different kind of recovery than the Step-based program that had pulled me from my addictions in the past. Because the medication I was using to control my cravings and manage my illness could be misused or diverted, it didn't fit the traditional model of abstinence-based sobriety. I was taking a drug—an opioid drug. Yet I didn't crave this one. I wasn't using it to get high; I was using it to get well. I was using it as a person who continued to be grateful for recovery.

What did that word mean for me now? What was "recovery"—this gift and goal that had saved me back when nothing else could? I had claimed and celebrated my identity as a man in increasingly stable recovery for more than two decades. I had gone to meetings two, three, four times a week for most of those years, and I had spoken about the life-changing power of the Twelve Steps to thousands of people. And throughout that time, even when my struggle with the pain pills drove me to distraction and despair, the call to service—to respond to those who needed help—had continued to keep me going. It may have been one of the few things that did.

I recognized how sustaining my Twelfth Step role in others' lives had been during these years. Now I had a whole lot more empathy for those whose struggles with opioids sounded so much like mine. But I still didn't know quite where I stood when it came to the assumptions at the heart of AA and its adherents.

After Suboxone erased my obsession and my craving for pills, I became hungry for understanding. My recovery had moved outside the clear boundaries I had once known and trusted. I had changed and thus my story had changed, but I was still speaking the old language and telling the old story. My insides still didn't match my outsides, and I wanted to make that right.

The more I pondered the triad of abstinence, sobriety, and recovery—three legs that had once formed the unshakable base for my life after *Broken*—the more urgently I needed to figure out how my new experience of recovery aligned with those practical principles. And the more I thought about it, in those heady weeks of early freedom from the pain pills, the more it seemed like I had an exciting new message to carry. I wanted to share my discovery with the world.

ONCE A MONTH, on a Saturday morning, someone from the pantheon of American celebrity bares their soul on the stage in the auditorium at the Eisenhower Medical Center next door to the Betty Ford Center, located in Rancho Mirage, California. The Awareness Hour, as this event is called, is more than a get-together for famous people in recovery. It's also something other than a giant Twelve Step meeting. The purpose of this event is to remove the stigma about addiction, which is why the speakers use their full names and the public is invited, free of charge. With their identities unveiled and in their own voices, superstars of professional sports, Hollywood actors and entertainers, best-selling authors, politicians, and musicians take the stage to tell their unabridged stories before an audience of several hundred people. The stories they share are symbols as much as statements. They reveal that recovery is real, tangible, and even—for those who believe in such things—miraculous.

Back in the summer of 2015, I had been invited by the organizing committee to headline the Awareness Hour the following February. The dead of winter is its most popular season—that's when the desert is filled with snowbirds from across the country. I was honored, even as I was aware I wasn't the first choice. I fit the budget, and I was available.

I had jumped at the opportunity. The Awareness Hour was a big deal. It presented me with an opportunity to reconnect with the Betty Ford Center's friends and advocates. Hazelden's 2014 merger with "The Betty," as the treatment center is affectionately called, hadn't been celebrated by everyone. Some feared that the identity forged by the famous First Lady's humility and grace would be eclipsed or altered by joining with the larger organization. A few of the California stalwarts had a hard time trusting that Hazelden, based as it was in the frozen tundra of Minnesota and operating multiple sites around the country, could grasp or appreciate the magic of recovery in the desert.

I was confident I could win over the audience. I looked forward to reminding them that Mrs. Ford herself had traveled to Hazelden's main campus in the early 1980s. She learned a great deal from the Minnesotans about how to set up and operate the treatment facility that would bear her name when it opened in 1982.

Back in 2015, I had also been excited about headlining the event because my boss would be in the room that day. Hazelden's senior management team and members of the board of trustees were traveling to Palm Springs for a board meeting on the same weekend. I had worked for Hazelden for twenty years at this point, but most of the top management staff had heard me speak only occasionally or not at all. I worried that they didn't always grasp or appreciate what I did. At times I felt like I didn't deserve my place in the lineup of senior execs. I wanted to dazzle them.

With the Awareness Hour, I had a rare and exciting opportunity to prove my worth, not just to these colleagues but to the whole organization. This was my chance, I thought, to share the joy and wonder I felt about being able to represent the place that had, in so many ways, saved my life. Even though I was taking Dr. Nixdorf's low-dose tramadol and struggling on and off with cravings for stronger painkillers when I received the invitation to speak, back then I believed I could give this speech blindfolded.

And now, half a year later and one month out from my life-changing first meeting with Dr. Frenz, I had even more to say. Buoyed by the miraculous way Suboxone had returned me to my life, I believed I could use this opportunity to share the good news about medication-assisted treatment. I would take the stage and "come out" for the first time, confessing to my misuse of addictive pain meds prescribed for chronic pain and describing how the medication that Hazelden Betty Ford offered its patients in trouble with opioids had changed the trajectory of one of its own vice presidents. I would be the face and the voice that would give a much-needed dose of legitimacy and authenticity to this controversial approach to treatment.

I COULDN'T WAIT. This speech gave me a chance to be open and honest about what had happened to me over the past three years. It seemed perfect that I would be on the stage at the Betty Ford Center. Before the merger with Hazelden, many of the treatment center's staff and constituents had been skeptical about the use of the very medication that had restored my recovery. If I could recover this way, as a committed Twelve Stepper, then surely it was okay for Hazelden Betty Ford to keep using it with patients addicted to opioids. Who could argue with living proof?

In the days leading up to the event, I could barely contain my excitement. Finally, with all eyes on me, I would dispense with the bobbing-and-weaving innuendo, the coded language and vague inferences that had bedeviled me for so long. I could put my years of hidden struggle into the service of something good. This was my opportunity to make my insides match my outsides again.

At last, I was the regular old William who could now say, honestly and forcefully, on a stage where so many others had shared their stories, that I had encountered and embraced a different kind of recovery. My colleagues would be amazed and delighted. Patients in the audience, many of them still dazed and confused in the early stages of recovery, would hear about my run-in with pain meds and how I overcame it. For patients with opioid use disorder, my willingness to speak openly about my ordeal would give them hope that there was a way out of pain and craving. Everything was coming together. I was confident my speech would be one of those memorable Awareness Hour moments that people talk about for years.

ONLY TWO PEOPLE had any idea about what I planned to reveal in my speech that day: my wife and Marv Seppala. I talked to Nell first, a few days before we left for California. With both undergrad and master's degrees in English literature, she loves to read and write. She's a confident public speaker, and she's also a recovery advocate who shares her story openly. Nell understands the importance of clear, concise messaging to drive the point home. Over our years together she has often been in the audience at my speeches and has always been among the first to stand up and applaud when I am finished. But when I've muddled my message or stumbled over an important point, she has never hesitated to fire away with sharp suggestions and critical feedback.

Still, Nell had never read my speeches ahead of time. I'm

usually wary about sharing even a paragraph or two with any-one before a speaking event, mostly because I'm slow to get the words on paper. The last thing I want is for someone to offer suggestions and give me more work to do. Also, the way the words read on the page is not how they sound in my head. I'm pretty good at fine-tuning or revising on the fly, even up to the moment when I stand in front of an audience. As satisfying as it can be to have the words written down and in hand, I feel better when I set the pages aside and speak from my heart. But this event was too big and too important for improvisation. I asked her to read the final draft of my speech.

I wanted Nell to see what I had written and affirm for me one last time that it was okay to break myself open in front of my colleagues and peers, telling a story that I had kept secret for so long—even from her. It had taken me until the day I returned home from my first visit with Dr. Frenz before I told Nell just how deep I had sunk. Then, over the weeks that followed, she had watched my light come back on as the Suboxone worked its magic in me.

"It's really good! You've got it!" Nell said after reading the speech, her smile fading when she saw the worried expression on my face. She gave me a hug. "This is a big deal, isn't it? Your talk will surprise a lot of people, but they can't help but be proud of you for having the courage to tell the truth and stand up for what you believe. Just be clear and direct—don't dress it up or dance around the facts. Speak your truth so that everyone in the auditorium understands what happened to you, why it happened, and how you got back on track. You cannot leave anyone guessing."

Nell had never liked my use of the phrase "run-in with pain meds." "What does that mean?" she challenged me more than once. "Call it for what it is—a relapse." That word still bothered me. "And don't talk about needing a 'medicine' or 'medication,'" Nell reminded me. That's how I had referred to Suboxone in a Twelve Step meeting we had attended together a couple weeks earlier. "Tell it like it is: Suboxone, a drug specifically created and rigorously tested to help people overcome addiction to opioid drugs."

When I talked to Marv the day before the event, he was not nearly as excited as Nell. I told him about the pain clinic, the tramadol, the craving that nothing could control. I shared the conversation I had with Dr. Giefer and his recommendation that I see Dr. Frenz, who prescribed Suboxone. "It's truly a miracle drug, Marv," I said brightly. "It changed everything for me—the pain, the craving, the scheming and deceiving, the denying and rationalizing. I see now, in a way I could not see before, why these medications are so critically important for our opioid-addicted patients. How did we help them before? Thank God you brought the COR-12 program to Hazelden Betty Ford!"

Marv frowned. "You'll want to be careful, William," he warned. "This is a hot-button topic not just in the field, but within our own ranks."

"People might be surprised, Marv, maybe even taken aback," I said, acknowledging his concern. "But I'm convinced this is the right path to take, right now. This audience needs to hear it."

When I arrived at the campus the next morning, the hallways were alive with enthusiasm, multiplied by the number of people who were there. It seemed like most of them had their eyes on me. I *was* the keynote, after all, and many of them knew me personally or they knew my work or my story. I was greeted with hugs and handshakes, and a few people had copies of *Broken* that they asked me to sign. For a moment I felt almost "too big for my britches," as my grandfather used to say when some celebrity or sports star sounded off or acted the part, and I smiled to nobody but myself thinking about Pa Pa Henry and feeling like a rock star again. I knew my self-image was blown way out of proportion, but it felt good. Really good.

I spotted Marv standing in the foyer of the entrance to the auditorium, near the tables of doughnuts and coffee. He waved me in his direction. He'd been waiting for me.

"I've been giving this a lot of thought," he said, "and I don't think it is a good idea for you to talk about your use of Suboxone. It's just not the right venue. Let me suggest you hold off for now. I think it might be a better idea to wait until we have a chance to talk more about what's happened when we're all back in Minnesota."

I was dumbfounded. Just minutes before the most important public speech I'd given in years, my friend and fellow traveler—but more to the point, the chief medical officer at Hazelden Betty Ford—was telling me to gut the heart and soul of my speech. The whole point of my presentation. The punchline. The memorable moment. When would this kind of opportunity ever come again?

Marv's expertise is unmatched. His wisdom is born of vast experience and careful thought. I was shaken. He was Dr. Marvin Seppala. In so many things, he knew better than me. Was he right again this time? How could this not be the venue for what I wanted to say? What better place? What better time?

I suddenly wondered if he had told anybody else what I had planned. Was I putting everything on the line here—even my job? I had never once been afraid of disclosing the details of my journey. My story was intended to help people by giving them hope, showing them that if somebody like me can make it, they can too. This had been the foundation of my whole career at Hazelden. We always said that hope is the bridge across the chasm of helplessness. Putting a face and voice to the story can be life-changing for people who struggle. Why should this time be any different?

I made my decision. "It's too late, Marv," I said. "I have to do this." I had been hiding my truth for too long and was tired of crouching behind my old story. I just couldn't do it anymore. I couldn't continue to be the man portrayed in *Broken*. It was time to share my new story. I needed to show my real self.

The auditorium was packed when I took the podium. I had the flutters. I wanted to do a good job. I knew that what I had to say was important, new, and necessary. So many of the familiar faces in the audience affirmed for me that this was the moment. Marv was sitting next to Mark Mishek. Nell was to the side with a group of her staff on the alumni team she headed. Jerry Moe, the legendary founder of the Children's Program at the Betty Ford Center, was in a seat toward the rear of the auditorium. Board members past and present were scattered throughout the first rows. I saw my dear friend Cini Robb, a member of the board from the Betty Ford Center who had said my initial friendliness to her helped her overcome her doubts about the merger. I recognized a few high-profile donors whose names graced the entrances to several of the buildings on campus. Then I looked toward the higher level of the auditorium where several rows were designated for current patients. It was hard to make out their faces in the dim light, but I could sense what they were seeking: hope. I hoped I had some for them.

I took a deep breath and started speaking.

■

10

Breaking Open

2016

There are two ways for the heart to break:
APART into many shards like a fragment grenade,
or OPEN into greater capacity so we can hold
life's inevitable tensions creatively, not destructively.

— PARKER PALMER

Marv was right, of course.

Dr. Seppala's wise counsel—that I reconsider using the very public forum that was the Awareness Hour to announce my newfound passion for Suboxone—fell on ears that were deafened by my ego and its grandiose assumptions. I had hoped my charisma as a speaker, along with a happy-ending story, would somehow allow me to escape judgment. I wanted my revelation about the miracle of anti-craving medication to help people who were suffering, of course, but I also needed it to somehow absolve me of all the wrong I had done in secret. I took advantage of the high-profile platform I had been entrusted with to leapfrog past the implications of my years of misusing painkillers while withholding my struggle from my friends and colleagues—not to mention my employer.

It didn't work out the way I had wanted.

In the room that day, the audience applauded generously. I wasn't even worried about the few who didn't stand to clap. Stepping away from the podium, I was surrounded by a press of people eager to shake my hand. "I've heard you a million times, man," remarked a gentleman who sounded like a Texan. "Never heard that part of your story; never knew you'd been through the same thing as me with the pills. Holy cow. Wow!"

A counselor I knew from Minnesota who had retired to the desert reached out with both arms, demanding a hug. "Today I'm more than proud of you." She explained how, years earlier, she had "lost" her own sobriety and didn't know how to explain her journey. "That part about there being more to recovery than sobriety is something I understood but couldn't explain until you just did. God bless you."

A middle-aged man and woman intercepted me in the parking lot.

"Our twenty-six-year-old daughter died a few years ago of an overdose of opioids," the woman said, her cheeks wet with tears. "The treatment facility she was in never mentioned the possibility of the medication you talked about today," the father added.

They walked away, hand in hand.

When I got back to the hotel, Nell greeted me with a tight hug. I was drained enough to drop onto the bed for a nap, yet I still felt the energy of the morning. I felt good—better than good—I had delivered big-time in front of an audience of people who mattered deeply to me.

The first inkling of trouble came as a voicemail on my cell

phone, from a friend back in Minnesota. "I was watching the live feed of your talk," he said. "You were great! But then the sound shut off and the video never came back."

Darn, I thought. *What a huge miss!* The very first time the Awareness Hour had been live-streamed on the Hazelden Betty Ford website, and somehow a technical gremlin had wreaked havoc on my big moment.

Other messages suggested that it was more than a technical error. There didn't seem to be a way to view a recording of the event at all. I opened my laptop to check the website. The talk was still advertised as available during and after the appointed time, but the link didn't work.

I called my colleague in charge of the website to ask what had happened and where I could tell people to find the link.

"I was told to disable it and take it off the website," he stammered.

"Why?" I asked, red flags flying in my head and sirens wailing in my ears.

"I don't know, William," he said apologetically.

Logging into my email triggered more internal alarms. In addition to a slew of congratulatory notes and a couple more questions about the live feed, one message caught my eye with its terse subject line: *Heads up.* Another note simply said, "People are worried about you."

FEBRUARY 27, 2016

The speech I gave a week ago today did not achieve my goals. I was confident my presentation would expand my platform for advocacy and affirm our mission—let

the genie out of the bottle too, in a process that I
controlled. Only that's not what happened.

I fell short—big time—and the bitter taste of my
failure is weird because usually I don't screw up on the
stage, especially in front of an audience of people who
really do matter to me.

If I do exactly as I am told I can emerge from the
jungle of glass shards without further injury to my
relationships. My job. My reputation.

In the weeks that followed my Awareness Hour speech, I came to understand that my self-revelation—as satisfying as it had felt to me and as enthusiastically as it was greeted by some in the audience that day—had caught too many others off guard. People with whom I worked closely were surprised and confused by what I had revealed about myself. Loyal colleagues who had assumed they knew me—work friends who had placed personal and professional trust in me—felt blindsided. They were concerned about my health. They were worried about my recovery. A few felt personally betrayed. It's no wonder someone decided to pull the plug on the livestream—nobody knew what was going on with me or what I was attempting to do on that stage.

Taken as I was by the miracle solution that had finally quieted and calmed my craving brain, I thought everyone would be thrilled. I was wrong about that. I had made assumptions about how my organization would respond to my presentation. The surprised, shocked, sometimes openly judgmental mishmash of reactions from friends and colleagues knocked me back on my heels.

I had said true things in my speech, just like I had offered versions of the truth throughout the years of my painkiller use, but I had also tried to control how people heard those truths. I had chosen a forum where I had the only mic and in which nobody could ask me questions or dig deeper into my story. Beyond being disrespectful, this was dishonest. Rather than responsibly sitting down in conversation with my superiors in Center City to explain what had happened with the pain pills and the facts and circumstances surrounding my use of Suboxone, I had hoped a grand and public gesture would sweep away the unsavory details of the previous few years. Instead of consulting the team of people I worked most closely with, I had abused their trust by assuming I knew best.

It was neither kind nor fair of me to invite these colleagues to celebrate a miracle comeback when I had been keeping my struggle with opioids a secret. It was not fair to present myself as a spokesperson for a still-controversial treatment modality without having been appointed as one. Doing so had damaged relationships with people who had respected me for years. My need to ensure my story continued to matter for the recovery movement and the organization I loved—my need to be seen, once again, as a shining spokesman of successful sobriety— foolishly shoved itself to center stage. I had thought I was brave and daring, when in truth I was reckless and selfish.

As powerful and positive as I believed my story about Suboxone was, it also involved those terrifying years of opioid use. I had scared or triggered or offended people, for reasons I hadn't known nor considered as I prepared my speech.

Once again, I had amends to make and learning to do. I

had to understand what others had heard and how my words had affected them. It was time for me to accept the humbling fact that I wasn't calling the shots and embrace the reality that I wasn't likely to find the answers I needed on a timeline that I got to determine. I had to let go of my desire to control this narrative and ditch my obsession about what others thought of me. The only way to counter my sharp impulsiveness was with a heavy dose of patience, something that is not one of my virtues. I needed to rebuild my credibility at work, and I was eager to get going on that, but it couldn't be on my terms. The words of my old recovery counselor took on a new significance for me in those days: "Moyers, get out of the way and let it happen."

IT WASN'T JUST my coworkers' responses that jarred me. In the months to come, Nell revealed that she was rattled too. "I want you off that medication, back to meetings and talk to your sponsor," she exhorted one afternoon. She sensed in my demeanor that I wasn't "right."

Nell was nervous that I might be straying too far from the tradition that had united us even before we became a couple. Like countless others, my wife is committed to Twelve Step recovery. She's pinned her twenty-five-year sobriety journey to the guidance and stability that those Steps continue to offer her. She's a regular at meetings, sponsors other women, and has worked in the addiction recovery field for a long time. A spouse on anti-craving medication who had failed to find relief through the AA path confused and scared her just like it had shocked so many others who cared about me.

As Nell gave voice to her worry, I realized what a challenge this was. My recovery story had changed, and I clearly didn't know how to tell it yet. Understanding and then crafting the best way to describe the ferocious power of the pain pills, the seemingly simple solution offered by Dr. Frenz and his prescription, and how this chapter of my life and my recovery was taking shape would take patience, care, and humility.

I needed to go back to the drawing board when it came to understanding how my new recovery narrative fit beside the one I had told in *Broken*—and how both connected to the mission of Hazelden Betty Ford. I had to take my role as part of a team more seriously. Yet there is one thing I did know: going backward wasn't an option. After years of self-loathing and shame, Suboxone had given me a remarkable new story. Hiding in half-truths was no longer the way I wanted to live and work. I just had to figure out who I was now and how to share it.

EVER SINCE THE DAY I discarded my prepared notes of figures and stats while giving a speech at the St. Paul Rotary Club luncheon in 1997 and instead shared an honest account of my own addiction to alcohol and other drugs, my personal story—and my willingness and talent in telling it—has been the backbone of my public advocacy work for Hazelden and beyond too. It didn't matter if it was on a stage in front of thousands of people or in a hospital detox at the bedside of a man whose alcoholism had left him desperate for hope. I was always ready to share the details of my own struggle from the depths of addiction to the freedom of living recovery. That story had reliably and meaningfully connected me to others, and I had been celebrated for telling it. But now, after so many years of being surrounded and supported and in the spotlight of attention, I felt uncertain and alone.

In the weeks and months after the Awareness Hour, with a renewed appreciation for the unintended impacts my words might have on audiences, I struggled to find language that would help me explain myself accurately and honestly. I was perplexed about how to describe my experience in ways that wouldn't alienate my listeners or get me in hot water at work. I worried especially about the audiences that are integral to my public advocacy. More personally, I dreaded disappointing the groups of fellow travelers who had been part of my own circle of fellowship and support. I knew there were people at work who now questioned whether my sobriety "counted." Maybe others would as well. Could I blame them?

FOR A WHILE I stuck to the story that had made me a popular keynote speaker at professional conferences for treatment counselors, healthcare executives, and advocacy organizations. I did not mention my battle with pain meds in interviews with the media either, though I was regularly asked to comment on the opioid epidemic and what the Hazelden Betty Ford Foundation was doing about it.

After having spent decades championing one set route to recovery—a route marked by milestone experiences on a tried-and-true, comfortably familiar pathway and demonstrated by my own sobriety journey—I felt tentative again, and I hated it. When I did try to tell the new story, it didn't come out of my mouth clearly. Sometimes I found myself tongue-tied and self-conscious. I'd get flustered about whether to say "run-in" or "relapse" while describing my battle with pain pills. I worried about what to say if people asked when I would stop taking Suboxone.

In the beginning I even had a hard time talking about my opioid experience with others who were struggling with the same drugs. Most of the people who sought out my help and advice did so for what they knew about my journey recovering from addiction to alcohol and cocaine, not for what had happened to me since. One woman asked to meet me for coffee. The mother of a twenty-year-old woman who had become addicted to heroin, she was stunned when I told her about how Suboxone had returned my life to me. "You mean you've got the same issue as my daughter?" She left shaken, uncertain if she could trust any advice from a recovering addict who was "using." She wasn't ready to consider that what had worked for me might help her daughter too.

That mother's shock and confusion rattled me. I knew she wasn't the only person I'd meet who felt as she did. Even if I somehow figured out how to put my experience into words, even if I could articulate my new perspective on how recovery related to abstinence and sobriety, I wondered whose wrath I'd incur. The fallout from my Awareness Hour blunder still stung. I anticipated pushback from strangers as well as friends. Traditionalists, old-timers, treatment specialists, and people who believed with every fiber of their being that the AA way of life was the one true pathway to sanity and stability would likely reject both the message and the messenger. Rejection meant more loneliness, more shame.

Still, I didn't give up. As the year 2016 progressed, I began to pick venues (or maybe they picked me) where I could try out my new story. There was more to me than what I had once shared, more to me than what people had read in *Broken* or expected from a national advocate who had made no secret of his commitment to peer recovery. Sometimes I feared being judged for using Suboxone. Sometimes I wondered if people would accuse me of abandoning the Twelve Steps and all they represented. Often, if I got rattled by a question or a tone or a sideways glance, I'd revert to acceptable lines of the old redemption story. Then I'd see on my calendar another chance to try again.

A COUPLE MONTHS after the Awareness Hour, I was on the road again. A multi-stop trip through Tennessee and Alabama would connect me with a handful of Hazelden Betty Ford's donors and key alums. I rarely plan these kinds of trips without also building in visits with local treatment centers. As someone who doesn't have clinical credentials, I invariably pick up useful insight while spending time with those who are doing this work. I enjoy observing and absorbing how other organizations and their executives think about and deliver care. The visits usually come with an invitation to meet and speak with the patients too. These opportunities are among the best parts of my job.

That day I was the guest of a faith-based organization in a rural community. This facility housed about thirty women and men who stayed a full year in treatment. The program included a working farm where patients raised their own food and built resiliency in early recovery. Church and the Bible were cornerstones of their treatment experience as well. I was deeply moved by their commitment and by their humility as we shared lunch.

I had been introduced as "the Yankee from Minnesota," but when I stood up in the middle of the crowded dining room, I set the record straight. "I'm a native Texan whose family came from North Carolina," I said. "And I loved every bite of your collard greens, black-eyed peas, and corn bread. But I won't be satisfied until I get my share of banana pudding on the counter over there." The shouts and cheers made me one of them. They applauded when the director announced I would be their guest speaker after the meal. While a team of patients cleaned the kitchen and dining room and reset the chairs for lecture, I met with staff to talk about the state of addiction care and what Hazelden was up to.

It didn't take five minutes for me to start squirming beneath the rapid fire of their questions.

"What's this I read about Hazelden using opioids to treat opioid addiction?"

"How can anyone ever keep a relationship with the Lord if they are on Suboxone?"

"Our program is living proof that addicts can get sober without prescription meds. Why do you guys at Hazelden give them to patients?"

I was queasy, but it wasn't the lunch in my belly. I could easily explain why we had altered our treatment regimen to improve outcomes for our patients with opioid use disorder. Besides, I reassured them, the COR-12 protocol involved weaning patients off buprenorphine. It was their implications I took personally. Each of their questions was a blade that cut to the core of who I was now.

I might have eased their doubts, or at least countered their arguments, if I had chosen to tell the truth. My truth. That I, too, love sobriety and rely on Twelve Steps that involve a Higher Power I know as God. That, thanks to this program of recovery, I never want to drink or smoke crack again. That the Trojan horse of narcotic pain pills that invaded my life and activated my brain turned out to be more than what God or the Bible or Twelve Steps or the Big Book could counter. That the medication I took every morning and evening helped me stay sober and keep claiming the gift of recovery every single day.

Instead, I failed. I shrunk. I didn't lie to them, but I laid aside the full truth. I left out the last and latest chapter of my story. Instead of revealing the rest of me, I showed them what I sensed they would accept. I did this out of fear of rejection and a sense of shame that the man they had invited—the man they met in *Broken,* perhaps—was not the man who arrived at their door to receive their hospitality and celebrate the miracle of recovery.

In the middle of a room surrounded by people like me, I felt alone and ashamed. Everyone was listening to me, nodding their approval, smiling or furrowing their faces when my words struck a chord. My old story of addiction and redemption held the group's attention for nearly an hour.

I left that day having exchanged hearty handshakes and hugs with people who were rebuilding their lives in good faith. I had done my work: delivered a message of hope and support.

Still, when the car door had closed and I was driving back down the gravel road toward the highway beyond, I thought, *This isn't working.* Anyone who knows anything about recovery also knows that hiding from the truth is perhaps the most dangerous pathway of all.

IN THE MONTHS after I began my Suboxone regimen, I began to have regular meetings with Dr. Frenz. These started as standard follow-up appointments, with a general inquiry about how I was doing and any necessary adjustments to my dosage. Apart from also resolving my lingering jaw pain, I experienced no side effects from the Suboxone. As the months passed, our meetings morphed into an ongoing, intimate, and edifying conversation. I peppered him with questions, relieved to be spilling my guts and emptying my brain to someone from outside the sphere of recovery as I had always known it. I relished our back-and-forth.

The years of pain pills had scrambled my assumptions about addiction and tested what I once believed about sobriety. The medication that I slipped under my tongue every day had silenced my craving brain. There had been no divine whisper, no arduous climb. The pills had lost their power; the snake was defanged. I was relieved and confused by this freedom. I was able to share my still-tentative wonder with Dr. Frenz. He did more than listen. He helped me understand what was happening.

Like every doctor I've ever known, David Frenz was smart, but he didn't flaunt his intellect or experience. He was provocative without being threatening, authoritative without being demeaning, friendly without being patronizing, and I never doubted, as he jotted notes on a pad held on his knee, that he was paying attention and making every effort to zero in on what mattered most to me.

"Would you say that I failed AA?" I asked one day. "Or did AA fail me?"

"That's a loaded question," Dr. Frenz replied, "but it really drills down into the commonly held idea that people fail because they are just not working the program hard enough or well enough."

I nodded and noted that "It works if you work it" is a common refrain in Twelve Step meetings. I shared how, over the years, I had seen people who couldn't stay sober or who relapsed as those who weren't committed enough. They simply needed to work harder, I had thought.

"I'm not willing to say that," Dr. Frenz said. "It's like telling a breast cancer patient, 'Well, you're just not working your breast cancer recovery right. Try harder.' Some people just have a bad disease and the off-the-shelf treatment plan doesn't work. That's part of it. The other part is—and you've heard me say this a bunch—substance use disorders are different. Same as with the cancer example: breast cancers can have mutations that make them resistant to some medications. Treating cancer requires a very specific and individualized approach. We tend to lump substance use disorders together, but they are different because the drugs are different. Alcohol, for example, has a favorable natural history and there are studies on this. A lot of people get better from alcohol use disorder on their own. There's a pretty high rate of spontaneous remission."

I was startled by his perspective. "You mean, 'A drug is a drug is a drug' isn't true?"

"It's not about being true or untrue," he said. "It isn't that simple. Opioid use disorder is its own unique diagnosis. This whole idea of trying to treat your opioid use disorder with something that might work for another illness but doesn't tend to work for opioid use disorder is—from a medical perspective—a mistake," he said. "That's why I think AA didn't work for you this time."

I leaned back in my chair, my mind racing.

Dr. Frenz continued, "There's a reason that we needed methadone in the 1960s. AA had been around since the late 1930s, and it just didn't tend to work very well for people whose problem was heroin. When methadone was first described as an effective treatment for opioid use disorder in 1965, people wondered, 'Well, why do we need this medicine?' And the answer is that we didn't have anything else for this disease."

He paused.

"So in your case I think 'fail' is a strong word. Too loaded with judgment. I just think, in this circumstance, AA was the wrong tool for the job."

The wrong tool for the job.

I felt turned inside out. AA had always been the right tool for the job of long-term recovery—the only set of tools I had been given. I had always believed that my own relapses, as well as the often sordid and always heartbreaking stories of slipping-falling-almost-dying that get told with tears, sobs, and shaking voices at AA meetings, were about personal failure. We who start using drugs again somehow stop being vigilant enough or passionate enough or dedicated enough. The failure was our fault, and the only solution we had was to start over and work harder. If we were going to prevent that next relapse—the next disastrous or deadly detour on our recovery road—then we needed to stop being lazy or self-indulgent and get serious again. The idea that the failure might not be in the person but in the procedure made my head spin.

AA had worked for me for a long time. The program of surrender and self-examination had saved me once—more than once. It still mattered. Against my fierce addictions to cocaine and alcohol, the Twelve Steps had been a refuge and a strength. They did the job. They gave me a sequence to follow and a ladder to climb. They gave me a community of support and structure—mentors and guides like Bob B. and Paul L. and Bob C. and so many more. They gave me a way to progress toward a better way of being—a way that led to life instead of death. I chose that path and experienced sustained sobriety—a gift I cherished and tried to share with as many others as I could.

But the opioids affected my brain differently than those other substances. The tools I was familiar with—the lovingly passed down instruments of AA—weren't enough when my brain was hijacked by painkillers. Then I needed something my previous life hadn't prepared me for.

THE ONE-STORY brick building had seen better days. I guessed that it had probably been a general store a hundred years earlier, serving its rural community in the hills of North Carolina. At some point in the last century, it had become an Elks Lodge. I cringed at the sight of the metal roof; I would be competing to be heard with the rain that continued to beat down. The American flag on the pole hung soggy and limp despite the gusty winds. At least the parking lot was full—always a good sign. I dashed through the rain to the front door and was greeted warmly by a phalanx of guests who had taken refuge beneath the small awning. The blue-gray cloud swirling around them confirmed that where there's smoke, there's usually a group of people in recovery.

I stepped through the door and handed off my raincoat, pleased to discover that the inside of the building was cozier than the outside suggested. The place had been renovated recently, with warm oak paneling, shiny chandeliers, and a small stainless-steel bar with tiny white lights lining a large rectangular mirror. Tables with floral centerpieces were set up. An older woman sat behind a stand-up piano in a corner, tapping out tunes I didn't recognize.

The only holdover from the old club was a massive elk head that seemed to be eyeballing me from across the room. Mounted to the wall directly above the podium, the creature loomed over the parquet dance floor. The combined effect of massive taxidermy, tinkling piano, and driving rain rattling the windows was vaguely surreal. I suddenly felt far from home.

As a public speaker, I've learned how to think on my feet. Often, in the minutes leading up to my introduction, some local connection or shared observation will present itself. Sometimes it's the weather; sometimes a current event or date on the calendar finds its way into the opening moments of a talk. *Tonight,* I thought, *it has to be this magnificent specimen on the wall behind me.* The opportunity to utilize a long-dead animal to bring my story to life for this crowd was too juicy to ignore.

As I mingled with the attendees, learning a little about their lives—what they did and where they lived—I began to feel more and more at home. The guests that night were happy to be there, together, warm and dry. They welcomed me with smiles. I reminded myself that these people were just like me; tonight was about celebrating the gift of recovery we shared.

"All the way from the renowned Hazelden center in Minnesota to our little community here in the foothills of rainy North Carolina," announced the emcee. "We are honored to have with us William C. Moyers." He paused for the smattering of applause before continuing.

"Mr. Moyers is a best-selling author, an advocate on the national stage who has made smashing stigma and helping people his passion; he's also an all-around good guy who has been walking the walk clean and sober, one day at a time since 1994. Mr. Moyers is here to tell his story and give us hope, so let's give him a Tar Heel welcome."

More applause as I stepped to the podium and settled in.

"Over the decades I've given thousands of talks, from big cities to small towns. From the Library of Congress to the National Cathedral. I've been in prisons and treatment centers, conferences and symposiums, grade schools and high schools and graduate schools," I said. "I was even on *Oprah* once, and *Larry King*." My cadence set the pace for what was ahead. "But tonight, here with you," I said, "I have an unprecedented opportunity." I paused for effect. "Never before have I given a talk with a guy like this staring over my shoulder."

The audience burst into laughter.

"I'm a bit intimidated, so please—pray for me."

More laughs.

I continued. "Most of us in here know exactly what it's like to be the elephant in the room." A grin spread across my face as I savored the coming punchline. "But an elk? No way."

I pointed to the table right in front of me. "Do me a favor and give me a heads-up if that thing starts coming at me from behind."

This time we all laughed together. An hour ago, I'd arrived frazzled, damp, and out of sorts. On the dark drive from Charlotte, I had wished I could be headed anywhere other than another roomful of strangers. Now the gift of shared laughter assured me this is where I needed to be tonight. I felt a glimmer of confidence. For the first time since my disastrous showing at the Awareness Hour earlier that year, I truly felt like myself again in front of a crowd.

I opened my well-worn original hardcover to read from the prologue of *Broken*. This had been the way I started hundreds of speeches in rooms like this nearly every week since 2006, when the book was first published. I could recite these lines with my eyes closed—in my sleep even—but I held the book in front of me to underscore the intimacy of the words as I read. This was my story. The man who had lived these things was now standing before them. For about five minutes I walked among the tables, alternately reading passages and speaking about what had happened to me on that miserable October morning in 1994, when two burly cops plucked me from the crack house in Atlanta and led me to where my father waited.

I read the last few paragraphs of what I had written and lived so long ago:

A hard, steady rain was falling as we approached the gray van parked at the curb. The sliding door opened, and I collapsed into the backseat.

My father was sitting in the front passenger seat. Turning around to look at me, he saw a thirty-five-year-old crack addict who hadn't shaved, showered, or eaten in four days. A man who walked out on his wife and two young children and ditched his promising career at CNN. A broken shell of a man, a pale shadow of the human being he had raised to be honest, loving, responsible. His first-born son.

Silence.

"You're angry," I said. I didn't know what else to say.

"That's hardly the word for it." His voice was harsh and cold, like the rain outside.

More silence.

"There's nothing more I can do," he said. "I'm finished."

All these years later, he tells me that's where the conversation ended. But whether I imagined it or not, I heard him say something else.

"I hate you."

And I remember looking in his eyes and speaking my deepest truth.

"I hate me, too."

After a beat, I closed the book sharply in my hand, the front and back covers snapping like a burst balloon. In the silence that followed, I walked slowly back to the podium where I put down the book. It had stopped raining, and the room was still. I looked out at the audience of men and women who had come through the night to hear me say something true. No one moved—not a cough or sneeze.

The people in that room recognized the weight of what I had just read in part because it is a very human story, but also because some version of that moment had happened to them too, or to someone they loved. The moment of terrible clarity when the truth finally crashes through the lies and the doubt and the fear and the anger and the sorrow and the grief. As hard and as hopeless as that experience is, it's the moment where something new can happen.

For a few more minutes I unfolded the rest of my old story to the audience, who remained transfixed as I walked back and forth across the floor. Down into addiction and up with recovery's moment of salvation—mine was the time-tested V-for-victory-shaped formula for hope, help, and healing. This was the story that people wanted to hear, and I had mastered telling it.

I don't know what made that night at the Elks Lodge so different. Maybe it was as simple as the remoteness of the location. We were in the middle of nowhere with nobody around who knew me professionally or personally, no media to report on the event. Maybe it was the rain and the darkness and the safety of this welcoming community. Maybe it was the jokes and the laughter. *Maybe far from home is the perfect place to start a new chapter,* I thought.

I was at a crossroads. I could keep providing these people with the rags-to-riches tale of addiction and redemption chronicled in *Broken*—the acceptable and approved narrative for a recovery success story—or I could tell them what my life was like now. I could tell the truth about myself.

"Once upon a time this is where my story ended," I said. I held the thick book over my head like the Baptist preachers of my childhood had elevated their Bibles.

"And my family and I lived happily ever after, right?"

I let the question linger.

"Hardly." I shook my head slowly.

"As we know, 'stuff happens' in life. It's called the rest of the journey, and some of it is hard," I said.

"And it doesn't always end up the way we want, or expect, or deserve." I nodded toward the glassy-eyed head on the wall behind me.

"The Big Book says that addiction is cunning, baffling, and powerful. I've learned that when it comes to my illness, it is also patient. Like a coiled snake it waits, and it waited for me too."

I could sense a shift in the audience. Some people were trying to anticipate what was coming next. Some had an idea. It was one of those few times as a public speaker when I had no doubt that people were listening to my every word. Nobody was checking their phone or whispering to a neighbor or dozing in their chair.

"A few years ago, I started taking pain meds after dental surgery," I said. "I always thought it was hard to stop drinking and smoking crack. My encounter with opioids turned out to be even harder. This brain of mine, fired up by the pain-killers, just wouldn't stop wanting, needing, hungering for the drugs—first for the pain in my mouth, and then for the pain in my life. The craving was fierce and relentless."

I spoke about the years I had hid the truth of my addiction to the pills. I described how I had kept the secret not just from the dentists and doctors who had tried to solve my pain problem, but from my employer, my colleagues, and my family. I described how ashamed I felt at meetings where people had once looked to me as a model of success in sobriety. I shared how fear had kept me quiet about my struggle, even as I had held on to my work as a recovery advocate and ambassador, even as I had continued helping others take steps toward treatment and health. I told them how torn up my insides were during these years, and how alone I had felt.

"Nothing worked," I said. "Not my will, not the Steps, not even God." I paused. "Then, finally, a doctor who knew what we were up against prescribed a medication called Suboxone."

I scanned the crowd. A few people seemed confused, or maybe just surprised. There were tears on some faces, smiles on others. Some in the audience looked down at their laps. Nobody laughed.

"These have been hard years," I said, "and very different from the story I told in here." My fingers drummed against the book where it lay on the podium. "Less drama, maybe. Fewer crack houses and more pharmacies." I stepped toward the tables again. "And here I am with you tonight, after all of this, still ready to talk about the gift of recovery.

"I've begun to learn that, for me, this great gift isn't measured or determined by the steps I take or the days I accumulate or the meetings I attend or the people I sponsor," I said. "It includes these things, maybe, but they're only part of something bigger. My recovery isn't a thing to achieve, like a grade in school." I pointed back to the book where it lay. "It's not a fixed point in time in the past, either—no matter how miraculous that moment seemed." I paused to take in the whole room. "It's also not a happier or more perfect moment in the future—some goal we strive toward along a path that's neatly laid out.

"Recovery is a journey," I continued. "It's a long and uncertain and *necessary* journey, and it is filled with ups and downs, hope and disappointment, mystery and wonder. There's nothing perfect about this journey, either. We have good days and bad ones—no matter how many miles we've walked through the years, and regardless of the medallions we've collected. We fail at the serenity we aspire to—sometimes for a day and sometimes for a season—but we keep going. We keep trying. We keep finding it and sharing it and losing it and then finding it again." I paused to take in the whole room. "The good news is that we don't have to do it alone."

I was out of breath. The people at the tables seemed out of breath too. It seemed like nobody had moved for the past forty-five minutes. I felt relieved and wrung out, both utterly spent and deeply strong. I stepped back to the podium to take a swig from a bottle of water. I wasn't quite done.

"Tonight is a first for me," I said, "and not just because of the taxidermy." A few chuckles. "I want you to know that I've shared myself and my story tonight in a way that's new for me." I picked up my copy of *Broken*. "What I've said isn't polished—heck, it's not the speech I came prepared to offer this evening. But in this room, well, you've made me welcome in a way I haven't let myself feel in too long. Standing here, I know I'm part of something bigger than me." I paused. "'We' is the first word of the Twelve Steps for a reason. And this . . . ," I opened my arms to include everybody. "*This* is the antidote to the loneliness of addiction and to the shame we feel when we lose our way on the journey. So thank you for listening, and most of all, thank you for including me in the community of 'we' here in North Carolina."

The chairs scraped back as everyone in the room stood to offer a standing ovation. I could see a few people in tears and felt my own eyes welling up. I was among people who not only understood what I said but accepted why I had to say it. I wanted to belong. I needed to belong. And right there, beneath the impassive ungulate on the wall, right then, in the circle of the lost and found, I belonged again—not the shiny image of perfection, not the character in the inspirational bestseller about redemption, but just me; just William.

My shirt was damp with sweat and my knees ached. Even as my lower back was stiff from standing, I could feel a surge of energy from somewhere above my stomach. I had found my voice once more. In that moment I could sense the shattered parts of my banged-up story drawing together again. I could see how my new chapter could continue to fit alongside my old story, how it could expand my recovery testimony with a new honesty and renewed authenticity. I felt again the deep release and relief that come with telling the truth at last.

AN HOUR OR SO later, as the crowd started to disperse and people headed for the exits, a middle-aged man dressed in a suit walked toward me. His cheeks were wet with tears and he used the back of his hand to wipe them away before extending his arms and giving me a big hug. He held me close for a few seconds and then stepped back, still holding on to my shoulder, his eyes locked onto mine as he told me his story. He was a successful lawyer in the community, a former politician who, like me, found recovery in 1994. Then, after a knee replacement, he got hooked on oxycodone.

"I had twenty years sober," he said, tears forming again. "Twenty good years before the surgery and the painkillers." He told me how, when he went back to AA seeking the friendship and support he had always found there, he was met with shame instead. "My sponsor said I had to start over. He said I was back to square one."

"That's bullshit," I said, suddenly overcome by anger and frustration. I felt the man's pain. His story was just like mine. AA had given him a pathway to recovery and a community where he felt accepted and secure. He lived an honest and decent life for decades before a struggle with doctor-prescribed narcotics laid him low. All those years in recovery didn't count anymore, he was told. He had to go back to zero and start counting the days, weeks, months, and years once again. What I had feared for so long—what had kept me hesitant and hurting for three years—had happened to him.

Realizing how frustrated I was, I took a deep breath and suggested we sit down. We pulled two chairs up to an empty table.

"It's not fair for me to get between you and your sponsor," I told him. "That's a relationship more important than what you and I can share in these few minutes." I took a breath, unsure exactly what I needed to say to this man in this moment.

"You and I have benefited from the Twelve Steps, yes?" I asked. He nodded. "The Twelve Steps not only helped us stop using," I said, "they're also a way of life that helps millions of us stay stopped." He nodded again. "And some people don't need anything more."

"That was me," he said. "Then the pills took me out."

"Me too," I said. "And then it turned out I needed to add something else."

"Hearing you share tonight really gives me hope that all is not lost for me," he said.

"It's not lost," I said. "And neither are you, my friend. You get to keep everything that got you here. And you get to keep going."

■

11

Becoming Whole

The world is perfect. It's a mess.
It has always been a mess.
We are not going to change it.
Our job is to straighten out our own lives.

— JOSEPH CAMPBELL

Nearly eight years have passed since that rainy night in 2016 when I walked out of the Elks Lodge in the hills of North Carolina. The initial steps I took that evening and the meaning I tentatively began to assemble from the rough and jumbled years of shame and self-doubt have stayed with me. Thanks to the gifts of time and space and sobriety, those early insights about how I might integrate my old recovery story with a new one have matured and deepened.

When I first attempted to write an account of this period of my life, beginning in 2018, I believed the story of my participation in the nationwide epidemic of opioid misuse and misery properly started in 2012, as I sat in the dentist's chair. For a long time, I thought my desire to take one more pill than the doctor prescribed appeared out of the blue and that my encounter with opioids interrupted the perfectly running personal system of reliable recovery that AA and the Twelve Steps had given me. I thought my problem with painkillers could be fixed through restoration—all I needed to do was get back to the place I was before.

It took a few years, a handful of drafts, and the help of an insightful editor for me to realize that "the place I was before" wasn't a particularly healthy or honest or sustainable way to live. I hadn't seriously considered how much the events that preceded my impulsive *plus one* moment prepared me to respond as I did to the painkillers. Revisiting the years that led up to that moment—years that included unexamined and unprocessed grief and confusion and exhaustion—helped me realize just how vulnerable I had become and how ill-equipped I was to care for myself with the recovery tools I thought I had mastered.

Writing this memoir prompted me to reflect on my prior definitions and practices of recovery and explore how my understanding was unfolding in new ways. I came to recognize that the story I had to tell wasn't simply a cautionary tale about the power of opioids or an inspiring narrative of reclaiming lost sobriety. It wasn't even primarily a story about the wonders of medication-assisted recovery. More than anything, it was a story of personal evolution and change. It was, and continues to be, a story about breaking open and growing up.

I'm grateful that, despite the many ways I regularly demonstrate my imperfections, I still have the capacity to learn and the willingness to do so. I'm also blessed to work for an organization that is committed to discovery and innovation as it advances its lifesaving mission. Like the Hazelden Betty Ford

Foundation has done since its founding in 1949, I recognize and celebrate the truth that I'm a work in progress. I don't ever want to stop growing or trying to help others find paths that lead to healing and wholeness and growth in recovery. In this final chapter I'll share some of what I'm coming to understand about these things in my own life. I'll start with what I'm learning about myself.

Progress, Perfection, Performance, and Persistence

My relationship with the program of recovery that became known as Alcoholics Anonymous started in the summer of 1989. It began with three weeks of enforced abstinence in a New York City psych ward. Once I transferred to an addiction treatment facility, where the Twelve Steps were framed under glass on the walls of nearly every room, my abstinence from alcohol and cocaine became the foundation of a pathway that promised me a restored and renewed life.

The "no half-measures" absolutism of the Big Book's program for living was a blessing for me when I had no boundaries. The structured shelter it provided turned out to be lifesaving. I needed a fence around me then, when I was still reeling from the influence of the drugs that had altered the structure of my brain and nearly killed me. I needed lessons, exercises, direction, and duties. With its rituals and customs and its emphasis on human connections, AA provided safe spaces and practical advice for creating a life without alcohol and cocaine. Its teachings and literature gave me a language to learn and a framework for understanding who I was and how I could change for the better. Within the strong walls of a well-tended program and under the care of people whose approval and acceptance made me feel worthwhile and loved, I came to my senses. My body began to repair itself. I got healthier.

The rooms of recovery, both in treatment and beyond, provided space for me to get well. They also gave me an audience I could perform for and please. In a place and among people where, as I saw it, there were clear winners and losers as well as wrong and right answers, I could figure out how to be right—or at least how to say the right things—and I could become one of the winners. Achieving fluency in the language and the mechanics of the Twelve Steps and the culture they created became, for me, another way to demonstrate my value.

It took several attempts at treatment and a few more years of frustration and failure, but I was eventually able to assemble the combination of luck, skill, self-awareness, and surrender that counts as success in AA. Encouraged by my accomplishment, and buoyed by the kudos that came with it, I dove gratefully into the comforting embrace of recovery culture, enthusiastically adopting its rigid borders and clear categories. I lived there, more or less comfortably, for a long time. It became my home and my work. My success at Twelve Step recovery from alcoholism and cocaine addiction served as the backbone of the redemption story I told in *Broken*. It filled my days with purpose and helped to make my life matter.

In retrospect, I believe that I adapted so well to the Twelve Step philosophy and AA culture back in the 1990s not primarily because these things offered me a path to freedom, but because they provided a fenced field in which I could make something of myself. Much like my experience chasing top grades in school, in AA I could work hard to become good at the subject at hand and thereby demonstrate my acceptability. Today I recognize more and more how quickly this overachieving, approval-seeking aspect of my personality attached itself to the curriculum of the Twelve Steps and found a home in the culture of incremental progress and reward that helps newcomers climb from chaos to stability. I see now how my need for approval compromised my early embrace of AA and how my flawed grasp of the program's deeper purposes and wisdom undercut its ability to help me when my life began to fray and unravel long before I started taking prescription opioids.

When the facts about my life stopped being able to supply what I thought it needed to show—the perfect picture of sober success—it felt like my very identity was under threat; certainly my public identity was. Instead of asking for help and admitting I was anything other than in control and on task and an acceptable model of on-track recovery, I stuck to the prize-winning script I had developed; it was a story people liked. I kept trying to make everything look okay in public, at home, and even in meetings. And rather than being a source of help and connection and compassion as it was intended to be, my membership in the fellowship of recovery became one more performance I felt I had to maintain.

The slogan "Progress not perfection" is intended to offer grace to the recovering person. Perhaps some hear it that way.

I hope they do. But I worry that people like me, who reflexively try to deny our need for grace—or our need for anything else for that matter—simply attach our perfectionism to the idea of progress. Most of the people I know who suspect they're perfectionists—myself included—aren't as concerned with *being* perfect as we are with *appearing* perfect. And since AA suggests that human perfection is impossible, we diligently go to work demonstrating how *perfectly* we're making progress. We want others to see us as people who've got all our shit together—people whose excellent and inspiring trajectory can be admired and charted along a steady upward line.

Beyond the early stages, when milestone celebrations help us build momentum and recognize the importance of our accomplishments, I believe recovery can and should be less about achievement than about persisting. It's about striving and surviving and continuing. Sometimes this will look like positive progress, and sometimes it may seem like stagnation or stuckness. That's just life. Our lives ought not be expected to follow the pattern of V-shaped victory. There is no unbroken climb.

Today, my recovery is not defined by a constant rate of success or by continuously productive progress. I believe success—much like sobriety—is an intermittent quality in life. Progress is no longer a thing I need to perform at. Progress just means I'm still alive. If I'm aware of what I need and want, I'm making progress. If I'm working to align my outer life with my inner one—and recognizing when these things are out of whack—I'm making progress. If I'm reaching out— both to offer help to others and to receive help for myself—I'm making progress. Perfection can go to hell.

Shame, Fear, and the Problem with Faking It

In her wonderful book *The Gifts of Imperfection*, researcher Brené Brown describes a crisis that reflects my experience. Writing about the tension between living *authentically,* which includes admitting and even embracing one's imperfections, and living for *approval,* which entails hiding or denying imperfections, she arrives at an illuminating conclusion. When you exchange your personal authenticity for others' approval, she writes, "You stop believing in your worthiness and start hustling for it."

I've been skeptical of my worthiness for a great many years. Dr. Brown's insight has helped me recognize that this self-doubt is connected to some moment, or series of moments, wherein I began to trade my authentic self for a version of me that would earn the acceptance and approval of other people. While I can't pinpoint the place in my life where this self-abandoning hustle started, I know it was early. When I was in second grade, I gave away all the nickels in my coin collection to the other children on the playground. Years later, strung out on a Harlem street corner, I bought ice cream for all the kids on the block. I noticed early on that people responded when I gave them something. They patted me on the back, they laughed and smiled. People liked me when I could make them feel good.

Those early lessons stuck. From handing out my nickels as a boy who hoped to make a friend to signing books and smiling when I felt like screaming, I've pretended and performed for most of my life, hustling to be what people want when they wanted it. External validation, acceptance, applause, recognition—I've been chasing these things since childhood.

My hunger for this approval followed me into sobriety. It matured with me as I became more in control of my passions and impulses. My choice to publicly share my status as a person in recovery and make it central to my professional life meant that my personal sobriety included performing a public role. I turned out to be good in the role—so good that people gave me standing ovations. They paid me lots of money for my inspiring story. They validated me. They invited me to speak and share my opinions. They looked to me for words of wisdom and an image of hope, and they thanked me when I delivered.

The aspects of my worthiness-hustling personality that contributed to my opioid addiction and kept me within its grasp—my failures of courage and honesty, my self-doubt, my impulse to protect myself by trying to control how others perceive me—remain part of me. The Big Book calls these "defects of character" and suggests that they're symptoms of an alcoholic's or addict's disease. While I certainly see the way my addictions affected my thinking and influenced my behavior, I'm unwilling to ascribe all my dysfunctions to the effects of the drugs I took or the booze I drank. Rather than calling them defects and working to purge these impulses and attitudes from my life, I'm learning to see and name them as the less helpful parts of my personality. I'm coming to understand and accept how many of these unruly aspects of who and how I am were part of that hungry hole in my soul way before my first hit on a joint or my first beer or line of coke.

For a long time, I've felt ashamed of these parts of my personality. And while my hustling and achieving have occasionally earned me temporary respites from that burden, I've also found shame to be a remarkably nimble and sticky force in my life. Fueled and fed by my deep fear of disappointing people, my shame jumps effortlessly from one perceived failure to another. In this story, even before I thought about popping a pain pill, shame attached itself to my affair, my inability to embody the man portrayed in *Broken*, my divorce from Allison, my worn-down teeth, my imperfect parenting skills, my failure to please my parents, and the dubious value I suspected I provided my employer and my colleagues. When the oxycodone I was prescribed after my dental surgery offered me a brief chance to rest from laboring under the weight of this heavy wad of sticky shame, I took it.

Then I took some more.

The painkillers erased the pain in my mouth. They also removed, for a few hours at a time, the deeper pains I had been carrying for decades. I've since learned that opioids—the painkilling pills that so powerfully captured me—have a unique capacity to relieve emotional pain. They do this as effectively as they address acute physical pain. This is part of what clinicians describe as the "profoundly reinforcing aspect" of opioids—a key reason people like me find these drugs so attractive and so hard to let go of.

At first the pills provided relief from the anxiety that drove me to constantly demonstrate my value, from the shame of doubting my worthiness, and from the persistent fear that I would somehow be exposed as an imposter or a fraud. Then, of course, they became themselves yet another source of shame and fear, soon compounded by my inability to stop wanting them.

Finding myself on the wrong side of the fence and far from the safe center that had kept me from death and given me everything good in my life was terrifying. The idea of failure—of losing the respectability and status I had acquired—filled me with shame. Perhaps more than anything else, this is why I suffered in silence for so long as I struggled with the pain-killers. It's also why I later hesitated to share my ongoing use of Suboxone with people I suspected would judge me as being un-sober. I worried that, rather than embracing me as a person who continued to desire and pursue recovery, some would consider me a still-active opioid user—someone who fell outside the boundary that divided the saved from the lost.

Following my revelations on the stage at the Betty Ford Center, some people doubted my recovery status. A few months later, someone accused me of being under the influence. One person went so far as to suggest that I should stop giving speeches and publicly representing the Hazelden Betty Ford Foundation until I had clocked at least a full year of sobriety—presumably from a date they would assign.

That experience of being judged and found lacking wasn't a first for me, and it very likely won't be the last. It's also not unique to me. The man I consoled that night at the Elks Lodge shared the same experience. I wonder how many others experience slights or even hostility, or fear that they will receive such treatment, from their fellow travelers if they stray from the conventional path.

Some might argue that there's a place for healthy shame or fear in recovery because the stakes are so high. If that's the case, I believe it's a small one and must be specific to the situation. Fear of legal consequences can keep you coming back to the safety and support of meetings. Shame and guilt about a past action or present behavior can generate energy for change. Healthy fear of what returning to active use will do to your body or your wallet or your marriage or your ability to keep your kids might be enough to give you another day without drinking or using.

You can get sober out of fear, and even stay that way for a while, but you can't build a sustainable recovery from addiction based on the power of fear—not fear of shame, not fear of disappointing people you respect. Fear itself will eventually fail you. When your fear of failure outweighs your faith in your essential worthiness, it will make you hide behind some kind of show. You deserve better than that. You deserve to be whole.

As I continue to learn about shame and reflect on the role of fear in my recovery, I've begun to think about another well-worn recovery slogan in a new way. When the phrase "Fake it till you make it" functions in your ears as it was intended—when that advice encourages you to get up every day and do things that support your healing even when you'd rather stay in bed—I think it's useful. If, however, you've been faking your happiness or your identity or your actions or your commitments for longer than you can remember, it's time to stop pretending. You will never "make it" by "faking it."

If you sense yourself hustling to demonstrate your worthiness from behind a mask, know that you can return to the authenticity that comes with honesty at any moment. Start by talking openly with someone you trust. Take it from a person who has faked and fumbled for way too long: don't pretend to be what you aren't, even if it's a person you used to be or a way of life that once seemed to fit like a glove.

My battle with shame continues. I am tempted daily to discount or doubt my worthiness. Hustling for approval and validation has become second nature to me, so slowing and stopping these things requires time and patience. Detoxifying from shame and fear can be a long process. Flushing my system from the effects of these persistent poisons continues to be a challenge for me.

That said, I am getting better at recognizing when the frightened, furtive, and shame-averse aspects of who I am are trying to run the show. I'm also working to understand them and become more skilled at countering or quieting their voices. I've even begun to offer these unruly parts of me a little compassion—after all, they've worked hard trying to keep me safe for many years. I hope this book is evidence of my ongoing aspiration to live a life of authenticity, even if I have more work to do. And even though asking for help is still hard for me, I'm relieved to know that I don't have to walk this road all by myself. I'm deeply grateful for my family and for the mentors and friends and fellow travelers who love me for who I am and who continually invite me to set aside the hustle and be a healthier, happier, and more whole person.

Miracles and Medicine

AA was founded at a time when, with a few notable exceptions, medical science was stymied by what to do with the intractable challenges presented by alcoholics and addicts. Facing the apparent failure of their arts, many doctors of that era simply opted out of attempting a remedy and returned the problem to their patients. The problem of chronic "inebriety" was deemed not a medical issue, but instead a problem rooted in moral weakness or a failure of will. The genius of the movement begun by Bill W. and Dr. Bob was its insight into the complicated reality of addiction—that the illness ran deeper than most medicine could reach. The two men sensed a need for a multilateral approach to healing, and so they named alcoholism as an issue that involved the spirit as well as the body and mind. Encouraged by the work of Christian revival movements, impressed by the insights of psychology, and inspired by their own spiritual experiences and epiphanies as they sought to become sober, they came to conclude that the alcoholic needed a spiritual solution. What would finally make the difference for each sufferer was the miraculous intervention by, ongoing connection to, and accompaniment of a Higher Power. Many in the medical world at the time dismissed this crucial insight as superstition or snake oil. They tuned out or washed their hands of it as outside the realm of what they knew or could prove or replicate.

Medical science hasn't slept in the decades since, however, nor has it stayed quite so stuck in its own certainty—and thank God for that. In 2024, the biopsychosocial understanding of addiction undergirds addiction medicine. It has produced breakthrough treatments that transform lives. And while science hasn't yet been able to locate or quantify the human soul, it keeps looking for opportunities to learn. I've found that those who study the phenomenon of addiction and provide care for people who labor to heal from substance use disorders recognize and respect the vital role that spirituality and connection play in human health and wellness. I'm blessed to work among many of these people at the Hazelden Betty Ford Foundation.

Today, I can happily attest to a pair of truths that once seemed impossible to reconcile: the program and fellowship of Alcoholics Anonymous saved me, and so did Suboxone. AA provided a place of safety and acceptance, and a path to follow. Even as my early attempts to learn and live them were hobbled by my approval-hungry heart, the Twelve Steps helped me understand how to be human and whole again after cocaine and alcohol had hollowed me out and ground me into pieces. Two decades later, Suboxone gave me a new kind of freedom. Opioids had invaded and overpowered what I thought was a secure sobriety and trapped me in a cycle of craving and chaos. Dr. Frenz's prescription gave me clarity and courage enough to reclaim my recovery and begin rebuilding my life with renewed honesty and passion.

These days I am careful with the way I use the term "miracle." I try not to limit my imagination of how and where a Higher Power is willing and able to work healing and wholeness. God arrives in our lives through diverse means. I find mercy in fellowship. I recognize blessing in the calls I make and the assistance I offer people who ask for help finding a path to healing. Grace arrives in conversations with close confidants as often as it does in a daily devotion. Physical therapy was, for me, a godsend. There is miracle in medications like Suboxone and methadone. I still go to meetings. I'm occasionally on my knees in prayer. I also keep taking my medicine.

Complexity and Complications

"Keep it simple" isn't always a helpful slogan. Some people even add "stupid" to the end, which seems derogatory to me, even when the speaker claims to be offering this remark out of love. Just like addictions, which are so often threaded through the hurts and holes in the addict's soul in ways and by routes that differ from person to person, recovery is complicated and personal. Denying this reality by ignoring or avoiding or downplaying these complications is a way of elevating theoretical people over actual ones. Oversimplifying recovery serves nobody well. Smoothing every story into a version that fits a single framework fails to do justice to the truth of our differences.

Everybody's addiction is complicated by something. This means their recovery will be too. However you choose to pursue recovery, you will be most likely to stick with its disciplines and enjoy its benefits if they are rooted in your authentic identity and address your particular needs and goals. It matters who you are and where you've been. It also matters what drugs you're trying to stop using.

The struggles I experienced in the years covered by this memoir were complicated by my personality—by the William-specific shape of the hole in my soul—and also by the specific way opioids worked in my brain. They were complicated still more by my role as a public face of the recovery movement, fed by the success of *Broken* in the early 2000s and by my job representing the Hazelden Betty Ford Foundation.

Other things that can and do complicate recovery include mental and physical health conditions, unaddressed trauma, racism and sexism, and homophobia. These factors and forces can make seeking and finding help for addiction—and finding support for recovery—more challenging. Stigma about addiction is part of this problem, but it's not the only obstacle.

We're currently in the beginning of a new and very welcome era in which addictions are understood and addressed as something more complex than a failure of morals, and recovery is seen as something more profound and holistic than maintaining abstinence-based sobriety. As we keep moving forward, building upon the foundation of this new framework, we're going to become aware of many other forces and factors that get in the way of people's willingness and ability to access help and discover a path toward recovery.

I'm a straight White guy in my sixties. I've got a track record of sustained remission from my addictions to alcohol and cocaine, and I'm gratefully recovering from an opioid use disorder with the help of prescription medication. Today, I enjoy a fairly stable sobriety, a healthy marriage, and a job that offers me flexibility and trust. I've got financial resources, networks of friends and family, and other privileges. Apart from my bad teeth, cancer-prone complexion, and a predisposition for substance use disorders, I'm physically and mentally healthy. All of this has made it easier for me to avoid some consequences of my addictions. My status has also afforded me access to all kinds of recovery resources and supports—in part because many of the resources and supports currently available have been developed and delivered by and for people much like me.

But I'm an outlier when it comes to who needs help—especially with opioid use disorder. According to a 2023 article in the *Washington Post,* "1 out of every 5 people who died of an overdose in 2020 usually worked in construction or restaurants." Compare that to people employed in the fields of education and computer work, among whom one in a hundred experienced a fatal opioid overdose. A separate article in the same paper identified fentanyl overdose as the leading cause of death for Americans aged eighteen to forty-nine. In my home state of Minnesota, American Indians were ten times as likely to die from a drug overdose in 2021 than Whites. The CDC reports a nationwide upsurge in overdose rates among Black men—a population notably underrepresented in and poorly served by traditional treatment centers like the one I work for. When it comes to getting professional help, only one in ten people with any kind of substance use disorder in the United States receives treatment.

Our challenge, as people who desire to share the gift of recovery, is not *keeping* things simple so much as *making* them so. If we're serious about sharing the gift of healing and wholeness with those who need it, we must work to make treatment and recovery from addiction simple *enough,* accessible *enough,* welcoming *enough* for complicated people with complicated lives. We need to do this so they, too, can find their way out of the clutches of addiction and find help growing in and with recovery. We can do this by changing our exclusive attitudes and working to remove obstacles.

My friend and colleague Andrew Williams has helped deepen my appreciation for the diversity that characterizes our common humanity. He has also opened my eyes to the perpetual inequities and injustices that have limited so much imagination about who needs and deserves addiction care and what forms that care can take. Andrew serves as the Hazelden Betty Ford Foundation's national director of diversity, equity, and inclusion—he's the first to hold this position in the seventy-five years of our organization's history. In a recent report to the staff, Andrew quoted the great revolutionary feminist poet Audre Lorde, who writes, "It is not our differences that divide us. It is our inability to recognize, accept, and celebrate those differences."

It's time to move beyond trite and dismissive platitudes about simplicity when it comes to addiction and recovery. We must learn to recognize and accept the complexity of the problems people face and the solutions we help them find. As we develop this capacity, as individuals, as friends and sponsors, and as institutions that seek to support recovery and provide care, we will become more able to celebrate the diverse ways people choose to get well.

I believe the most effective way to discover what prevents people from seeking help or pursuing recovery is by paying attention to individuals and the stories they tell. We will learn by listening as people express their needs, share their hopes, and trust us with their fears. We will serve people well by taking their needs and desires and concerns seriously and then fashioning treatments and approaches to care that respond directly to those issues. Only then will we be able to help individuals construct a recovery that fits their unique lives—a recovery that works for them, no matter how it looks or how their solutions and goals and methods might differ from our own.

Abstinence, Sobriety, and Room for You and Me

I used to believe that abstinence and sobriety were achievements, the first to maintain and the second to safeguard. The program of Steps and Traditions that comprised the curriculum in each of my stays in treatment defined abstinence and sobriety and recovery in stark and simple terms. The first priority was abstinence. It was the nonnegotiable outer boundary that separated an active user from the realm of recovery. Continued abstinence from the substances that had captured and controlled me was critical to achieving sobriety, which was defined as the freedom from needing and wanting those things. Sobriety—alternately described as a divine gift or a self-disciplined duty—was offered as the only foundation strong enough to support the gift and burden of ongoing recovery.

When I asked Dr. Frenz who or what had failed when it came to my painkiller problem—me or the Twelve Steps—he declined to answer. Instead, he invited me to see the whole program of the Twelve Steps as a set of potentially useful tools rather than an inviolable system of solutions for every addiction. His invitation gave me permission to reimagine the uses of abstinence and the significance of sobriety. Once upon a time, I saw the Steps as a sacred program and the only way to recover from a substance use disorder. Today, I see them as tools that can help a person get well. But they're not the only tools available or the only tools that are effective. Abstinence is about stopping. Sobriety is about learning to live well without the substances and what they did for you. Recovery is bigger than both.

I'm still exploring what all this means for me personally

and for my more public work and advocacy. In this, my friend Susan Cheever has been a help. Her groundbreaking biography of Bill Wilson, *My Name Is Bill*, is a treasure for anyone interested in exploring the roots of the recovery movement he helped birth. In it, she identifies the paradoxes that so many of us grapple with after we have put down the drink or the drug that led us to ruin. She also notes how Bill himself made space for learning and change in the daily pursuit of wholeness and a more integrated life.

> In one way, an alcoholic who stops drinking is a walking miracle, a man or woman whose life has been so changed that the addiction that twined through all of his or her behavior has been removed. But what if this miraculously recovered alcoholic is a chain-smoking gambler who continues to snarl up the family finances and endanger his or her own health and the health of the family? There are no answers to these questions, of course, only paradoxes, balances, daily readjustments. In embracing the two sides of each of these questions in his writings, Bill Wilson left room for each alcoholic to find his or her own accommodation with recovery.

As I approach the midpoint of my sixties as some version of the "walking miracle" that Susan describes, I marvel at the way my recovery has endured for the past thirty-five years. I also contemplate what it has meant for me, even during the periods when abstinence proved impossible or my sobriety stretched thin or my flaws caused me to founder.

I still believe in the promises that the AA pioneers wrote

about in the Big Book almost a hundred years ago. But now I am reconciled to the truth that there is no predictable path to the newness and freedom and happiness that are among the gifts that come with recovering from addiction. That's not to say I don't recognize that we discover and claim these gifts by working toward them—the life we're living is not a theory, of course; it requires action—it just means that there are as many ways to pursue these rich rewards as there are people who want to make them part of their lives.

My own children have faced challenges with substance use, and they have found pathways that continue to work for them. Each has a different approach, and all are different from my own. I am proud of my kids, and I celebrate their persistence and the solutions they've found for living life on life's terms. There are many routes to well-being.

I find solace in the gracious idea that there is room enough in the great house of recovery for everybody who wants to claim it whenever and however they're able to do so. I'm confident that we can work out the details and find language to helpfully describe our paths as we journey together.

The Journey and the Clock

I have come to accept that no matter how dearly we'd like to believe there's a single true route to recovery, there is no sure-fire way to get well and stay that way. As tempting as it may be to imagine recovery as a puzzle we might finally solve or a contest we can win or lose, these ways of thinking discount the truth that recovery isn't so much a static state of "being in" as it is a process of continually becoming.

For this reason, I think that recovery remains best described as a journey. For me and for many, it has been and will be a path we pursue all our lives. It's a journey of adaptation, discovery, and growth. Mine is the ongoing, daily effort to live a responsible and decent and connected life liberated from the substances, situations, attitudes, and habits of heart and mind that have proven their ability to break my spirit and empty my soul. I'm still learning where this journey will take me and exactly how to walk it.

By now it's probably clear that my recovery hasn't been plotted along a very straight line. I've been an inefficient and irresponsible traveler at times. I'm prone to wander, and, truth be told, I tend to tire quickly. Shiny things tend to distract me, and I'm often spooked by scary situations. I flee from pain and seek out pleasure. I'm not proud of these sections of my story, but at least they're honest assessments; I know who I am. In addition to my occasional ineptitude, I hope my persistence is evident as well. Despite my setbacks and stumbles, I keep going. I try new things. I keep learning, seeking, and striving. I'm still at it.

While I wouldn't presume to know the right course for anyone else, what I do feel confident about suggesting is this: If your program or method of recovery stops working one day, you can change it. When some event, circumstance, or substance invades what you thought was a secure sobriety and breaks apart the supports that once kept you safe, you have the chance to rebuild it. It may look different than it did, and that's okay. I believe that if you ask for help, you will encounter mentors, partners, doctors, and neighbors who can help you reimagine what's possible. I know these people exist because I work with them every day at the Hazelden Betty Ford Foundation.

If you find that what you've always known or done isn't effective as you face a new challenge or crisis, try something else. Adapt and adopt. Add supports like medication or therapy. Don't be afraid to seek what you need and don't fall into the trap of thinking that you've somehow failed. Purity isn't the point—this is about staying alive. Don't be shy about demanding the help you need. Keep an open mind. Be teachable. Trust the professionals. Get second opinions. Ask for the evidence. Your journey is ongoing.

For a long time I marked the start of my journey by the date I took my last hit of crack cocaine. Most measures of sobriety start the clock at a point like this and award weekly or monthly or annual medallions as, and if, a person's streak of success continues. These keepsakes have begun to matter less to me than they once did. Same with my sobriety date.

At the time of this writing, I've been pursuing recovery for 12,669 days. My lifelong recovery clock started on August 6, 1989, when I shakily stepped through the admissions entrance into St. Vincent's Hospital in New York City. On that warm Sunday afternoon, saddled with shame and sluggish from drugs, I grudgingly admitted that I had some kind of problem. I wanted a way out of the trouble I was in. I wanted a way beyond the misery I felt. I wanted a future that was so very different from the painful place I had fallen into.

Today, I recognize that my history of recovery runs along a broader timeline than can be captured by a single sobriety date. Instead of pegging my story to the final drink or drug I ingested, I mark the start of this ongoing journey in a different way. In my mind, recovery begins the moment you first want to get well. Including my years of relapse and regret in my recovery story helps me recall how strong I can be. Calling to mind the months and moments of hard travel reminds me who was there to help and guide me on my journey. The map I look at these days includes valleys as well as mountaintops, strenuous climbs as well as stretches of ease and rest and delight.

For a long time, I carried my inspiring recovery story as a thing I had to live up to—much like my famous last name. I was grateful for it, even if I resented the standard it set and the shame and judgment I felt whenever I wasn't able to make my life match it. Now I'm embracing the still-unfolding story of my life and my recovery as a thing I get to live into—an adventure that I get to keep pursuing at whatever pace and level of success brings me the deepest and most authentic peace.

If you need to connect your recovering life to a timeline or a date on the calendar, it doesn't have to be the date of your last drink or hit or binge. Pick the moment that you decided you wanted to get well. Mark your journey from the place you began to turn your face and your heart toward the possibility of freedom and away from the pain or paralysis that had you in its grip. The moment you choose might be weeks or even years before you finally managed to stop drinking or using. New life—if that's the metaphor that works for you—is not about scorekeeping. It starts with hope and desire. Recovery grows from that moment, and it rarely grows or goes in a straight and uninterrupted line.

The only requirement for beginning this journey is to believe that it is possible. This belief starts with hope, and it is sustained by the love and support of those who travel with us. As you pursue your recovery journey, do it with a spirit of freedom and adventure. It's okay to be a work in progress. It's okay to be a person with needs that don't fit the mold. It's okay to have cracks and scars and wounds that might still be mending. Becoming whole won't happen all at once. It's the journey of a lifetime.

■

Epilogue

In February of 2013, I found myself onstage at the 92nd Street Y in New York City. The Y is known for hosting readings, panel discussions, and other public events that let thought leaders share their perspectives on current events or other topics. I was there to talk about my latest book, *Now What? An Insider's Guide to Addiction and Recovery.*

Joining me were my parents, Judith and Bill Moyers, and author and biographer Susan Cheever, who agreed to moderate the conversation. The auditorium was packed with 800 people. Not even the threat of a Nor'easter snowstorm had kept them home. Addiction never takes a break, so people are always looking for answers, regardless of the weather.

Audience questions are the heart and soul of events like this. What people ask from the floor often connects abstract or theoretical statements or ideas to real life—and it happens in real time. Knowing this, as well as knowing how asking people to raise their hands or approach microphones can be daunting for some, I had proposed passing out index cards as people entered the auditorium. Attendees would write down their questions anonymously and pass them forward to Susan, who would read them aloud. Then one of the four of us onstage would respond.

Twenty minutes into the event, Susan already held a stack of cards several inches thick. "Now we'll stop for just a moment and let's address a question," Susan said. I watched as she drew the first card from the middle of the stack. In a moment her casual smile turned into a slight frown. Instead of reading aloud the question on the card, she passed it to her left—to my father.

I've never known my dad to not have an answer for anything. He made a career and earned a worldwide reputation as someone who was eager to explore life's most intricate, confounding, and perennially relevant topics. But as he scanned the card with furrowed brow, I could sense this question might be beyond him. Dad passed the card to my mother, turning to her for help as they've done for each other since they were married in 1954. Even Mom's reassuring smile faded as she considered what was written on the card she held. After a few seconds, she handed it to me, the last person on the stage.

I read the card and took a deep breath. Here was a question like none I had ever been asked before, at least in such a public setting. Ten short words formed a single sentence on the card. It's a sentence that summarizes the stakes that so many of us who struggle with addiction or mental illness or both have asked ourselves, usually in the darkness of despair.

I read the question aloud.

"What do you do if you don't want to live?"

In that moment it felt as if there were nobody else in that jam-packed auditorium except the two of us. Me, who held the question in my hand, and the person out there somewhere in the darkened hall who was anguished enough to ask it and was now awaiting an answer. Somebody, despite what they were suffering, or maybe because of it, had made the trek through New York City's uncaring and impersonal streets to the shelter of the 92nd Street Y, perhaps in a final bid to hear a word that offered an alternative to their own desperate solution.

I read the card a second time.

"What do you do if you don't want to live?"

It seemed like an eternity had passed since my mother had handed the question to me. *Do I have an answer? How do I answer?* I couldn't sound glib. Clinically, I might pretend to have an answer, but out of my mouth it couldn't possibly sound convincing—and besides, what if I was wrong? For a split second, I wanted to pass. I considered telling the questioner to come and see me after the event. But I knew it is only in that moment of total openness that people are ready to change. In an hour, whoever had worked up the nerve to write and submit this question might not be open to an answer. They might have disappeared back into the night's darkness. I had to answer now.

Then it hit me. Why my parents and Susan Cheever and I were there on that stage. Why the event was sold out. Why people had taken time away from their busy lives to show up and sit still for ninety minutes. Why it was being broadcast on the public radio station in New York.

I took a breath before I spoke.

"Turn to the person next to you and ask for help."

I knew that auditorium was filled with people who cared. Those with firsthand knowledge of the wanton, destructive toll of this illness, either in their own lives or those of their families. Counselors and therapists, social workers and clergy, nurses and doctors who treat addiction down in the trenches. Administrators or executives who run facilities. Scientists and researchers who study it. I knew the odds favored there was an answer, or at least an empathetic heart, sitting next to the person who had scratched their question on that card.

A rippling wave of emotion flowed through the audience. I heard gasps and whispers. The stage lights made it impossible to see much except the dark outlines of heads and shoulders in the crowd, but I sensed that somewhere, somehow, my response had resonated in the room. I hoped it had found the person who had made the plea. After a few moments, we carried on with the rest of the program.

An hour later when it was over there was the usual rush to the stage by people who wanted to say hello, offer their own sentiments, or, in the case of my father, get an autograph. One woman made a beeline toward me. I could see her coming, holding a scrap of paper. "Mr. Moyers," she said, "I'm a psych nurse and I'm in recovery. The man sitting next to me turned and told me his name. He's the one who asked the question! I wrote down his cell number. But afterwards he bolted." She pressed the paper into my hand. "Please call him."

It had worked.

Nell and I finally made it back to our hotel room around midnight. As I sat on the edge of the bed, I unfolded the scrap of paper like I would open a box marked *Fragile, Handle with Care*. Then I dialed the 917 number.

"Hello," a man's soft voice answered. "Hello, who is this?"

"Hi, it's me, William. William Moyers," I said. "Is this the person who wrote the question?" It was hard to believe that, in a city of fifteen million souls, two people who had never met but forged a sudden bond in a full auditorium had found each other. We were actually connected and really talking—on the first try. There was a long pause from the other end of the line. I spoke again. "Can I help you?"

That night, over the course of an hour-long telephone conversation, Don G. and I got to know each other. He told me about surviving several suicide attempts, the last of which had left him with serious injuries that led to a dependence on opioids he could not escape. Don shared his struggle with mental health challenges and isolation. "I came to the Y tonight on a whim, really," he said. "I have wanted to die for too long, but tonight, hearing you and your parents, I want to live more. Can you really help me?"

I could. Don didn't have health insurance and almost no money, but I helped him access a scholarship to an outpatient program not far from where he lived. We never did meet in person, instead relying on phone calls and instant messages to stay in touch over the years. Don continued to struggle with his sobriety, yet every time we signed off, he reminded me of how much had changed in his life since the night we first connected. His last email message to me was in August of 2021.

In the midst of the pandemic that had isolated so many of us from each other and from the connections that help keep us healthy and whole, Don wrote:

> I want you to know you didn't waste anything helping me throughout the years. You planted a lot of seeds that may not have kept me sober then, but helps me to stay alive because I've had hope ever since that night at the Y. I'm going to stay living in this world of recovery as long as I can. I promise you. Many thanks, Don.

As I was finally finishing this book, I reached out to my friend Don once again. I wanted to tell him about the book and talk about the journey he and I shared. I wanted to let him know I was thinking about him. My messages went unanswered. Finally, an internet search revealed that he had died, apparently of an accidental opioid overdose, about eight months after his last email to me. Don was forty-one years old.

We can't always keep the promises we make, but I believe we can continue to hold on to hope. And we can share that hope with others who wrestle and wonder and wait for healing in their lives. This work is never wasted.

■

Acknowledgments

Like everything else that's complicated and worth it in my life, this book is the result of the power of "We." Including:

Marc Olson, my editor at Hazelden Betty Ford, who took on this project just over a year ago and made this book everything that it is now. Thank you, Marc, for your many literary talents and wise insights into who I am and how to make my story matter to our readers. You were right; "We got this!"

Andy Lien, for seeing this story as a book worthy of the Hazelden Betty Ford imprint. Your decision to give me a chance to work with Marc was a brilliant move.

Publishing's all-star team also includes editorial project manager Cathy Broberg, whose attention to detail and language proved invaluable in the transformation of manuscript to book.

Dr. Joseph Lee, the president and CEO of the Hazelden Betty Ford Foundation, who, over a quiet meal in Chicago in 2021, shared with me his vision for the future of the organization we both serve. Only then did I understand how my story reflects the transformative spirit of what's possible for our mission in the years to come.

Moira McGinley, my indefatigable colleague, whose advocacy for this project allowed me to push on despite my other duties. Without our colleagues Stephanie Bates and Amelia Grant, I doubt I could have pulled it off. Ann Schumack was also instrumental in helping me balance this project with my other priorities.

Kathy Ketcham, who wrapped her heart and soul around the reams of raw material scattered across my journey, especially my journals, to assemble the narrative that pointed us in the right direction.

Brad Martin, whose generous, selfless spirit has sustained me for many years now. The earliest iteration of this book was born at his home at Blackberry Farm, where I've always felt at home away from home thanks to his team, Bobbi Swann and Judy Bledsoe.

Cini Robb, my kindred "fellow traveler" who walks her walk with a generous passion for helping thousands of people like us.

Amy Williams, my agent. Amy always knows what is best when it comes to sharing my story on the page.

Pamela Dorman, who first believed in the power of my story in my first memoir, *Broken* (2006), and Jeramie Orton, who helped to find my voice for this work.

Dr. David Frenz, whose wisdom is like the sky; it covers everything for me.

Of course, my wife Nell Hurley is the anchor in my life. Her love renewed me when I was nearly empty and sustains me one day at a time for a long time now.

Thank you. Together WE did it!

■

Notes

Note: The number that begins each note indicates the page in this book where the cited material appears.

CHAPTER 1

17 | "Even today, only one in ten people with a diagnosable substance use disorder seeks treatment for it.":
US Department of Health and Human Services, "SAMHSA Announces National Survey on Drug Use and Health (NSDUH) Results Detailing Mental Illness and Substance Use Levels in 2021," news release, January 4, 2023, https://www.hhs.gov /about/news/2023/01/04/samhsa-announces-national-survey -drug-use-health-results-detailing-mental-illness-substance-use -levels-2021.html.

CHAPTER 2

42 | "Author Beverly Conyers notes that even people who are committed to recovery can be separated from their values . . .":
Beverly Conyers, *Find Your Light: Practicing Mindfulness to Recover from Anything* (Center City, MN: Hazelden, 2019), 10.

CHAPTER 3

59 | "I find it a hopeless undertaking indeed . . .":
From a letter to Mark Whalon, quoted in Susan Cheever, *My Name Is Bill: Bill Wilson—His Life and the Creation of Alcoholics Anonymous* (New York: Washington Square Press, 2004), 179.

60 | "In their book *Beyond the Influence* . . .":
Katherine Ketcham and William F. Asbury, with Mel Schulstad and Arthur P. Ciaramicoli, *Beyond the Influence: Understanding and Defeating Alcoholism* (New York: Bantam, 2000), 195–96.

CHAPTER 5

118 | "That year, healthcare providers wrote 259 million prescriptions . . .":
US Department of Health and Human Services, Centers for Disease Control and Prevention, *2018 Annual Surveillance Report of Drug-Related Risks and Outcomes—United States,* Surveillance Special Report, August 31, 2018, https://www.cdc.gov /drugoverdose/pdf/pubs/2018-cdc-drug-surveillance-report.pdf.

118 | "Between 1999 and 2010, sales of prescription opioids . . .":
Congressional Research Service, "The Opioid Crisis in the United States: A Brief History," November 30, 2022, https:// crsreports.congress.gov/product/pdf/IF/IF12260.

118 | "Only after the Centers for Disease Control and Prevention recognized and named . . .":
US Department of Health and Human Services, Centers for Disease Control and Prevention, "Prescription Painkiller Overdoses at Epidemic Levels," news release, November 1, 2011, https:// www.cdc.gov/media/releases/2011/p1101_flu_pain_killer _overdose.html.

118 | ". . . and released prescribing guidelines in the following years . . .":

US Department of Health and Human Services, Centers for Disease Control and Prevention, "CDC Releases Guideline for Prescribing Opioids for Chronic Pain," news release, March 15, 2016, https://archive.cdc.gov/#/details?url=https://www.cdc.gov/media/releases/2016/p0315-prescribing-opioids-guidelines.html.

118–119 | "During the year I received my first prescription for an opioid pain medication . . .":

US Department of Health and Human Services, Substance Abuse and Mental Health Services Administration, Center for Behavioral Health Statistics and Quality, *Results from the 2012 National Survey on Drug Use and Health: Summary of National Findings*, NSDUH Series H-46, HHS Publication No. (SMA) 13-4795. Rockville, MD: Substance Abuse and Mental Health Services Administration, 2013, accessed via https://www.samhsa.gov/data/sites/default/files/NSDUHresults2012/NSDUHresults2012.pdf.

119 | "It wasn't until October of 2017 that this crisis was declared a public health emergency. . . .":

US Department of Health and Human Services, Administration for Strategic Preparedness and Response, "Declarations of a Public Health Emergency," last reviewed September 15, 2023, https://aspr.hhs.gov/legal/PHE/Pages/default.aspx.

CHAPTER 10

270 | "A hard, steady rain was falling as we approached the gray van . . .":

William Cope Moyers, *Broken: My Story of Addiction and Redemption* (London: Penguin Books, 2007), 3–4.

CHAPTER 11

285 | "When you exchange your personal authenticity for others' approval, she writes, 'You stop believing in your worthiness and start hustling for it.'":

Brené Brown, *The Gifts of Imperfection: Let Go of Who You Think You're Supposed to Be and Embrace Who You Are* (Center City, MN: Hazelden, 2010), 9.

294–295 | "According to a 2023 article in the *Washington Post*, '1 out of every 5 people who died of an overdose in 2020 usually worked in construction or restaurants'":

Andrew Van Dam, "The Depressing Relationship between Your Job and Your Odds of Drug Overdose," *Washington Post*, October 6, 2023, https://www.washingtonpost.com/business /2023/10/06/jobs-likely-to-overdose/.

295 | "A separate article in the same paper identified fentanyl overdose . . .":

Julie Vitkovskaya and Courtney Kan, "Why Is Fentanyl So Dangerous?" *Washington Post*, updated April 10, 2023, https:// www.washingtonpost.com/nation/2022/11/03/fentanyl-opioid -epidemic/.

295 | "In my home state of Minnesota, American Indians were . . .":

Minnesota Department of Health, "Drug Overdose Dashboard," last reviewed September 15, 2023, https://www.health.state.mn .us/communities/opioids/opioid-dashboard/index.html.

295 | "The CDC reports a nationwide upsurge in overdose rates among Black men . . .":

Kumiko M. Lippold, Christopher M. Jones, Emily O. Olsen, and Brett P. Giroir, "Racial/Ethnic and Age Group Differences in Opioid and Synthetic Opioid–Involved Overdose Deaths among

Adults Aged ≥18 Years in Metropolitan Areas—United States, 2015–2017," *Morbidity and Mortality Weekly Report* 68, no. 43 (November 1, 2019): 967–73, https://doi.org/10.15585/mmwr .mm6843a3.

298 | "'In one way, an alcoholic who stops drinking is a walking miracle, a man or woman whose life has been so changed . . .'":

Susan Cheever, *My Name Is Bill: Bill Wilson—His Life and the Creation of Alcoholics Anonymous* (New York: Washington Square Press, 2004), 236–37.

About the Author

William C. Moyers is the vice president of public affairs and community relations at the Hazelden Betty Ford Foundation. As the organization's public advocate, Moyers carries the message about addiction, treatment, and recovery to audiences everywhere. Using his own story, Moyers highlights the power of addiction and the promise and possibility of recovery from it. He has appeared on *The Oprah Winfrey Show, Larry King Live, Good Morning America,* and National Public Radio. His work has been featured in the *New York Times,* the *Washington Post,* and *Newsweek.* William has written four books, including *Broken: My Story of Addiction and Redemption,* a *New York Times* bestseller that remains in print. Moyers was born in 1959 in Fort Worth, Texas, and was a print reporter in the 1980s and a journalist for CNN until 1995. A year later he joined the staff at (then) Hazelden and has been there ever since. Moyers and his wife, Nell Hurley, live in St. Paul, Minnesota. Between them they share four adult children.

About Hazelden Publishing

As part of the Hazelden Betty Ford Foundation, Hazelden Publishing offers both cutting-edge educational resources and inspirational books. Our print and digital works help guide individuals in treatment and recovery, as well as their loved ones. Professionals who work to prevent and treat addiction also turn to Hazelden Publishing for evidence-based curricula, digital content solutions, and videos for use in schools, treatment and correctional programs, and community settings. We also offer training for implementation of our curricula.

Through published and digital works, Hazelden Publishing extends the reach of healing and hope to individuals, families, and communities affected by addiction and related issues.

For information about Hazelden publications, please call **800-328-9000** or visit us online at **hazelden.org/bookstore.**

Also by This Author

Broken

My Story of Addiction and Redemption

Broken tells the story of what happened to William Cope Moyers between then and now—from growing up the privileged son of Bill Moyers to his descent into alcoholism and drug addiction, his numerous attempts at getting clean, his many relapses, and how he managed to survive. Beautifully written with a deep underlying spirituality, this honest and inspiring account proves the spiritual insight that we are strongest at the broken places. 384 pp.

Order No. 2751

Now What?

An Insider's Guide to Addiction and Recovery

Addiction and recovery insider, expert, and best-selling author William Cope Moyers answers the question "Now What?" for addicts and their loved ones. Covers every step of the journey from contemplation through intervention, treatment, and recovery. 208 pp.

Order No. 3982

You May Also Like

Craving

Why We Can't Seem to Get Enough

Omar Manejwala, MD, translates the neurobiology of this phenomenon into real and accessible terms, explaining why we just can't seem to get enough. He then gives us tools and guidance to find satisfaction without giving in to our cravings. 216 pp.

Order No. 4677

If You Want What We Have
Sponsorship Meditations

Written as conversations between sponsor and sponsee, these daily meditations explore the concerns, dilemmas, and struggles involved every day in recovery. Provides insights for sponsors on mutual trust, compassion, and what is important in recovery. 420 pp.

Order No. 5669

Find Your Light
Practicing Mindfulness to Recover from Anything

Author Beverly Conyers has guided hundreds of thousands of readers through the process of recognizing family roles in addiction, healing shame, building healthy relationships, releasing trauma, and focusing on emotional sobriety, as well as acknowledging self-sabotaging behaviors, addictive tendencies, and substance use patterns. With her newest work, Conyers shows us how the practice of mindfulness can be a game-changing part of recovering from any- and everything. 168 pp.

Order No. 3591

The Gifts of Imperfection
10th Anniversary Edition

For over a decade, Brené Brown has found a special place in our hearts as a gifted mapmaker and a fellow traveler. She is both a social scientist and a kitchen-table friend whom you can always count on to tell the truth, make you laugh, and, on occasion, cry with you. 240 pp.

Order No. 1060

For more information about Hazelden publications,
please call 800-328-9000
or visit us online at **hazelden.org/bookstore**.